Tending Iowa's Land

◆ ◆ ◆

A BUR OAK BOOK

Holly Carver, series editor

Tending Iowa's Land

Pathways to a Sustainable Future

Cornelia F. Mutel, editor

UNIVERSITY OF IOWA PRESS
IOWA CITY

University of Iowa Press, Iowa City 52242
Copyright © 2022 by the University of Iowa Press
uipress.uiowa.edu
Printed in the United States of America
Design and typesetting by Sara T. Sauers
Printed on acid-free paper
ISBN: 978-1-60938-873-7 (pbk)
ISBN: 978-1-60938-874-4 (ebk)

"Iowa's Life and Land: A Brief History" was previously
published, in somewhat different form, in *Compelling Ground:
Landscapes, Environments, and Peoples of Iowa* (Ames: Brunnier
Art Museum, Iowa State University, 2021).

Cataloging-in-Publication data is on file with the
Library of Congress.

For the future healers of Iowa's land.

◆ ◆ ◆

Our greatest responsibility is to be good ancestors.

—JONAS SALK

WE STAND now where two roads diverge. . . . The road we have long been traveling is deceptively easy, a smooth superhighway on which we progress with great speed, but at its end lies disaster. The other fork of the road—the one less traveled by—offers our last, our only chance to reach a destination that assures the preservation of the earth. The choice, after all, is ours to make.

—RACHEL CARSON, *Silent Spring*

CONTENTS

Introduction

❖ ❖ ❖

AROUND THE YEAR 2000, I STARTED WRITING WHAT I was sure would be my final book: a natural history of Iowa. I wanted to tell the story of how my home state, in the previous two centuries, had morphed from a wildland that sustainably embraced thousands of kinds of interacting organisms into a much simplified and tightly managed landscape of cities, roads, and farms. I acknowledged that many of Iowa's finest features had been lost in that transformation. Our deep rich soils, unpolluted slow-moving waters, dependable climate, and complex native biodiversity had all been compromised. But my book was mostly a love song for Iowa as it once was and as I still thought of it: ripe and rich with nature's beauty and possibility, a model of resilience.

Following that book's publication in March 2008, I gave talks across the state describing how we can replant prairies, restore savannas, and invite soils and waterways to reenter functional partnerships that nurture both. Three months later, one of the most destructive floods in our state's modern history sent the Iowa River ripping through Iowa City, where it surged through the homes of friends and closed my University of Iowa workplace for two months. Before the floodwaters receded, I was invited to edit a book on the science of the 2008 flood. "Okay," I thought, "the need is great and the cause is good. One more final book..." I spent several months asking experts to write chapters on the flood's causes, damages, and broader implications. That book was published in 2010.

About that time, I agreed to help edit a science-based report for the state legislature, "Impacts of Climate Change on Iowa 2010," published early in 2011. As I sat through a year's worth of group meetings with the academics who would write the report's chapters, I finally grasped a truth I'd long avoided: Iowa has major environmental problems. Human-caused alterations of soils, hydrology, and native ecosystems had reached the point where any one of these could take us down a road of no return. And now our changing climate was putting all those environmental challenges on steroids.

Stimulated by anxiety, I decided I must write yet one more book: this one on climate change. To make it palatable to lay readers, I interthreaded writings from my heart—a personal memoir and nature journal—with fact-based snippets of climate science. To do the latter, I needed to learn far more about climate change than I had ever wanted to know. The resulting book—again to be my last—was published in 2016.

I didn't realize that by then I had learned too much. With all my research and hobnobbing with experts, I understood what was plaguing Iowa's environment at the moment as well as the history of our major modern ills and the predictions for our future. I also knew many of the experts who were doing groundbreaking analyses and discovering potential solutions to our problems. I realized all too well that several of our environmental problems needed immediate attention. I believed that an introductory-level sourcebook that summarized our major problems and their solutions could help educate Iowans and just might help energize remedial action. Teachers told me that it would be welcomed as a text.

But was I the one to compile such a necessary resource? I debated that question with myself for a few years. Then I got to work. This book, which will surely be my last, is the result.

My first tasks called for developing a structure and finding authors. The book's basic organization was easy. Four natural amenities had attracted nineteenth-century Euro-Americans to Iowa: deep rich soils, clean water and abundant streams, a stable climate favorable for growing crops, and an incredible abundance and diversity of game and other wildlife. These four amenities went on to define Iowa's agricultural wealth and nurture the state's development, which in turn produced Iowa's four major environmental challenges: degraded soils, polluted and flooding waters, climate change, and the loss of biodiversity. These topics determined the book's four sections: "Soil," "Water," "Air," and "Life."

I then sought Iowa scholars who specialized in one of these fields, well-established scientists with a lifetime of experience in research and teaching. These contacts helped me identify individual chapters, and many agreed to write a chapter. From the start, the tremendous diversity of subject material served as a constraint. The book would need to be limited to our most crucial environmental concerns rather than becoming a comprehensive sourcebook.

In addition, I wanted the chapters to be friendly, inviting, and accessible to all readers regardless of their background or training. Thus I encouraged a relaxed, nontechnical writing style with straightforward scientific explanations, and I asked authors to mix first-person stories about their lives and work with factual information. One more desire: I wanted the book to convey facts but also to awaken each reader's sense of activism and commitment—to instill a can-do attitude. Empowering readers to aspire to making a difference became an important goal.

Unfortunately, remaining active and involved can be difficult nowadays, when multiple environmental problems are trending in the wrong direction. I feared that a litany of problems might overwhelm readers, sending them spiraling downward into depression and fear. For readers to see our problems as challenges or even as opportunities, they had to retain a sense of hope, which generates the energy needed to work toward resolution and healing.

And indeed there is reason to hope. In truth, although our environmental problems are worsening, we largely know how to solve them. It's not solutions that we are lacking, it's the collective will to enact them. A resilient future remains within our grasp. However, we must acknowledge that the farther we travel down our present course, the more we lose control over our options; at some point a sustainable future may pass beyond our grasp. We urgently need to replace despondency with committed action at all levels.

How could this book help feed hope and fuel activism? For a start, I asked chapter authors to remain truthful but to write in an upbeat, positive tone and conclude with hopeful approaches and solutions to our problems.

I then went a step further. Early in the book's creation, I realized that many of Iowa's environmental heroes were ordinary citizens. I felt that their stories could inform and inspire similar efforts. And so I sought out Iowans who have reshaped life in our state: movers and shakers who farm, rehabilitate land, promote renewable energy, and the like. I asked them to write short essays about their motivations, experiences, and accomplishments. The resulting dozen affirmative essays interlace with the book's longer science-based chapters.

I also wanted to give readers a mental picture of how a well-functioning world might look and operate. So I redirected the fourth chapter in each section to become a vision for the future. I solicited authors who routinely gaze outside the box to consider how soil degradation, polluted and flooding waters, excess atmospheric heat, and lost native biodiversity could each be returned to health and balance. What would the world look like if we recognized the critical importance of healthy, well-functioning ecosystems and addressed these problems in the right way? Then I asked each author to write an answer to that question through personal stories as well as facts.

The four vision authors exceeded my expectations. Lisa Schulte Moore writes about the exciting innovation of regenerative agriculture practices and the potential for these to become Iowa's norm. Thomas Rosburg sketches an expansive plan to increase habitat for Iowa's thousands of native species, which Larry Weber mirrors in his water-focused vision of land-use priorities. And Gregory Carmichael proclaims the need and potential for listening to today's students and redesigning college-level climate change education accordingly.

These vision chapters at the end of each section are the book's shining stars. They invite readers to dream of larger-than-life end points. Will we ever achieve these visions? We have made some progress toward reaching them, but we still have a long way to go. None of these visions, however, is unrealistic. Each is possible if we have the willpower to give it a try. In any case, these chapters encourage us to think and act big. I'm convinced that each time we do so, our actions feed our personal hopes even as they encourage better and more positive results.

Dare I make one more wish? Could I hope that this science-based book reaches inward to touch hearts and values as well as minds and spirits? Because that's what I feel we need to lift our current dilemmas from the backs of our descendants: a change of heart, a recommitment to the common good, a society-wide shift in assumptions and expectations. A realization that profit and productivity cannot take priority over quality of life and Earth's long-term ability to sustain life—a realization that a healthy and well-functioning Earth capable of perpetuating life must be our ultimate driver and our destination. Such inner transformations may not be easily discerned. But I hope that readers will be better prepared to walk into the ever-changing future with more courage, recognizing that our major decision now is whether we proactively combat environmental challenges or instead allow them to control our lives.

From the beginning, I unapologetically founded all information and interpretations on science rather than on opinions or anecdotes. Said another way, the book's factual information is based on meticulously collected data interpreted by well-trained specialists and on numerous rigorous research studies that have withstood the challenges of time and the probing of other trained scientists. Such careful scientific work is imperative for charting our future and guiding the difficult environmental decisions we will need to make in the years to come.

Once authors started to send me their chapters and essays, relationships among them began to emerge. I noticed, for example, that about half of the book focused on nature and the other half on agriculture. This made sense here in Iowa, where over four-fifths of our land is in agricultural use.

But I knew that for many Iowans, the relationship between nature and agriculture remains fraught with dissension. Agriculture, especially Iowa's industrial-scale commodity agriculture, appears to emphasize productivity and profitability without considering the necessity of nature's services, such as moderating floods and providing habitat for wildlife, or without factoring in the decline of long-term sustainability. Environmentalists, generally outsiders to agriculture, may appear to naively make unreasonable demands that may limit a farmer's financial survival.

I wanted this book to propose a middle ground. Chapter authors met the challenge by describing proposals and movements capable of benefiting both agriculture and nature—such as the regenerative agriculture movement and the 30×30 proposal for preserving nature's essential ecological services in a human-transformed world. Such efforts are becoming more visible. For example, in 2022, the majority of states had either passed or had pending soil health legislation.

This book builds a bridge that connects natural and agricultural systems in order to move Iowa's land and water toward environmental health. Its authors outline multiple ways for agriculture to reincorporate biological diversity and its self-generated resilience into farming systems, both above the ground and in our soils. This merging of biodiversity and agriculture for the benefit of both has become the overriding theme that unites the book's chapters, essays, and recommendations. My hope is that its many stories of environmental quandaries and accomplishments will stimulate hope and action and perhaps even a change of heart, all leading us to work together toward a more positive future.

And now, before closing, one final story about preparing this book. When the project was in its youth, while direction and substance were still searching for shape, I woke early one morning from a hazy dream about circles. In my mind's eye, numerous small circles looped together to form bigger circles, those stringing together into a network of circular interconnections.

I quickly realized that this was a picture of my book's subject matter. Each problem discussed herein interacts with and often intensifies the other problems: the repeated plowing and degradation of soils create runoff that pollutes water, the upended organic matter releases carbon dioxide emissions that exacerbate climate change . . . Around and around we go.

But as I mentally played with this complex conglomeration, I realized that these interactions among problems also created solutions. Because each time we address one problem, we also help solve others. When we lower carbon dioxide emissions, we lessen climate change's enhancement of flooding. By holding eroding soils in place, we reduce water pollution and enhance soil health. In this way, we can multiply the results of our efforts, and each of our small solutions can contribute to a better whole. We all, in our daily lives, can nudge Iowa toward greater environmental health.

Return one last time to my early morning reveries. As the sun rose outside my window and the circles spun around my head, they became a vision of my emerging book's structure and import. The book's many chapters became connected circles of ideal nature, degraded by a problem for which realistic solutions were suggested.

The four book sections became the same: circle stories of problems described and resolved, paradise lost and regained. And the book as a whole spoke of today's interconnected environmental problems awaiting resolution by returning biodiversity and its healing processes to Iowa's working and natural landscapes.

As I lay there, I thought of the myriad actions favoring environmental integrity that are waiting to be taken by each of us—be we teacher or student, parent or child, scientist or science skeptic, legislator or activist. Each action, be it large or small, top down or bottom up, is needed for us to move forward successfully. Together these actions can help Iowa—the state said to be more altered through human activity than any other—achieve a more sustainable and resilient future.

And so I offer this circle story to you, the book's readers. Your future, my future, Iowa's future are yet to be determined. They lie in the hands of each one of us. How do we embrace this truth? By learning about the problems and living the solutions. Doing so, we can each begin, one day, one year, one paragraph at a time, to do the right thing for our land and for our collective future. Turn the page. Let this book be your beginning.

Tending Iowa's Land

◆ ◆ ◆

Iowa's Life and Land

A Brief History

Cornelia F. Mutel

IN THE MID-1800S, my ancestors left their homes in Europe's German Confederation to settle in America's midwestern wilderness. Family legend places my mother's great-grandmother trekking alone several miles down a woodland trail to the land office where she filed the family's farmland claim. It's said that she sang the entire way to ward off any threats of danger and to still her soul.

I love the image of a woman walking fearlessly through primeval oak woodlands, seeking protection with song, just as I love family tales of the newly arrived clan assembling half-buried stick structures on hillsides to repel the howling wolves. But I question the story's veracity. What self-respecting family would scrape together the fees to board ship for America, only to send its daughter alone into danger?

I also question my ancestors' premise that they laid claim to vacant wilderness. During their struggles for survival, did they recognize that other people had occupied that land for thousands of years? Did they question, as they cleared the trees, what would happen to the native animals and plants then thriving there? Or consider that each action has a cost, each taking a giving? That each problem solved spins new quandaries to be confronted? Or are these questions only to be asked in hindsight?

The story of Iowa's land transformation and the disappearance of our prairie wilderness can be told from many perspectives, for example, its economic costs and benefits, cultural and technological evolution, or the fate of the displaced. My particular story focuses on the environmental gains and losses of replacing Iowa's complex prairies with farms modeled after those of eastern states and Europe, some of which have evolved into today's industrialized operations. I focus on agriculture. How could I do otherwise, when agriculture claimed vast expanses of the richest topsoil on earth, soil from which newly imported seeds emerged even before the

1

ancient prairies had completely disappeared. Iowa was, from the start, an agricultural state.

Even though this landscape benefited its new arrivals, doing so initiated a cascade of unintended consequences that unraveled the land's functional integrity, stability, and sustainability. With the first cut of the plow through Iowa's deep prairie roots, the landscape's native functions, which had ensured vibrant life in abundance, started to fade. This was the genesis of the environmental problems that today demand our attention.

But today's environmental dilemmas need not prevail. We Iowans are capable of acting wisely and with conviction, of changing direction and healing the natural and agricultural worlds that surround and sustain us. How might we do so? Perhaps understanding where we came from and where we are today will help. This is my hope. This is my story.

IOWA: MAY 31, 1833. PRAIRIE RETROSPECTIVE

The dawn sun lay low on the eastern horizon, a golden globe spreading light and heat across the dew-laden tallgrass prairies—all 28.6 million of the almost 36 million acres of future Iowa. Breezes set flowers and grasses in motion. Bees, beetles, and flies commenced the nectaring that would ensure flower pollination and seed production later that summer. Bobolinks, dickcissels, and horned larks sang on the wing. Prairie-chickens nested everywhere in the thick grass. Gray wolves followed loose groups of roaming elk and bison. Where wetlands prevailed, clusters of shorebirds whirled over hundreds of nesting ducks and geese. Even whooping and sandhill cranes joined the throng. The huge diversity of animals joined ranks with hundreds of kinds of flowering plants, each species feeding others and assuring the survival of the whole.

A heavy rain had fallen the previous night. Its moisture had quickly been absorbed into air pockets in the spongy prairie soils built up through millennia from sunlight, water, and atmospheric carbon, soils created and safeguarded by the prairie's deep, dense root masses. Those underground waters oozed downhill into sedge-covered swales where slowly coursing streams might gradually rise or fall but seldom flooded adjacent land. Making and protecting soils, cleansing water and tending its flow, decomposing wastes, sequestering carbon, these and similar beneficial processes that we today call ecosystem services were part of the landscape's operating instructions. While governing the land, they also provided homes and food for the thousands of species of animals and plants whose interdependencies over centuries had woven self-sufficient communities. Thus the ancient prairies—among the most diverse and complex of North America's ecosystems—remained stable, regenerative, and ultimately sustainable.

Usually little changed on the tallgrass prairie other than the seasons. And so May 31, 1833, passed without fanfare. There was no announcement that the following morning, a new culture would start wiping the land clean and laying upon it a different template. Nothing foretold the fact that the future of the native prairie inhabitants was about to be rewritten. Nothing warned that the ecological functions that had tended the land would start a slow but inexorable unraveling that would challenge the lives of its plants and animals as well as threaten the well-being of its future inhabitants.

IOWA: JUNE 1, 1833, TO 1900. PLOW-DOWN

Iowa was officially opened to pioneer settlement on June 1, 1833, even though the land was not vacant. Native Americans—the Oneota and Ioway, more recently the Meskwaki, Sauk, and others—had lived here for thousands of years. Beyond regularly regenerating the prairies with fire, they had not transformed these grasslands in any major way.

The new settlers arrived hungry—for food, for land to grow the food, for a place to call home. They struggled to survive, using farming techniques like those they had known in the East and imported seeds, livestock, and tools that were familiar to them.

I try to imagine how the first settlers might have responded to this land where grasses were tall enough to tickle cattle's ears, insects droned incessantly, and wildflowers and wind stretched to the horizon. Did wildlife rustling unseen through nearby vegetation inspire fear? Awe? Curiosity? Some of each?

Whatever the settlers' responses, work awaited—building shelters for their families, readying the land for crops. The arduous task of plowing the prairie was first performed with heavy cast-iron plows pulled by teams of oxen. But plowing was soon revolutionized by John Deere's much lighter steel moldboard plows. Plowing the prairie also helped eliminate the frightful wildfires that consumed everything in their reach. The earliest settlers completed most farm tasks with hand tools often made by their users. But as the century progressed, these were increasingly relinquished to horse-drawn mechanical devices that eased farming and increased productivity: the reaper, grain drill and thresher, corn planter, two-row cultivator, and others. By the 1870s, barbed wire was being used to fence pastures. That same decade, new technologies including clay tiles enabled farmers to create more cropland by draining wetlands and marshes; drainage tiles were especially useful in north-central Iowa's prairie-pothole region.

The prairie landscape provided royally for settlers. Small game supplied meat and skins. Low-flying flocks of passenger pigeons, dense enough that a single shotgun blast dropped several from the sky, were so plentiful that the birds were fed to hogs, which also snouted for acorns in the oak woodlands that were most abundant in eastern Iowa. Cattle grazed on lush prairie pastures. Corn seeds dropped into the fertile soils yielded bountiful crops. Trees furnished firewood and much-needed construction materials.

The prairies also afforded surpluses that could be sold for cash. Within a few years of settlement, longboats were transporting grains and cured pork downstream to Mississippi River towns. By the 1860s and 1870s, refrigerated railroad cars were carrying tens of thousands of Iowa's prairie-chickens, shorebirds, and waterfowl to Chicago restaurants and markets. From the start, the farmers' livelihoods were tied to market economies and evolving technologies, two influences that continue to shape the state's agriculture today.

As the population soared and humans remade the landscape, the frontier rapidly retreated westward. Civilization followed close on its heels. By the end of the century, a period shorter than a single lifetime, agriculture dominated the state to its western border. Iowa's transformation was more rapid and complete than that of any other state. What were its environmental costs?

Most obvious was the loss of the prairie's biodiversity and its associated stability, resilience, and sustainability. But what were other effects? Searching for answers, I page through drawings of farms in A. T. Andreas's *Illustrated Historical Atlas of the State of Iowa*, published in 1875. Many of the sketches present a pleasing synthesis of neat farmsteads interspersed with croplands, woodlots, and prairie pastures grazed by cattle, horses, and pigs. I recall my grandmother telling me of childhood forays with her sisters through their farm's flower-strewn grasslands and oak woodlands, returning home with bouquets for their mother. Surely on many such farms, some native ecosystem services remained to tend the land.

Then I come upon a sketch that clearly displays emerging environmental problems. All signs of native prairies and woodlands are absent. Instead, the entire print is covered by row crops and cattle pastures except for the house and barn in the picture's center. Densely occupied cattle lots stretch from the barn down a hillside into a cornfield that borders a deeply entrenched, bare-sided creek several feet wide—a sure sign of rainwaters rushing downslope and cutting into the valley bottom. In its race downhill, any rainfall would surely wash both cattle manure and loose soil into the creek, polluting the once-crystalline waters. The prairie's original infiltration hydrology, which had once coaxed slow-moving water into airy, cleansing soils, had flipped to speedy surface-water flows, resulting in water pollution, flooding, and soil erosion.

Less obvious problems probably existed on Iowa farms in the 1880s. Overgrazed prairies would have been seeded with introduced pasture grasses by then, and the suppression of fire would have allowed the invasion of woody shrubs, both in prairies and in open savannas with their widely spaced oaks. Soils would have become compacted and would have lost some of their organic matter, which would decrease their fertility and their ability to catch and hold water. These and other incipient environmental challenges may not have been abundant in the 1800s, but they lay in wait, garnering the force to emerge in full strength during the following century.

IOWA: 1900 TO 1950. MUSCLES TO FOSSIL FUELS

By the turn of the century, Iowa's vast prairies had been largely erased from the land and the original woodlands were logged or in decline. Much of the vast wilderness, with its myriad associations of native plants and animals, had been replaced by a few dozen imported crop and livestock species, occupying orderly fields, farmsteads, and villages. Gone were the dangers of prairie wildfires and large predators, the gray wolves, mountain lions, and black bears, along with bison and elk, some birds, and many other life-forms. These had been replaced by cattle, hogs, work animals (mostly horses), and domestic poultry.

In exchange for the prairies, agriculture characterized by small family-owned and family-operated farms was at its apex. In 1900, Iowa boasted an all-time high of 228,622 farms and 1.66 million rural residents. Both numbers have since declined. Ten years earlier, in 1890, Iowa had been considered settled when it had claimed at least 15 people per square mile in each county. And ten years later, in 1910, 97 percent of the state would be identified as developed for agriculture.

However, agricultural Iowa looked and functioned far differently from the way it functions today. I'm gazing at a 1910 photograph of the eastern Iowa countryside. Everything seems to be small. Farmsteads are numerous and close together. Undersized fields of crops—likely corn, alfalfa, oats, and other small grains—intermingle with fenced pastures grazed by cattle, hogs, and horses. These sweep over the gentle hills, patterning them with pleasing diversity. A hayfield dominates the forefront, its variation in the sizes and textures of plants identifying it as native prairie, something uncommon by that time. Trees shade the farmsteads, woodlands cloak the distant hillsides. The scene is friendly and inviting. I can imagine half-hidden pockets where dragonflies swarm, frogs and toads lay their eggs, songbirds build their nests, and pollinators fly from one native flower to another. It brings to mind stories of my grandfather about this time, exchanging his Sunday pastoral garb for more comfortable clothes, pulling on his boots, and taking off for an afternoon of botanizing. I recall my father, a small-town boy, telling me about his rambling hikes a quarter century later along fencerows and across frozen swamps with his friend Arnie. All three felt the urge to explore wild natural areas and they still found plenty of places to do so.

All three also lived in a world far better tended by nature's services than today's world. The perennial croplands and interspersed pastures and hayfields performed, to some degree, the same functions as native prairies. They covered the soil year-round and decreased its erosion. However, as in the century before, heavy rains still washed topsoil from fields of row crops, downcutting streams that sometimes overflowed to flood surrounding farmland. Iowa's topsoil continued to thin and, along with pasture manure, sullied the state's once-clean waters.

One additional environmental problem lay in wait: climate change.

Scientists had first described the process in the 1800s: increasing atmospheric carbon dioxide from burning fossil fuels prevents the sun's heat from escaping the planet's atmosphere, and this is inexorably raising Earth's average temperature. However, until 1900, Iowa's farms had boasted a tight, self-contained cycle of renewable energy: agricultural machines were powered by work animals that ate from and fertilized the pastures they inhabited. Iowa had thus sidestepped fossil fuels and the creation of greenhouse gas emissions with a few exceptions—the burst of carbon dioxide released from decomposing prairie roots when the prairie was first plowed as well as methane from ruminant cattle. That changed between 1900 and 1950, when Iowa's work animals were replaced by tractors that burned fossil fuels from Texas and the Middle East. With this energy switch, agriculture adopted the modern world's climate-altering energy sources as the norm. Meanwhile, the ongoing addition of new farming implements such as mechanical corn pickers, planters, balers, and cultivators and the adoption of gasoline-powered vehicles for transportation continued to increase Iowa's use of fossil fuels.

This energy switch produced one last casualty: it speeded the demise of Iowa's wet hay meadows—the last of the extensive prairies that had been preserved as a source of hay. Between 1900 and 1950, as work animals disappeared and wet hay meadows were drained, over 90 percent of Iowa's remaining prairies were cultivated for annual row crops. With these acts of draining and plowing, Iowa's native prairies became functionally extinct—they were relegated to small pockets in settlers' cemeteries, road and railroad rights-of-way, inaccessible snippets unsuitable for farming, and western Iowa's Loess Hills. Native woodlands survived in greater abundance, although most by then were degraded and overgrazed. This destruction of native plant communities furthered soil erosion and water pollution. It also decimated the landscape's inbred resilience. Meanwhile, today's largest environmental crisis, climate change, was tightening its grip on Iowa.

IOWA: 1950 TO 2020. INTENSIFICATION AND SPECIALIZATION

When I was a child in the 1950s, our egg man, Mr. Schmidt, would stop by every Friday afternoon to drop off a few dozen eggs and, if we were lucky, announce that he'd have roasting chickens the next week. Once a year, he'd invite us and his other customers to a picnic at his farm, where we feasted on fried chicken, sweet corn, and an assortment of salads and desserts brought by others. It was quite a banquet, but what I relished most were the farm animals—the pony and retired workhorse nickering for treats, the chickens that provided our eggs, a few sleeping pigs, cats scampering about the barn, dairy cows speckling the distant pastures. I'd gaze enviously at the Schmidt kids who were helping serve the food: they got to live with these animals, ride the pony, frolic with the cats, maybe even bottle-feed hungry calves. They could run off to play in the nearby woodlands or splash in the creek. What I would have given to be one of them!

Mr. Schmidt's establishment was the midcentury edition of the diversified family farm that had characterized the Midwest since the 1830s. With its several types of crops and livestock, the farm fed a family and produced a surplus to sell for cash. But unlike earlier farms, it had lost nearly every vestige of its original native biodiversity along with many of the landscape's ecological functions. The farm's perennial crops and pasturelands would have helped hold the soil in place and safeguard water quality. But its row crops encouraged the same environmental problems that began in the previous century: soil compaction and loss to erosion, water pollution, and flooding and other signs of altered hydrologic processes. And with the farm's increasing dependence on fossil fuels to power an expanding array of equipment, agriculture added its own greenhouse gas emissions to those from industry and other sources, helping intensify future climate change.

In the coming decades, increasing mechanization—including astounding new technologies, tools, and procedures—joined hands with government policies, economics, market pressures, vertical integration of farming operations, and the constant search for greater productivity and profit to convert many diversified midwestern farms into industrial-scale businesses striving to maximize production of one or two uniform commodities. This transformation has intensified Iowa's existing environmental problems even as it has added new ones. Factors contributing to this transformation would have included nitrogen fertilizers and other farm chemicals, livestock confinement operations, and the increasing dominance of corn and soybeans.

For over a century, soil fertility had been maintained by manure, nitrogen-fixing crops of legumes, and crop rotation. But after World War II, inexpensive nitrogen fertilizer's ability to increase crop productivity encouraged its rapid adoption. Since then, the use of this synthetic fertilizer has continued to multiply until, by 2016, 150 pounds or more were commonly applied to each acre of corn. In addition, new insecticides and herbicides offering solutions to crop diseases and weeds became commonplace on the farm. The problem? Not all these additives are completely used or broken down before they wash downhill and into water bodies. Today's rivers run heavy with a brew of nitrates from nitrogen fertilizers and smaller amounts of other synthetic farm chemicals. The nitrates feed toxic algae blooms in Iowa's water bodies and the growing Dead Zone in the Gulf of Mexico. Pesticides drifting through the air can damage neighbors' crops or nearby natural areas.

Since the 1800s, pasture-raised hogs had been a given on Iowa farms, where they converted corn to meat and manure. But by the 1980s, concentrated animal feeding operations, CAFOs, began to transform hog farming into a large-scale industry where hogs are raised under controlled conditions. Today Iowa grows more than twice the number of hogs as any other state, with many spending their entire lives in CAFOs that house thousands. In addition to their odor and the health problems they cause for workers, CAFOs' concentrated manure when poorly managed can spill or leak into waterways, leach into the soil, and wash into floodwaters. Like nitrogen fertilizers, the millions of tons of livestock manure created each year threaten Iowa's water quality.

In the late 1900s, as profit margins narrowed and farmers were pushed toward greater specialization and economies of scale, pastured livestock declined on many Iowa farms. In response, the forage crops, pastures, and hayfields that once diversified the landscape were no longer necessary. Since the mid-1900s, many of these perennial-covered agricultural fields have been converted to corn and soybean row crops. This conversion intensified in the early 2000s, when corn prices rose because of the crop's use for the biofuel ethanol (which in 2021 used over half of Iowa's corn crop). Today, in many places, farms with thousands of acres of corn and beans, which are highly dependent on chemical additives, stretch to the horizon without interruption. Because row crops cover the soil for half of the year or less, these monocultural expanses readily funnel eroding topsoil along with chemical fertilizers and pesticides into nearby drainages.

Runoff from these crops is largely unregulated and is a significant cause of Iowa's worsening water pollution.

Today, over vast sections of Iowa, efforts to thrive in a business where profit margins have dwindled have pushed farmers toward greater economies of scale—that is, toward ever-larger and more specialized fields, machinery, and CAFOs. On farms thousands of acres in size, everything has been pushed to its limits, as if our landscape were an inanimate factory.

Iowa's farmlands and their inhabitants are living entities that are now showing signs of collapse. We have lost over half of the depth of our topsoil; our water quality is among the worst in the nation; our floods are increasing in size and number. And in places Iowa's biodiversity has evaporated. Craig Childs, in his 2012 book *Apocalyptic Planet: Field Guide to the Everending Earth,* describes spending a long weekend in a large Iowa cornfield searching for animals. Other than six very small insects, animal life had been erased—suggesting that such extreme obliteration of animal life might also be happening throughout the two-thirds of Iowa now covered by corn and beans. This is ironic for prairielands that just 200 years ago boasted one of our planet's most diverse ecosystems. Add to this fact the irony that Iowa's fertile topsoils have become water pollutants and that our formerly clean waters now pose hazards to our health, and it becomes obvious that we must address these problems.

These trends define the extremes of Iowa agriculture today but not their totality. Regenerative cropping and grazing systems are used by some farmers and are described in several of this book's chapters and essays. I know of farmers with good-sized corn and bean fields who have constructed wetlands, planted pollinator strips, installed bioreactors to capture soil nitrates, and placed prairie buffers in and along their croplands. Broadly speaking, these farmers are reintroducing the prairie's complexity and diversity to their lands in order to rebuild some of Iowa's original ecosystem functions. Other farmers grow organic crops for the market or to feed free-range hogs, beef and dairy cattle, poultry, and lambs. Many small farmers are growing organic vegetables and eggs for local farmers markets, restaurants, and Consumer Supported Agriculture customers. Amish communities have maintained their traditional low-tech lives and diverse farms in Iowa since the mid-1800s. The organization Practical Farmers of Iowa helps a variety of farmers who are resisting the trend toward super-specialization and striving to reestablish landscape resilience and sustainability.

In addition, many Iowans are passionate about preserving and restoring native prairie and woodland remnants or planting new ones. My husband and I, for example, are using prescribed fire and selective cutting to restore our eighteen-acre oak-hickory woodland near Iowa City. The return of diverse understory grasses and flowers has brought us joy beyond measure. And I have friends who, by joining with others, have bought large tracts of marginal farmland that they are returning to native prairie and savanna communities.

All these individuals and projects present alternative models for Iowa's future. They all address our environmental problems on a local scale. But how broad are their effects? I consider our sons, nice Iowa kids, growing up here thirty years ago. They swam in farm ponds and paddled in rivers, diving in when they needed to cool off. Last summer I repeated a favorite paddle with my grandkids, only to realize that the river water looked like melted chocolate and smelled like a sewer. After I remembered a friend who had ended up in intensive care from a river-transmitted infection, our trip became a litany of warnings: don't splash the water, no hands in your mouths, don't jump in . . . Whatever became of the Iowa I loved?

Do individual regenerative farming and conservation projects make a difference? Much of this book is dedicated to answering this question affirmatively and sketching visions for an environmentally healthier future, one that we *can* achieve if we do the right thing. For now, my brief answer is yes: whenever we reintegrate Iowa's original biological diversity and native self-sufficiency into Iowa's landscape, including its agricultural lands, we start to reverse our environmental problems and rebuild a healthier landscape. But we need many more such projects, and they need to be larger. We still have much to do.

Before you read this book's first chapter, let's consider the relationship between climate change and agriculture, which Eugene Takle and Gregory Carmichael explore in chapters 11 and 12. The link between the two is palpable but can sometimes seem contradictory. Iowa's agricultural fields both contribute to climate change—agriculture generates about 30 percent of our state's greenhouse gas emissions—and help solve the problem by "growing" wind generators. Increases in precipitation, flooding, and extreme weather caused by climate change damage crops and farmlands, but warming temperatures lengthen the growing season and sometimes increase yields. In addition to producing its own problems, climate change intensifies existing agricultural problems such as soil erosion and nitrate runoff. With current climate trends, models predict that by midcentury recent increases in productivity will have disappeared and we may be facing food shortages on a global scale.

Agriculture can play a major role in mitigating climate change through carbon farming, a term applied to any farming practice that draws carbon dioxide from the atmosphere down into the soil, where the carbon is stored in soil organic matter. Reducing methane from livestock also needs attention. Any efforts to lessen climate change will decrease other environmental problems as well, and building healthier soils will improve the landscape's ability to buffer extreme weather events.

Sometimes, when I'm weary, I walk a mile to the Iowa River, close my eyes to the sun and wind, and imagine a ghost flock of passenger pigeons coming my way. I hear a distant buzz from the south that grows louder as the birds approach, and suddenly they are passing overhead, obscuring the sun, their chatters and clucks deafening, billions of passenger pigeons on the move, once the most numerous bird on earth, now extinct. After a few moments of envisioning their spectacular flights, their miles-wide nesting colonies, their embodiment of nature's capabilities, their life force beyond compare, I return home renewed.

Iowa's nineteenth-century settlers, pulled forward by personal needs, market economies, and technological innovations, managed to survive and flourish in this new land by converting the prairie into an agricultural cornucopia. I am here, writing about their efforts, only because of their successes. But while I recognize this, I wish my forebears hadn't cleared the prairies quite so thoroughly or expected the land to give them its all. I wish they had left more nature-dominated pockets and fencerow refuges, more swales and corridors to pour pollinating insects and insect-eating birds out to surrounding lands, to cleanse polluted water, to grab eroding soil, to capture and hold carbon dioxide. To allow nature to do what it does best: create a diversity of function and life that also nourishes our spirits and beautifies our land.

Today's economic pressures, technologies, and economies of scale continue to push industrial-scale farming forward. But need this be so, or could we choose a different track? Might we now attach a regulator to those temptations, considering their environmental costs as well as their financial benefits? In past years, agriculture moved forward without our knowing the long-term consequences of farming practices. But we no longer have that excuse. Today we can see many of the environmental results of our actions, the destructive power of many of the problems we've helped produce. And we have proven alternative models to follow, including restorative options and techniques. We have an obligation to do better. Our need therefore is to harness the agricultural community's ability to adapt, which has guided Iowans for nearly 200 years, and redirect it toward a different end point: long-term sustainability, which encompasses long-term soil and landscape health as well as productive and profitable farms and rural communities. This is a goal that we can all aspire to.

Where do we start? This book suggests many pathways forward. The ideal template was established centuries ago by our native prairies. Wherever and whenever we can, we ought to return associations of deep-rooted prairie plants to the land. Where that is not possible, we should return associations of nonnative perennial plants. In addition, wherever healthy native remnants survive, be they prairies or wetlands or woodlands, we must work to preserve and restore them. With time and wise implementation of these practices, we will create conditions where nature and agriculture can start to restore each other.

Many farmers have adopted various conservation practices, but conservation programs are unlikely to be wholeheartedly adopted on a voluntary basis. We need federal, state, and local regulations and programs to push them forward. We need Iowa's largest farms, whose acres magnify environmental problems the most, to adopt solutions with determination. And that requires strong environmental policies, adequately funded monitoring and conservation programs, government incentives, and coordination of efforts. The choice is between accepting such regulations and programs or continuing to damage our environment. Because the land's degradation will not disappear on its own, an agricultural change of course is our only option.

Martha, the last passenger pigeon, died in 1914 in the Cincinnati Zoo. We cannot bring her species back. But we *can* cleanse Iowa's water and staunch the loss of its topsoil. We *can* return wildflowers and wildlife to parts of our state, heightening the beauty, resilience, and self-sufficiency of Iowa's landscape. And we *can* toil to limit climate change's worst repercussions. Doing so will be best for our land, even more so for our health and our spirits, and most of all for all those yet to come.

Section I

♦ ♦ ♦

SOIL

♦ ♦ ♦

AS A LOVER OF PLANTS, I'VE ALWAYS DELIGHTED IN SOIL: its earthy fresh smell, the way moist soil crumbles through my fingers, its soft cushiony feeling under my feet when I walk through the woods. But truth be told, I've also ignored or underappreciated soil, thinking of it as dirt when our boys tracked clumps into the house or our dog lumbered inside with a muddy bone she'd just unearthed.

I suppose most of us don't often think about the ground under our feet, even though soil is the ultimate source of nearly all our food and fiber. Even though healthy soils help control our climate, cleanse our water and govern its flow, and moderate flooding. Even though soils are the genesis of the aboveground natural world that I relish.

Iowa's prairie soils, when first farmed by Euro-Americans, were nothing less than miraculous. This ancient earth had been thousands of years in the making. Year after year, prairie plants had used sunlight, atmospheric carbon dioxide, and water to synthesize carbon-rich compounds that were then stored underground. Long-rooted prairie plants pumped organic carbon deep underground into windblown silt deposits with an abundance of micronutrients. Here in Iowa these elements constituted the perfect union for producing the richest soils on the planet, friable black topsoils an average of fourteen to sixteen inches deep.

The topsoils included far more than plant roots. Soil, when healthy and fully functional, is infused with life. In fact, the diversity of life-forms in healthy soils exceeds that found aboveground. Billions of microorganisms can be found in a single tablespoon of healthy soil. Insects, spiders, earthworms, fungi, protozoans, nematodes, reptiles, mammals, and many other creatures form a complex self-regulating and self-sustaining ecosystem—an entire wilderness, thriving unseen and unacknowledged, just below our feet.

These pre-1800 soil communities fed and fostered the prairie's lush growth and healthy biodiversity both above and below the ground without any of the fertilizers or pesticides we use today. Microorganisms feed on dead organic matter and release nutrients that in turn feed living plants; soil health, fertility, and productivity are thus intimately tied to organic matter and diverse soil life. And Iowa's tallgrass prairies generated a plethora of organic matter century after century, in the process maintaining the living soil systems that carried out multiple environmental functions. About half of the soil volume was made up of pockets of air and moisture, which aerated and watered plant roots. These absorbent porous soils also cleansed water and provided remarkable storage for water, which moderated flooding. They controlled pests and diseases by maintaining a balanced biological community. Dense prairie plants and their roots held the soil in place, preventing erosion. Prairie plants also captured and drew down atmospheric carbon dioxide that was then stored in the soil. And—most astonishing—the more this remarkable living sunlight-fueled engine ran, the healthier, deeper, and more productive the soils became.

I now understand why Iowa's original prairie soils have been called our state's black gold. Healthy soils are priceless and precious, a fundamental natural resource as vital to life as water and air. Our healthy, porous prairie soils produced Iowa's initial resilience and shaped our state's agricultural prominence. They became the basis for Iowa's culture and economy. But today we have lost on average over half of the once-richest soils in the world and degraded those that remain. Once gone, these living soils cannot be easily or rapidly replaced. What's more, degraded, dead, and compacted soils have generated or contributed to all of Iowa's other environmental problems.

Our number one task when considering our agricultural future should be preserving and restoring our remaining topsoils. That means fostering biologically diverse soil communities underground and (among other actions) integrating biologically diverse plantings into agriculture aboveground. Because Iowa's soils interact so closely with our state's hydrology, climate, and diverse life-forms, doing what's good for soils will also help our crops, water, air, native biodiversity, and future. It all begins with the soil.

This section focuses on what's happened to our soils and how we can recoup their resilience and health, thus moving agriculture down the path to long-term sustainability. With over 80 percent of Iowa's land dedicated to agricultural use, the agricultural focus is a given. However, readers should note that soils can also be degraded by other intensive land uses, including cities and roadways.

Kathleen Woida's opening chapter describes Iowa's original thick and fertile topsoils, explaining that they were formed, protected, and held in place by the prairie's continuous cover of plant material. The breaking of that cover through plowing initiated the unraveling of this miraculously sustainable soil complex. Major resulting problems included severe soil compaction and loss of natural fertility, which ironically continues to be compromised by the synthetic nitrogen fertilizers that are toxic to many soil microorganisms, fertilizers that we continue to apply to replace lost soil fertility. Other far-reaching implications are decreased porosity, ongoing erosion and pollution, reduced productivity, and steadily decreasing topsoil depth—all of which add up to a soil crisis that presents a serious threat to Iowa's rural communities and overall economy. Woida concludes that "today's conventional farming techniques continue to degrade Iowa's soil ecosystems," but that the regenerative agriculture techniques discussed in chapter 4 are proven to rebuild porosity, organic matter, and soil health. A major transformative movement toward these goals is "absolutely necessary for restoring Iowa's physical and biological environment" and bringing back soils that once again are self-sustaining.

Woida's chapter is paired with an essay by Ken Fawcett, a fourth-generation row crop farmer who for decades has steadily introduced conservation practices into his 2,000 acres of cover crops, trees, prairie plantings, and corn and beans croplands. Fawcett traces the evolution of his family's farm and farming techniques since 1853. "I have always looked to the future," he writes, and doing so has fared both him and his land well.

Next, Keith Schilling reveals the complexities of soil erosion, one of agriculture's greatest problems that has helped rob us of over half of our topsoil. He gives us a short history of erosion in Iowa and then describes its two dominant processes: topsoil washing downslope in shallow sheets from unprotected agricultural uplands and, lower on the slopes, concentrated flows that carve gullies and channels and collapse streambanks. Erosion not only robs us of a nonrenewable natural resource, it also turns our precious soil into our most voluminous pollutant: water-borne sediment. Schilling defines erosion as a once-natural process that has been greatly intensified and accelerated by human use. While we might address upland erosion with conservation practices such as grassed waterways, no easy solutions exist for most streambank erosion. Both forms are continuing at nonsustainable levels—we are losing far more soil than we are rebuilding. Iowa's already-high erosion rates are now being magnified by climate change's increase in precipitation and extreme rainfall events.

Seth Watkins, another fourth-generation farmer, describes what he's gained by permanently converting his erosion-prone farmland from row crops to a cattle operation. Not only has he improved his cattle's well-being, health, and forage, he also has decreased pesticide and fertilizer use, enhanced native biodiversity and water quality, increased profitability, and given his children "a future filled with abundance, opportunity, and hope."

Christopher Jones's chapter follows with an erudite explanation of the modern intensification of midwestern agricultural systems, which has also intensified soil degradation: the creation of synthetic nitrogen fertilizers, herbicides, and insecticides; the confinement of livestock in mammoth concentrated feeding operations; and the establishment of an ethanol market for Iowa's corn, which in 2021 soaked up over half of Iowa's corn crop. These creations sparked the replacement of Iowa's mid-twentieth-century integrated crop and livestock farms with vast monocultures of corn and soybeans, sometimes sprinkled with massive cattle, hog, or poultry confinement structures. Jones explains the history of these extremely simplified farming systems, concluding that while decisions were not made with negative outcomes in mind, these changes have meant more bushels of corn and soybeans and more protein but also more water pollution, more biodiversity loss, more soil degradation, and more greenhouse gases emitted to the atmosphere—in other words, more of the problems discussed in this book. We now need strategic thinking that "articulates environmental goals and makes decisions with those goals, and not just the number of bushels, in mind."

Levi Lyle then shares how he has kept his family's berry crops purposefully small to "align my farming practices with what I felt was right." His essay includes thoughts on maintaining an intimate connection with the land, melding these thoughts with explanations of cover crops, organic farming, and his concerns about protecting nature, family health, and community. He hopes to be part of a "shift from an extractive agricultural paradigm to one of regenerative economics."

All these writings acknowledge the challenges associated with modern agriculture, many of which intensify our problems and none of which bodes well for long-term sustainability. But the story does not end here. Just as we are today restoring health and diversity to nature preserves, so too can we restore health and biodiversity to our agricultural landscape and farmed soils. Both forms of restoration help return ecosystem services and long-term resilience, self-sufficiency, and productivity to Iowa's land.

Lisa Schulte Moore talks about such restorative measures in her vision for the future chapter on the regenerative agriculture movement. She explains how our two main crops, corn and soybeans, have a common weakness: they cover the soil only for half of the year or less. The rest of the time, soils are exposed to nature's forces with significant negative effects on soil health.

"Regenerative agriculture" is an umbrella term for rejuvenating living, complex, organically rich soils and, in the process, addressing our multiple environmental problems as well as our economic concerns. While Schulte Moore includes stories of diverse regenerative operations, the basic principles remain the same: maintain continuous crop residue and living plant cover on the soil, minimize soil disturbance, raise livestock in addition to crops, diversify plantings wherever possible, and plant especially fragile soils with perennial species—preferably prairie species, although other perennials can also produce a functional restoration. Schulte Moore strives to make these restorative practices and the rejuvenated soils they produce the norm rather than the exception. Although these practices are growing in popularity, Iowa's soils and landscape cry out for far greater adoption of regenerative agriculture on farms of all sizes and types.

Today farmers around the planet are facing environmental problems with agricultural intensification similar to our own. If Iowa were to export techniques for regenerative agriculture, as we have done with other agricultural technologies, our model could positively influence food production systems around the world. Like it or not, we are part of a global economy and ecology with far-reaching implications. What we do here affects billions of humans and other organisms.

CHAPTER 1

The Root of Our Problems

Iowa's Degraded Soils

Kathleen Woida

TAKE A SUMMER DRIVE around our state when the crops are high, and chances are that what you see through your windshield will look lush, green, and fertile. And if you think about it at all, which is unlikely for most of us, you will probably assume that the soils hidden from view are healthy and thriving as well. But in most cases, this is an illusion. Before the crops were planted—after the winter snows had melted, the soil lay bare, and the spring rains came—you would have seen eroded soil accumulating at the base of most hills and too often washing into a stream or lake. Erosion and the pollution caused by flowing water traversing the land—called runoff—are major environmental problems in Iowa. But just why does Iowa have such runoff and erosion problems? Well, the truth is that runoff is largely the consequence of a less visible but widespread and serious environmental problem: degraded soils, resulting from years of unsustainable farming and grazing practices and, on a smaller scale, urbanization. Damage to our soils is ongoing and is causing immediate and worsening problems.

For twenty years, I worked as a geologist in Iowa for an agency of the U.S. Department of Agriculture called the Natural Resources Conservation Service. Studying soil and evaluating soil erosion and soil health across the state were important parts of my job as well as my life's work. A few years ago, I was working with colleagues from one of our field offices in northeast Iowa, sampling soil to take back to the lab for analysis. In one field we visited, the farmer had been planting seed corn for decades using conventional methods, which entail multiple passes over the field with heavy equipment. These are the same methods used on about half of Iowa's cropland.

The soils in this particular field had endured so much tillage and traffic that they were severely compacted. We had a difficult time even excavating an intact block from the surface for later study under a microscope. Because of the compaction, very little rainwater could penetrate the soil. Instead, most of it flowed over the surface, cutting ugly rills and gullies every spring—narrow channels through which water, sediment, and farm chemicals could race downslope. In fact, the land was damaged enough that the Natural Resources Conservation Service determined the landowner was out of compliance with his U.S. Department of Agriculture contract, by which he had received federal payments in return for a promise to use conservation practices on his acres. The situation was tense for those involved but not unfamiliar; badly degraded soils may be the norm in our state. In this chapter, I will explain the two critical ways in which Iowa's soils are suffering. Their inability to absorb rainfall, as this story illustrates, is one. The other is the loss of natural fertility, which has left soils unable to support robust plant life without the addition of massive amounts of chemical fertilizers, which in turn are causing widespread water pollution. Without question, human activities are the cause of this degradation.

THE SOILS WE STARTED WITH

It wasn't always like this. Before Iowa was settled by Euro-Americans in the 1800s, the sight of a patch of bare ground at any time of the year would have been rare except in creek bottoms. The land may have looked desolate after a prairie fire, but its thick fertile soil and deep roots brought forth new growth within a week or two. Indigenous people would have seen water running off the land only when snowmelt flowed across frozen ground. Erosion would have been uncommon because the prairie soils that had formed over thousands of years were covered by vegetation year-round.

Most of these soils had formed in the silty sediments called loess, which strong winds had picked up in major river valleys, carried eastward, and dropped onto the land some 15,000 years ago. Younger soils in north-central Iowa formed in sediments deposited by glaciers as recently as 13,500 years ago. It may not seem like it to you, but such numbers are recent in geological terms, so these untapped deposits were still rich in crucial mineral nutrients.

Over time, the soils called Mollisols, which formed under tallgrass prairie vegetation with its dense, deep roots, developed an average of fourteen to sixteen inches of fertile black topsoil that soaked up rainwater like a sponge. ("Topsoil" refers to the dark soil at the land surface that is richest in organic matter and plant nutrients.) The soils called Alfisols, which formed under deciduous trees, had thinner topsoil but were still one of the world's most fertile soil types. These two soil types probably covered more than 90 percent of Iowa's land before 1800, and they were the most productive soils on the planet.

Iowa's remarkable soils attracted settlers who began to work the land a few acres at a time. At first, change was slow. But in 1837, John Deere invented a steel plow that could cut through tough prairie roots much faster, and the number of acres a farmer could cultivate increased dramatically. Plowing inverted slices of the sod, eventually killing the prairie vegetation and leaving the soil bare for much of the year. By 1930, Iowa had lost nearly all its tens of millions of acres of tallgrass prairie to agriculture, and our state had become the most transformed landscape in the country. This drastic change quickly resulted in tremendous agricultural production, but it also led to a severe decline in the health of Iowa's soils.

Today Iowa's prairie-generated topsoils are only six to eight inches thick on average, having lost at least half of their former depth to erosion and the oxidation of organic matter from tillage. Many are only an inch or two thick. Eroded and compacted soils are at the root of many of today's environmental problems. Thinner, more compacted topsoil absorbs and stores much less water, leading to runoff as well as severe stress on crops during periods of drought. Such topsoil is also much less fertile because of the loss of organic matter teeming with plant nutrients. Today most of Iowa's cropland soils under conventional cultivation would produce very low corn and soybean yields without the addition of commercial fertilizers and animal manure.

Now let's examine what is causing this damage to Iowa's soils in more detail.

DAMAGE TO SOIL POROSITY

So why do Iowa's soils absorb so much less water than they once did? The amount of water that can infiltrate and be stored in a given soil depends on two things—soil texture and soil structure. Together they determine porosity, which is the amount of pore space in the soil. Soils consist of mineral particles of different sizes (from large sand grains to tiny clay particles), organic matter (living organisms and their remains), and pore spaces that hold water and air. The particle sizes in a soil define its texture—for example, loam, silty clay, loamy sand, and the like. The shapes and sizes of the particles also determine how tightly they can pack together and how much pore space exists between them for water to enter. For example, water infiltrates sandy soils much faster than clayey soils, as you can probably guess, because sandy soils have greater porosity.

Soil structure is produced by the aggregation of soil particles into discrete units called peds. Over the course of many decades, the action of earthworms, soil insects, and microbes, along with repeated episodes of wetting-drying and freezing-thawing, causes peds to form. They can be anywhere from a millimeter to a few centimeters across. The pore spaces between peds provide most of the room for air and water, so anything that breaks up soil peds destroys porosity and reduces the ability of the soil to absorb and store water, leading to the problems of runoff and water stress for plants.

Texture doesn't change much over the life of a soil, but human activities often destroy soil structure and porosity. In Iowa, the most widespread of these damaging activities is tillage—plowing and disking—of cropland soils. Tilling the soil to prepare a seedbed has been the norm for decades and is still the preferred method on nearly half of Iowa's cropland.[1] Tillage implements break up many of the soil peds, and by turning the soil the implements also bring buried peds to the surface, where raindrops hitting the ground at more than twenty miles per hour pulverize them. The destruction of soil structure in the top six inches or so, called the plow layer, leaves very little porosity to allow rainwater to enter the ground. The plow layer ends up being a structureless block that then requires more tillage just to break it up into clods before seeds can be planted. Damage by tillage is made even worse when it takes place in fields that are too wet, because the peds basically get churned into mud. Unfortunately, because Iowa's spring rainfall amounts have been increasing with climate change, farmers have found themselves tilling wet fields much more often.

When I have shown Iowa farmers photographs of their topsoil taken under a microscope, they've often been shocked at how little pore space is visible in the solid mass of soil particles making up their plow layer. Tiny pores might constitute as little as 5 percent of the soil volume. For comparison, I show them a photograph of a healthy topsoil of the same soil type, which typically displays 30 to 40 percent porosity and numerous large pores for water to move through. Seeing is usually believing.

Tillage doesn't just destroy soil peds, it also reduces porosity and infiltration of water by compacting the soil. Many Iowa cropland soils have what is called a plow pan, a dense zone two to four inches thick just beneath the plow layer, the result of downward pressure from years of tillage. Over time the entire topsoil can become compacted by the weight of farm machinery, which has been increasing as farms have grown in size. A full grain cart can weigh almost forty tons, and as it trundles across a field it crushes any remaining peds and obliterates most pores, greatly reducing porosity. This of course leads to runoff and pollution. The tremendous amount of runoff from fields during heavy rains is also a major contributor to the state's worsening problem of flooding.

DAMAGE TO SOIL FERTILITY

The second major problem with today's soils is their loss of fertility, which has led to the use of more and more chemical fertilizer on corn and soybeans. As astounding as it sounds, farmers in recent years have been applying nearly 4 billion pounds of chemical fertilizer to Iowa soils annually, as well as excessive amounts of manure from the thousands of concentrated animal feeding operations.[2] As a result, many of Iowa's lakes and streams are polluted with the nitrate, phosphorus, pesticides, and fecal bacteria delivered by runoff.

The most important natural contributor to soil fertility is organic matter. You can think of this organic matter as consisting of three things: the living, the dead, and the very dead, usually called humus. The dead portion consists of actively decomposing plant parts and is the primary food source for living creatures like earthworms, insects, and microscopic organisms. Humus, on the other hand, is thoroughly decomposed and is typically more than a thousand years old. It consists of tiny particles that are very good at attracting and holding nutrients for gradual use by plants.

Much of the damage to natural soil fertility is due to the erosion of topsoil, which is rich in organic matter. But even if erosion magically stopped, the fertility of Iowa soils would continue to suffer with every pass of the plow or disk. About 60 percent of organic matter consists of organic carbon, and when tillage exposes organic matter to the air, some of its carbon is lost because it joins with oxygen to form the gas carbon dioxide. (Ancient humus, the least renewable type of organic matter, is especially vulnerable to oxidation.) The carbon dioxide escapes into the atmosphere, where it contributes to global warming. In chapter 11, Eugene Takle looks at the many impacts of climate change on agriculture already happening in Iowa.

In addition to supplying most of the nutrients needed by plants, organic matter improves infiltration of water and is also extremely good at holding on to water, keeping it available for plant use throughout the growing season. In fact, the amount of organic matter in the topsoil is the most important control over crop productivity. And the living portion, interacting with the nonliving matrix of minerals and dead organic matter, plays an indispensable role in driving the whole system. A healthy soil might contain up to a hundred thousand kinds of organisms, a diversity of life many times greater than that found aboveground!

We can group soil organisms according to who eats whom, and they come in all sizes, from microbes to small rodents. Earthworms are the most visible indicator of a healthy soil ecosystem, and a scarcity of earthworms is almost certainly a sign of depleted organic matter. All it takes is a shovel to find out. Earthworms are natural tillers, pushing and eating their way through the soil, creating pore spaces in the process and leaving behind waste products rich in the nutrients needed by plants. But microscopic organisms may be the most essential ingredient of a fertile soil. As these microbes decompose organic matter, they release nutrients to plants that are otherwise not available, such as nitrogen—usually the nutrient in shortest supply. The subject of natural soil biology is very complicated, but suffice it to say that while soils are amazingly efficient natural systems, humans have been harming them for many decades.

Year after year, today's conventional farming techniques continue to degrade Iowa's soil ecosystems. When soils are left bare for months at a time with no roots in the ground, many of the organisms starve. Anhydrous ammonia and pesticides applied to fields kill most of those that have survived. Compacted soils deficient in both water and air are inhospitable to soil microbes, which are aerobic organisms in need of both. Microbes have also suffered from Iowa's increase in rainfall over the past couple of decades because they shut down in saturated conditions low in oxygen.

The key to healthy soils is managing them in a way that increases porosity and builds organic matter—the most important ingredient in a strong, self-sufficient soil ecosystem. A very healthy soil ecosystem requires only sunlight and rainwater to thrive, and there are Iowans successfully farming several hundred acres who have not applied nitrogen to their fields for decades. A healthy soil is also self-regulating because it supports diverse organisms that keep pests under control.

One of the most important ways to sustain the soil ecosystem and build organic matter is to keep living roots in the ground for as much of the year as possible by planting fall cover crops immediately after harvesting a cash crop. The roots of cover crops also go a long way toward improving soil porosity and infiltration. To protect soil structure in the topsoil, it is important to disturb the soil as little as possible by reducing field traffic and practicing forms of conservation tillage. Eliminating tillage altogether—a practice called no-till—leaves all the crop residue on the surface to protect soils from heavy rainfall and erosion. In addition, there are many benefits to planting diverse cash crops rather than planting corn year after year with an occasional crop of soybeans (the Iowa norm). For example, instead of relying on the anhydrous ammonia that is toxic to soil microbes and causes water pollution, planting a legume crop like alfalfa or clover in rotation adds green manure that is naturally rich in nitrogen.

These are a few of the ways we can stop degrading—and start rebuilding—the health of soils in Iowa. This chapter focused on cropland—which covers about 72 percent of our state—but soil degradation is also common on much of Iowa's grazing land and certainly in most urban settings. Lisa Schulte Moore in chapter 4 presents a much fuller picture of what Iowa could look like under a system of stewardship that emphasizes the preservation and regeneration of our land. Such a transformation is absolutely necessary for restoring Iowa's physical and biological environment.

The good news is that change has begun. About one-third of Iowa's cropland is currently under no-till each growing season, and Iowa farmers have planted nearly a million acres of cover crops in recent years. You may be encouraged to learn that the seed corn farmer mentioned at the beginning of this chapter became a willing soil health convert and has been practicing no-till and planting cover crops on more of his acres every year since 2013. He now encourages others to join him in farming for healthy soils. Several hundred farmers across the state currently do just that. Of course, it is going to take a majority of farmers jumping on board to make a real and lasting difference, but I am hopeful that this quiet soil health revolution will continue to unfold.

NOTES

1. Natural Resources Conservation Service, *2017 National Resources Inventory: Summary Report* (Washington, D.C.: USDA–Natural Resources Conservation Service and the Center for Survey Statistics and Methodology and Ames: Iowa State University, 2020), https://www.nrcs.usda.gov/wps/portal/nrcs/main/national/technical/nra/nri/results.

2. National Agricultural Statistics Service, *2017 Census of Agriculture: United States Summary and State Data* (Washington, D.C.: U.S. Department of Agriculture, 2019), https://www.nass.usda.gov/AgCensus.

Farming for the Future

Ken Fawcett

I AM A SEVENTY-TWO-YEAR-OLD fourth-generation farmer in eastern Iowa. I work with my wife, Helen, nephew Kent, and son-in-law Troy to raise corn, soybeans, cover crops, trees, and prairie grasses and wildflowers on around 2,000 acres of some of the most fertile land in the world. It is amazing to me that the world's cultivated acres have remained relatively constant but that the world's farmers are producing so much more food through the technology available today.

When my ancestors arrived on this farm in 1853, their method of transitioning the native prairie to agriculture was through cutting, clearing, and plowing it. Turning the landscape black and barren was the only practical way to grow profitable crops. Tilling repeatedly until neither a cornstalk nor a bit of straw remained on the surface was the symbol of a good farmer. At that time, it was also the only way to control weeds, insects, and crop diseases. But it came at a catastrophic cost.

Exposing soil to sun, wind, and air releases carbon from soil organic matter into the atmosphere at an alarming rate. After the prairies were cultivated, the native soils lost up to half of their organic carbon. On average, half of our topsoil has eroded down the hills and into the valleys since the plow was introduced as a tillage tool. I vividly remember May 21, 1957, the day I stood by the middle branch of Wapsinonoc Creek after a violent thunderstorm, watching torrents of muddy water carrying our soil, seed, and fertilizer off the farm. Seeing the eroded soil leave the farm for the waterways was a powerful lesson to me as a young boy.

In the 1960s, we had all our land in a crop rotation. The cycle started with planting oats that we sold to Quaker Oats in Cedar Rapids. The oat straw provided bedding for our hogs, sheep, and cattle. The oats acted as a nurse crop for growing hay for at least two years: alfalfa, red clover, or bromegrass hay, feed for the ruminants. These crops protected the land to some degree. However, the inevitable plow then returned to prepare the soil for two years of corn, restarting the rotation cycle again. The plow was a necessary but destructive tool.

In 1971, we began conservation tillage and ditched the plow for a straight-shank Glencoe Soil Saver chisel, which left more than half of the crop residue on the land's surface and tilled vertically to increase infiltration of rainwater. We soon began experimenting with no-till, and by 1988 we began to plant crops with no tillage at all. This saved soil, nutrients, and moisture and began to replace carbon in the soil.

As cattle and grain markets continued to change and the need for forage diminished in the 1980s, the move toward more intensive rotation of corn and beans became widespread. We own less than 25 percent of the land we farm, and making this switch gave us a competitive return per acre for our ten landlords. We have grown a diversity of specialty corn and soybeans in an attempt to increase returns. These included seed corn for Pioneer, high-starch corn and tofu soybeans for the Japanese, and specialty soybeans to produce trans-fat-free Asoyia oil. We currently raise white corn for Quaker Oats grits and other breakfast cereals.

In the 1990s, we started reintroducing native biodiversity onto our farm. Contour buffer strips, once grasses, are now planted in pollinator mixes with short prairie grasses and thirty varieties of prairie flowers. We planted prairie grass filter strips along streams and native trees in the riparian buffers where cattle once grazed. Since 1986, we have planted over 15,000 trees.

Early in the twenty-first century, we started using cover crops to benefit the soil. This exciting and challenging practice allows us to protect and hold the soil year-round. We have grown rye, oats, wheat, radishes, and clovers as cover crops. Seeding methods have included airplanes, helicopters, fertilizer spreaders, drills, and air seeders. Cover crops obviously protect soil from wind and water erosion and can increase carbon sequestration, weed control, and water infiltration. Cover crops do not necessarily show an annual profit. Improving soil health does, however, ensure that my land will be productive for future generations.

Modern agricultural production relies on nonrenewable energy sources. It was not always that way. In the 1800s, power for farmwork and transportation came from the land. A good portion of a typical farm was devoted to raising the oats, hay, and pasture grasses needed to feed the horses, oxen, and mules that provided power to plow, disk, harrow, plant, cultivate, harvest, haul, and transport people and products. Many farm families made a living meeting the transportation needs of their city cousins. That started to change at the end of the nineteenth and the beginning of the twentieth centuries, when farm-grown renewable energy began to be replaced by fossil fuels, first by coal that powered steam engines, then by petroleum that powered internal combustion engines.

The shifts in cropping systems that accompanied the near-elimination of work animals, among other factors, threw farmers into decades of overproduction and resulting government controls. Now, with improved technology, the energy tide is turning once again. In 2020, we installed renewable energy sources on our farms. Through a net metering agreement with our utility company, our solar installation provides 100 percent of our electricity needs, including heating, air-conditioning, and pumping water at our home farm. We also generate 75 percent of the electricity we need for grain conditioning. Each month when I open my electric bill and see that I've generated more energy than I've used, I look to the future with hope. With renewable energy, rural America can once again achieve the energy independence of our great-grandparents.

Today's precision agriculture technology involves satellites, computers, engineering, biology, genetics, and much more in a way that gives accuracy, control, and efficiency to my farming operations. Precision agriculture technology helps me eliminate waste by accurately placing seed, fertilizer, and other materials in the quantity and location needed for optimum efficiency based on the soil and yield potential of the ground. We take soil samples every four years in GPS-controlled three-acre grids, and these provide the variable-rate placement of fertilizer to produce economically optimum yields. Our nitrogen is combined with a stabilizer to prevent leaching and denitrification. Genetically modified seeds have eliminated insecticide use and reduced herbicide use. All our crops are now planted into the past year's crop residue without any tillage. Cover crops add other plants to the rotation, enhance the soil, and help control pests. We have doubled our farm's yields of corn and soybeans since I started farming in 1971.

I have always looked to the future and enjoyed trying out new farming practices. I look forward to using technologies now in development, such as biologicals—naturally occurring substances that when applied to crops can provide pest protection, improve plant health, and increase productivity—and seeds and robots that will increase yields, cut the use of fertilizers, and reduce the use of pesticides. GPS mapping of every square foot of ground to rate farm productivity has already identified areas better suited to other crops as well as fragile and sensitive areas that should be set aside for conservation purposes. I believe that biodiversity should be part of every farm plan written by our state and federal agencies.

I also know that agricultural technology is very portable. Technological developments made and tested here in Iowa can be exported around the world to help increase food production, improve the lives of agricultural workers, and reduce pollution and the emission of greenhouse gases. Farmers and rural communities can provide the future food, fuel, and raw materials we need while protecting the environment. But I also realize that it will take everyone's collaboration, cooperation, and commitment to find our path to the future.

CHAPTER 2

Slurries of Sediment

The Problem of Soil Erosion

Keith E. Schilling

AS A RESEARCH GEOLOGIST, I've been working on interactions between water and the landscape for more than thirty years. But I didn't understand the nuances of soil erosion—the movement of soil particles by water—until I began walking through the reconstructed prairies and stream channels at Neal Smith National Wildlife Refuge outside of Prairie City, Iowa, starting in the mid-1990s. I was tasked with monitoring the effects of large-scale prairie plantings on the movement of water and soil in the 12,000-acre Walnut Creek watershed. My colleagues and I measured stream discharge (surface-water flow in the stream) and sediment (water-transported soils) in Walnut Creek for ten years and compared that monitoring record to a parallel monitoring record for Squaw Creek (now Ioway Creek), which has a watershed adjacent to Walnut Creek's but dominated by row crops. We expected to corroborate what previous research and modeling studies had predicted: converting about 40 percent (more than 5,000 acres) of the Walnut Creek watershed from cropland to tallgrass prairie had substantially reduced the export of sediment from that watershed. But do you know how much difference in annual sediment export we found between Walnut Creek and the agricultural Squaw Creek? None. No difference at all. To say that this was unexpected would be a gross understatement.

As I began to consider this seemingly inexplicable outcome, I realized that making sense of it required a better understanding of how soil erosion occurs in Iowa and how it has changed since Euro-American settlement began almost 200 years ago. What I found was that soil erosion processes were more complex than I had previously thought and that, as with many of Iowa's environmental problems, once-natural processes had been greatly intensified and accelerated by human use. This chapter is the tale of my journey of discovery.

To begin, it is important to understand that soil erosion is a natural process. Precipitation falling on the ground and flowing downhill naturally picks up soil particles and moves them from one spot to another. Long before humankind arrived on the scene, mountains and hillsides eroded and their particles were carried by flowing water to eventual deposition in oceans. Some eroded particles ended up on floodplains where rivers naturally meandered across wide valleys. Rivers eroded soils on the outside bends of their channels and deposited soils on the inside bends where water slowed down. However, with Euro-American settlement in Iowa and the establishment of large-scale agriculture, the natural process of soil erosion was greatly exacerbated.

Soil erosion occurs in two main ways. In the first, sheet and rill erosion, rainfall splashes on exposed soils and detaches particles from the soil surface. Flowing runoff then carries the particles downslope in a shallow sheet of water or in tiny channels called rills. The amount of sheet and rill erosion at any given site is highly dependent on the amount and intensity of rainfall, the texture and permeability of the soils (that is, their ability to soak up water), the slope of the land, and plant cover. Sheet and rill erosion is greatest under intense rains falling on steep, fine-textured soils with little to no vegetative cover. Such erosion in Neal Smith's planted prairies would be much less than that under row crops, because the prairie vegetation intercepts rainfall and provides surface roughness that slows runoff year-round. In contrast, land under row crops is bare for most of the year, so there is little to slow the runoff of water and soil.

The second form of erosion, channel bed and bank erosion, occurs when water flowing in sheets and rills becomes more concentrated and carves ephemeral gullies, small channels, and rivers. Soils erode because the energy of the flowing water plucks materials from the channel sides and bed. Sometimes the flow of water causes the channel sides to become unstable and soils erode as a slump or catastrophic failure. Soil erosion from concentrated flow can be seen in the development of ephemeral gullies at the edge of fields or in stream channels with bare exposed banks. Less obvious is erosion from the channel bed beneath the flowing water. All types of bed and bank erosion result from water's ability to detach, destabilize, and move soil particles.

While there are other types of soil erosion in nature, including erosion by wind and larger mass movements of soils and sediments down hillslopes, the dominant erosion types in Iowa are sheet and rill erosion and channel bed and bank erosion. Together, soil erosion from these two processes accounts for most of the sediment exported from Iowa's watersheds.

A HISTORY OF SOIL EROSION IN IOWA

When Euro-American settlers first arrived in Iowa, they encountered a gently rolling landscape covered by approximately 80 percent tallgrass prairie underlain by thick soils rich in organic matter. The prairie soils functioned like a natural sponge—allowing water to quickly infiltrate and storing rainfall, slowing runoff, and lessening erosion from raindrops. An early settler commented that "on fully vegetated lands practically no erosion occurs except possibly during storms of unusual violence, and then the erosion is seldom serious."[1]

Settlers soon began to plow the substantial prairie soils, unfortunately with little understanding of soil erosion. Deep moldboard plowing was done every year, often up and down rather than across hillslopes, and these plowings unleashed a tremendous amount of sediment. Ironically, most of the sediment eroded from upland areas was the same valuable topsoil that had sustained life on the former prairie. Estimates vary, but one study suggests that pre-1900 soil erosion completely removed this fertile topsoil from one-third of the farm ground in the Corn Belt states of North and South Dakota, Minnesota, Iowa, Missouri, Wisconsin, Illinois, and Indiana.[2]

The topsoils transported from hillsides tended to be deposited downslope in flat areas such as floodplains, which with time built up a thick blanket of what we call postsettlement alluvium. You can see this material today as a gray to light brown layer of silty sediment at the top of many exposed streambanks. I measured this postsettlement alluvium along Walnut Creek's banks, where it was an amazing two to six feet thick. The great magnitude of Iowa's soil erosion can also be seen in fields where the soil color on hillsides and convex slopes is now reddish and yellowish brown—the color of the deeper soils that once lay underneath black topsoils—while lowland areas are black with deposits of rich upland topsoil.

Return to Iowa's early erosion patterns. The first runoff from newly plowed slopes entered small stream channels and swales that had been naturally sized to accommodate the prairies' smaller and steadier flows. Early surveyors for the U.S. government's General Land Office in 1847 described Walnut Creek as a clear stream ten links wide (a total of about 6.6 feet) and six to twelve inches deep. But soon postsettlement's larger and faster flows began to deepen and widen the shallow prairie creeks. By 1905, Walnut Creek was said to have undergone "considerable downcutting," with the stream channel forming a "narrow gorge with precipitous walls."[3] Today the Walnut Creek channel averages about thirty to forty feet wide and more than ten feet deep.

Stream channels were also purposefully altered by Iowa's early farmers, who straightened and channelized—by cutting a new stream channel—many meandering creeks and rivers so they would shed water more quickly. This practice also squared up farm plots for easier cultivation. Channelization further accelerated water's downcutting and widening processes. Altogether, a massive amount of soil erosion occurred from the time of settlement to the early 1900s. We are still paying a high price for this legacy in many of our watersheds today.

The U.S. Department of Agriculture's Soil Conservation Service was formed in the 1930s and given the responsibility for reducing water and wind erosion of the nation's soils. Due to an extended drought and plowing of the fragile grasslands that left the soil surface exposed with no protective plant cover or residue, massive dust storms swept through the southern Great Plains during the Dust Bowl. This prompted the government to work with landowners to introduce soil conservation efforts to prevent wind and water erosion. Practices designed to reduce sheet and rill erosion were slowly implemented across the Corn Belt over the next few decades, including practices that are now standard for many farmers such as contour plowing (across rather than up and down hillsides), the construction of terraces and grassed waterways, and reduced tillage.

I can verify that these practices were implemented slowly because as part of the Walnut Creek project, I looked at regional air photos taken from the 1940s through the 1990s and didn't see any substantial use of conservation practices until the 1960s. However, there is evidence that the slow march toward improved soil conservation has been successful. In another study, my colleagues and I estimated annual sediment export in the Raccoon River using daily river-monitoring data from 1916 to 2009. We found that sediment concentrations were much higher from 1920 to 1950 than they are today. Concentrations have declined steadily since this time, even as the amount of water in the river has increased, and we attributed this mainly to improved soil conservation.[4]

The success of conservation practices in reducing sheet and rill erosion can be underappreciated if we forget where we started, but it is also clear that much more implementation is needed.

THE PROBLEMS WITH SOIL EROSION TODAY

Although it has decreased since the 1800s, soil erosion continues today and still presents multiple problems. Continued erosion of topsoil from agricultural fields reduces crop yields and necessitates the use of more and more fertilizer to compensate for losses in productivity. The U.S. Department of Agriculture says that soil erosion is "tolerable" if the maximum rate is less than five tons per acre per year, but consider the rate of soil formation in Iowa. We know that the majority of topsoils in the most recently glaciated part of Iowa—the north-central Des Moines Lobe—began forming at least 4,000 years ago, when tallgrass prairie interspersed with woodland became dominant. By the time of Euro-American settlement, topsoils were fourteen to sixteen inches deep. This suggests a rate of soil formation many times slower than the USDA's tolerable rate of soil loss, which was estimated several decades ago on the basis of best-informed judgment rather than rigorous research. In fact, many agronomists and soil scientists suggest that this tolerable rate is on the order of five to ten times greater than erosion rates that are actually sustainable. Indeed, new monitoring technology and modeling are able to better estimate soil erosion rates across the state, and in 2007 more than 6 million acres of soil were eroding at twice the sustainable rate of formation.[5]

Once it enters waterways, the transported soil, now termed sediment, is the most voluminous pollutant in Iowa, and it is considered by natural resources managers to be Iowa's most important water pollutant because of its significant impacts on biological species and processes. By filling wetlands, ponds, and reservoirs, sediment decreases the clarity of drinking water supplies and recreational waters and interferes with the growth and reproduction of fish and other aquatic life. More recently, suspended sediment in rivers and streams has been recognized as the primary carrier of phosphorus, which attaches to soil particles (see chapter 6). Phosphorus is an important nutrient for plant life, but high concentrations in rivers, lakes, and estuaries—like the Gulf of Mexico—work together with nitrate to stimulate excessive phytoplankton and algae growth and contribute to the development of oxygen-depleted dead zones.

Despite statewide adoption of conservation practices that reduce sheet and rill erosion, we still have a sediment problem in our rivers and streams. Increasingly, scientists are realizing that a large proportion of this sediment is due to channel bed and bank erosion. As I noted earlier, this type of erosion is a natural geomorphic process that typically occurs at the outside bends of meandering rivers. As a rule of thumb, you might expect 20 percent of a meandering river to have bank erosion on its outside bends. However, my colleagues and I recently estimated that the percentage of eroding bank lengths in Iowa rivers was 41 percent, more than double the natural rate, which suggests that this type of erosion is occurring at an excessive rate in the state.[6]

Why is this happening? Severe runoff from poorly managed agricultural fields and other factors such as stream channel straightening, removal of riparian vegetation, artificial drainage from subsurface tiles and ditches, urbanization, and an increase in heavy rains have led to greater and more energetic river flows. These higher flows have caused Iowa's river channels to deepen and widen and generally become more unstable. Unstable and poorly vegetated banks often fail and slough off into the water.

Along with researchers from Iowa State University, my colleagues and I have been using erosion pins to measure the rate at which streambanks are eroding in the state. Not a glamorous or high-tech tool, erosion pins are essentially rebar pounded into bare banks that are visited at regular intervals to measure how much has become exposed. By measuring erosion pins at several hundred streambanks across Iowa, we've estimated that streambanks in wadeable streams are receding about four to five inches per year and can recede more than fifteen inches per year in some locations. In larger, nonwadeable rivers, streambanks can erode even faster. We have concluded that sediment derived from streambank erosion is a major contributor to sediment export in several watersheds in Iowa, with streambank contributions ranging from less than 10 percent to 80 percent of annual sediment loads, depending on local conditions and streamflows.

Gullies are a type of channel bed and bank erosion that appear on hillslopes where runoff from fields coalesces into flowing water. Because they are ephemeral, typically enlarging after a large rainfall runoff event, they have been mapped less frequently than streambank erosion sites associated with flowing streams. Finding gullies in the landscape often depends on their size and how much they are repaired by farmers year by year. Some gullies can be hard to see if covered by grass or trees but believe me, you know one if you've fallen into it!

Researchers are becoming convinced that Iowa's soil erosion and sediment export is a combination of sheet and rill erosion, ephemeral gully erosion, and channel bed and bank erosion. This conclusion helps us understand the initially confounding results from the Walnut Creek monitoring project. When I evaluated upland areas in the Walnut Creek watershed, it was clear that replacing cropped fields with native prairie at Neal Smith did indeed reduce sheet and rill erosion substantially. However, when walking the stream channels in the watershed, we observed that channel bed and bank erosion was severe in many areas. In fact, approximately half of the stream channels were found to be severely eroding. When these features were examined in the Squaw Creek watershed, only 16 percent of the streambanks were eroding, but sheet and rill erosion was more dominant. Although the reasons for the differences between the two watersheds are complex, they relate to factors such as spatial patterns of channel straightening, riparian buffering, and land-use and cropping history.[7]

In the end, the two watersheds were exporting the same amount of sediment, but the sediment came from two very different sources. The Walnut Creek watershed was dominated by streambank erosion, while the Squaw Creek watershed was subjected primarily to ephemeral gully and sheet and rill erosion. Side by side, the two watersheds clearly displayed the two major types of erosion we now see across Iowa.

WHERE DO WE GO FROM HERE?

The problem of soil erosion and sediment transport in Iowa's rivers isn't going to go away anytime soon, so what can we do about it? We need to keep reducing soil erosion at its source, that is, in the upland cropped areas where sheet and rill erosion still dominates. When I look back on the past fifty years or so, it is amazing to see all the conservation practices that have been installed across Iowa's agricultural landscape. In rolling terrain, terraces, grassed waterways, contour cropping, riparian buffers, and various forms of reduced tillage are relatively common, especially in southern and western Iowa. However, much cropland still does not display any visible conservation practices, and this unprotected cropland is providing a disproportionately large share of the upland soil erosion.

New remote sensing and modeling efforts reveal that sheet and rill erosion will continue to be an issue into the future, especially with the increased frequency and intensity of the large rainfall events anticipated with climate change. Along streams and rivers where channel bed and bank erosion dominates sediment export, stream channels are now deeper, wider, straighter, and more prone to erosion than at any time in their history. Stream channels will continue to evolve and adjust to the historic changes imposed on them since the 1830s. It will take time for them to regain stability.

At this point, the restoration of river and larger creek channels (such as Walnut Creek) should be left to natural processes. Active restoration efforts such as armoring streambanks or installing meanders are terribly expensive and are not likely to work until the channel's hydrology is normalized. Again, in the face of climate change and increasing precipitation, rivers will continue to become more energized, their larger flows undercutting and eroding banks and further slowing channel recovery.

In contrast, some restoration efforts can be successful with smaller creek channels. I am encouraged by new approaches that focus on using natural processes—such as woody debris and both natural and analogue beaver dams—to stimulate stream evolution and readjustment without other human alterations. Thoughtful placement of low-head dams or weirs could also mimic and augment natural processes occurring in the stream. In areas prone to gully formation, grade stabilization structures, small dams, and farm ponds are often used to stop gullies from eroding upstream. These practices slow the pace of channel bed and bank erosion occurring across the landscape.

While soil erosion is a natural process that occurs everywhere soil and water meet, it has been greatly intensified and accelerated in Iowa since Euro-American settlement began in the 1830s. Our challenge will be to lessen the negative consequences of our current land management practices, increase the implementation of soil conservation practices, and give soils and stream channels time to recover from their historic disturbances.

NOTES

1. K. E. Schilling and P. Drobney, "Hydrologic Recovery with Prairie Reconstruction at Neal Smith National Wildlife Refuge, Jasper County, Iowa" (Washington, D.C.: U.S. Fish and Wildlife Service, 2014), https://www.iihr.uiowa.edu/igs/publications/uploads/2015-04-30_13-04-00_hydro%20synthesis%20report%20-%20final%20(print%20over)%20-%2004-23-2014%20(2).pdf.

2. E. A. Thaler, I. J. Larsen, and Q. Yu, "The Extent of Soil Loss across the U.S. Corn Belt," *Proceedings of the National Academy of Sciences* 118, no. 8 (2021), e1922375118.

3. Schilling and Drobney, "Hydrologic Recovery."

4. See C. S. Jones and K. E. Schilling, "From Agricultural Intensification to Conservation: Sediment Transport in the Raccoon River, Iowa, 1916–2009," *Journal of Environmental Quality* 40, no. 6 (2011): 1911–1923, and G. Villarini, K. E. Schilling, and C. S. Jones, "Assessing the Relation of USDA Conservation Expenditures to Suspended Sediment Reductions in an Iowa Watershed," *Journal of Environmental Management* 180 (2016): 375–383.

5. C. Cox, A. Hug, and N. Bruzelius, "Losing Ground" (Washington, D.C.: Environmental Working Group), 2011, https://static.ewg.org/reports/2010/losingground/pdf/losingground_report.pdf.

6. C. F. Wolter, K. E. Schilling, and J. A. Palmer, "Quantifying the Extent of Eroding Streambanks in Iowa," *JAWRA: Journal of the American Water Resources Association* 57, no. 1 (2021), doi:10.1111/1752-1688.12902.

7. K. E. Schilling, T. M. Isenhart, J. A. Palmer, et al., "Impacts of Land-Cover Change on Suspended Sediment Transport in Two Agricultural Watersheds 1," *JAWRA: Journal of the American Water Resources Association* 47, no. 4 (2011): 672–686.

Working with Mother Earth

Seth Watkins

MY NAME IS SETH WATKINS. I am the fourth generation of my family to care for Pinhook Farm—named after an oxbow on the Nodaway River by my grandfather's flour mill that looked like someone bent a pin into a hook—which was established by my great-grandfather James Shambaugh in 1848. My 3,000-acre farming operation is three miles southeast of Clarinda in southwest Iowa in a landform region known as the Southern Iowa Drift Plain. Pinhook Farm's primary revenue comes from the approximately 600 beef cows, their calves, and yearling cattle that graze our pastures. This is the most appropriate use of my farm's rolling land, which is vulnerable to erosion.

During the Great Depression of the 1930s, World War II, and the farm crisis of the 1980s, all of Pinhook Farm was put into row crops, either to meet the short-sighted goal of higher profits from grain or, in the 1980s, because cows were a liquid asset and could be used to make payments on variable rate loans with 22 percent interest. But my farm is not well suited to corn. Thus, over time, I have worked to restore its woodlands and perennial forage. To prevent my farm from ever being converted to crops again, I partnered with the Iowa Natural Heritage Foundation via the USDA's Agricultural Conservation Easement Program to establish a permanent easement that ensures that Pinhook Farm will remain a pasture farm forever.

Farmers often feel intense pressure from industry and society to maximize production. The fact that we are called producers instead of farmers says a lot. The truth is that until a blizzard in 1998, I farmed with a total focus on production. My attitude was that modern technology and determination could conquer anything Mother Nature threw my way. I noticed things that bothered me, such as muddy streams and diminishing numbers of birds and wildflowers on our land, but it was easier to ignore these problems when I focused on productivity.

One farming practice that had always concerned me was having my cows calve in February and early March. Industry wisdom was that by getting calving out of the way early, I could dedicate my labor to planting corn in April and I'd have larger calves to sell in fall, which to an agricultural economist probably looked good on paper. However, seeing a muddy shivering baby calf on a snowy March day never looked good to me.

The 1998 blizzard that transformed my farming struck on March 11 in the middle of calving season. Within hours the temperature dropped from 60 degrees to below zero, with fifteen inches of snow and sustained winds of forty miles per hour. For three days I worked around the clock sheltering cows and calves. This miserable experience was the inspiration I needed to trust my instincts and ask the most important question of my career: Why am I working against Mother Nature? What I really wanted was clean water, healthy soil, and happy cows. If the experts were right and I went broke because of my new approach, so be it. I'd had enough. I just wanted to do what was right by the cows and the land.

My first major change was moving my calving season from February to April. This small shift made wonderful things happen. The warmer April weather reduced my costs for fuel, equipment, and feed. Allowing the cows to express their natural instincts by calving on warm green pastures instead of in cold muddy lots reduced their stress and increased their productivity. Instead of going broke, I found that I had happy, healthy cows and a more profitable farm, and I had kickstarted a beautiful relationship with Mother Nature.

Sustainability is about continuous improvement. Over time, I worked to build a farming system that reduced my reliance on fossil fuels, equipment, synthetic fertilizers, and other farm chemicals. In their place, I enhanced the biodiversity and natural resources that truly sustain my farm.

The following practices have had the greatest impact. I have eliminated my grazing cattle's access to streams, ponds, and riparian areas. Instead, I pump water into upland watering tanks. By keeping cattle out of waterways and riparian areas and consistently providing them with clean water, I have increased the weight of seven-month-old calves by as much as fifty pounds each. In 2021, this resulted in additional revenue of about $87 per calf. Clean natural waters and untrampled riparian areas also create wonderful habitat for diverse insects, amphibians, and native plants.

I now rotate my cattle from one pasture to another. This rotational grazing allows pastures to rest and recover. Roots grow deeper, sequestering more carbon and improving the porosity and water-holding capacity of my soil, which makes the land more resilient to drought. In addition, moving cattle out of a pasture while the forage remains longer than six inches enhances the health, quality, and quantity of my forage.

One last effort—diversifying my pasture forage plants—has produced multiple benefits. The diversification began soon after I decided to have my cattle calve in April, which meant that I had to breed them the prior July or August when southern Iowa is at its hottest. The problem with this? Kentucky 31 fescue, now the dominant pasture grass in much of the Midwest, has many fine qualities. But in hot weather it produces a mild toxin that raises a cow's temperature slightly and decreases breeding success.[1] The solution? By introducing clover to my pastures and halting broadcast applications of herbicides, I was able to dilute fescue's influence and solve my conception problems. Diversifying my pastures with clover, which has a much higher protein content than grass, has also improved the quality of my forage, resulting in heavier, healthier cattle.

Because clover is a nitrogen-fixing legume, adding it also eliminated my need to fertilize pastures with synthetic nitrogen, which reduced my costs. In addition, the diversification forced me to eliminate broadcast spraying of my pastures, a typical management procedure that kills weeds but also eliminates plant biodiversity. Now I spot-spray only selected problem plants—multiflora rose, thistles, and thorny brush—which preserves the clover and other beneficial forbs and grasses that were naturally reappearing in my pastures. Reducing spraying also decreased my costs. Thus, by greatly reducing the use of synthetic fertilizers and farm chemicals, I've reduced my input costs by about $300 per cow, enhanced biodiversity, and improved my herd's forage and the quality of the water that leaves my farm.

One final point. My cows are the reason I can tend and restore the land and its natural resources while still making a profit. My cattle graze my multispecies cover crops in the winter, making these conservation plantings economically viable. In addition, grazing cattle has inspired me to diversify my corn-soybean rotation with oats and clover, which provide the cows with winter feed. And I have been able to retire fragile land that is not appropriate for row crops or grazing, putting it instead into native prairie plantings, which I have been doing as part of Iowa State

University's STRIPS research program. These practices are essential to protecting the natural resources we all depend upon. I fully understand that cattle can be harmful to our environment. But when it comes to regenerating our natural resources, it's not the cow, it's the how. Proper grazing is a big part of Iowa's long-term sustainability.

Focusing on stewardship and following nature's lead have made my farm more sustainable, profitable, and ecologically sound. It is also becoming more socially responsible: I feel that my farm is helping fight the increased poverty in our rural communities, with their declining and aging populations, and support public health issues associated with drinking water contaminated with farm chemicals. Farming with nature regenerates and protects the natural resources we all depend upon, and I trust that it will give my children a future filled with abundance, opportunity, and hope.

NOTE

1. Craig Roberts, "Tall Fescue Toxicosis" (Columbia: University of Missouri Extension, 2000), https://extension.missouri.edu/publications/g4669.

CHAPTER 3

Pushing the Limits

The Intensification of Agriculture

Christopher S. Jones

IF, LIKE ME, you are of the boomer generation, your childhood image of the Iowa farmer may have been something like this: fit and rugged, brown as a berry, manhandling animals with gnarled and meaty hands before hitting the fields on a John Deere model 60, stomping off the boot dust just before a sundown meal of fried chicken and apple pie, followed by an exhausted collapse into bed with 5:00 a.m. coming on fast. A generation or two prior—all that with no tractor. There was at least one house on each section and overalls-clad farm kids hopped on and off school buses headed for town. The big city of Des Moines was a destination only once a year—for the Iowa State Fair—maybe twice if your school made it to the world-famous Iowa Girls State High School Basketball Tournament.

As much as we may want to hang on to those images, farming and farm life in Iowa have trended away from them. Sixty or a hundred years after the fact, we may be tempted to think that a gradual process resulted in the production systems we see today as we drive across the countryside: tidy fields of only corn and soybeans, cattle in muddy feedlots instead of green pastures, many millions of hogs made invisible by the buildings that now house them, often on the horizon away from main thoroughfares. However, while the transition to Iowa Agriculture Version 2022 may have been continuous, it was not smooth and gradual. The evolution of Iowa farming has been like the evolution of much of life itself—punctuated—in this case by technological and economic forces that changed and intensified our farming systems. Many of these changes relate to energy—human and animal energy replaced by that of fossil fuels and their derivatives: fertilizers and other chemicals. These changes have meant more bushels and more protein but also more water pollution, greater loss of biodiversity, more soil degradation, and more greenhouse gas emissions.

Fritz Haber was a German Nobel laureate in chemistry who, in the years just prior to 1910, devised a process to synthesize ammonia from atmospheric nitrogen gas using hydrogen and a metal catalyst at high temperature and pressure. Prior to this, all terrestrial nitrogen on Earth had as its origin either oxidation of atmospheric nitrogen by lightning or fixation by bacteria in symbiosis with legumes. Haber's invention was first used to make explosives. It took another German Nobel laureate in chemistry, Carl Bosch, to upscale and industrialize Haber's procedure so that mass production of inorganic nitrogen fertilizers was possible. As a result of their efforts, Haber and Bosch unwittingly sparked a population explosion and almost single-handedly altered one of Earth's most important biogeochemical cycles, thus intensifying agricultural production in Iowa and around the world.

Following World War II, the increasing availability and affordability of inorganic fertilizers generated by the Haber-Bosch process made them a viable alternative to the organic nitrogen generated by legumes. About the same time, soybeans were emerging as a desired commodity crop. Thus, even though soybeans don't need nitrogen fertilizers, using inorganic fertilizers for nitrogen-hungry corn went hand in hand with the adoption of soybeans as Iowa's second cash crop. By the mid-1990s, oats and other traditional crops had virtually disappeared from the landscape, and our food animals—cattle, hogs, and poultry—were eating mainly corn and soybeans.

An acre of Iowa corn went from receiving an average of 16 pounds of commercial nitrogen in 1960 to 122 pounds in 1968 (it was about 190 pounds by 2020).[1] Soybean acreage increased 213 percent during this same time.[2] Iowa's cake had been baked, and our state's diverse farms with their integrated crop and livestock systems became an endangered species. The scientific literature is clear on this: while modern corn hybrids very efficiently use inorganic fertilizers, a greater portion of the nitrogen leaches beyond their roots compared to the organic nitrogen of legumes. This leached nitrate ends up in aquifers, drainage tile water, and ultimately Iowa's lakes and streams and the Gulf of Mexico, catalyzing the Dead Zone where aquatic life can't exist. In this new and intensified system, inorganic fertilizers are often applied long before corn can use them, and some are inevitably lost. The modern quest for the almighty bushel of corn does not tolerate a shortage of nutrients, resulting in the overapplication of inorganic fertilizers across Iowa.

PESTICIDES

Annual weeds have been the bane of farmers for centuries. Ironically, many of the weeds that plague Iowa farms were inadvertently brought here as seeds in the pockets of immigrant farmers. Some of our early crops—alfalfa and the clovers especially—suppressed or crowded out weeds by forming a near-turf-like ground cover. Corn, on the other hand, required bare soil for at least part of the year, and thus weed seeds found a favorable habitat in cornfields. The early remedies were iron and steel, that is, the iron and steel implements that disturbed the soil and disrupted weed growth. This worked well enough, but the resulting soil erosion was severe and many of our small river valleys are filled with eroded soil from a century of tillage. Following World War II and concurrent with the emergence of the chemical industry, farmers began to use herbicides to help eliminate weeds. Many of these early chemicals were toxic not just to weeds but to birds and other animals as well. Alachlor, Dicamba, 2,4-D, and Atrazine were a few of the early herbicides, some of which are still in use.

A new strategy for weed control had its beginnings in 1970. That year, Monsanto chemist John Franz and his team synthesized glyphosate, commonly known now as Roundup. The chemical is a broad-spectrum herbicide, meaning it can kill a lot of plant species. It's been especially effective on the annual grasses and broadleaf weeds that have been a drag on crop yields for centuries. Glyphosate became one of the most important chemicals in human history when other Monsanto scientists were able to genetically modify annual crops in ways that left them invulnerable to the herbicide. It quickly became the dream chemical for agriculture, annihilating everything in its path that didn't have the DNA antidote that was inserted into canola, alfalfa, cotton, sorghum, wheat, sugar beets, and, most importantly for Iowa, corn and soybeans. Roundup-ready soybeans were developed in 1996, and farmers loved this weed-control formula so much that by 2005, an astounding 87 percent of all U.S. soy contained the magic genes. Herbicide use on corn has grown from 11 percent of U.S. acres in 1950 to 95 percent in 1982.[3]

Safer and easier to use, Roundup seemed to be less toxic to humans and farm animals than many of the older herbicides it displaced. And it very likely did have some peripheral environmental benefits because it reduced the need for weed-control tillage, which reduced erosion. On the other hand, it was so effective that it possibly contributed to the decline of milkweed, which of course is necessary for the life cycle of the monarch butterfly. But on the whole, it's undeniable that Roundup let Iowa farmers intensify the production of the row crops corn and soybeans. Oats, alfalfa, and clovers, once common crops in Iowa, became a thing of the past for most farmers.

What about insecticides? Farmers have battled insects for millennia, using chemical insecticides all the while. But the move to mainly cash crops made insect infestations more problematic. Monocultures of certain crops like corn and an overall decline in biodiversity on Iowa farms gave insects like the European corn borer and corn rootworm the opportunity to thrive. Early Iowa insecticides included mainly formulations of arsenic but also sulfur, kerosene, mineral oil, and a few others. Some Iowa groundwater is still contaminated with arsenic from these early attempts to kill insects.

The post–WWII chemical industry gave farmers new and more potent poisons like DDT and the organophosphorus family of insecticides. In just five years, from 1947 to 1952, the USDA registered 10,000 new insecticides. These chemicals proved profitable for farmers—every dollar spent produced three to five dollars in extra revenue from increased crop yields.[4] But these chemicals took a toll on the environment and continue to do so. In 1962, Rachel Carson wrote poignantly in *Silent Spring* of the price paid by birds and other wild creatures in our quest for the almighty bushel.

As with weeds, scientists began looking to DNA for the key to open new doors for insect control. In the late 1990s, genetically modified, insect-resistant corn hybrids were approved for use.[5] DNA from a naturally occurring soil bacterium was inserted into corn DNA. Before that time, caterpillars of European corn borers and other insects fed on corn, damaging the plants and leaving them vulnerable to other pests such as fungi. Now, with the genetic modification, corn plants produce a toxin that is effective in controlling the insects. Bt-corn, named after the donor bacterium, now dominates the corn market with about 82 percent of the seeds containing the genetic modification.[6]

The latest major development in pest control is the use of seed coatings to protect soybean and corn seeds while they lie ungerminated in the ground. The neonicotinoid family of chemicals is used to coat the seeds and protect them from insects before the plants emerge. Environmental concerns plague these chemicals as well: they have been detected in drinking water supplies, and they have broad unintentional impacts on a wide range of species, causing, for example, immune suppression in bees and fish.[7]

While many will say that genetic modification for pest control has been an overall environmental good, there can be no doubt that it has also enabled farmers to intensify corn and soybean production at the expense of other crops and overall plant biodiversity, including native plant diversity. Synthetic chemicals, many of which are derived from and applied with equipment powered by fossil fuels, have replaced tillage and hand weeding (especially of soybeans), and these chemicals have had both direct and indirect consequences for the environment.

THE CONCENTRATION OF LIVESTOCK

The emergence of tractors, soybeans, and commercial fertilizers made the presence of work animals and their food crops—oats, alfalfa, and clovers—unnecessary on farms. This enabled many Iowa farmers to intensely focus on corn and soybean production. Demand for animal protein, however, continued to increase along with world population and income levels. With fewer farmers wanting or needing livestock, those who continued production greatly enlarged and intensified their operations. This is especially evident in Iowa with hogs, the state's primary livestock animal. In 1980, 65,000 Iowa farmers raised a total of 13 million hogs; by 2002, the number of hog farmers had dwindled to 10,000, but total hog numbers had increased to 14 million. The average number of hogs being raised by an Iowa hog farmer at any single time has skyrocketed from 200 to 4,700 in the last forty years.[8] And bear in mind that a hog reaches market weight in six months, so the actual number raised in a calendar year is double this.

This dramatic shift in production has resulted in many hogs being concentrated in certain areas of the state as well as in a geographic alignment with buyers, packinghouses, and feed and equipment suppliers and haulers. Similar scenarios have also played out with cattle and poultry. Hogs are raised most notably in northwest, north-central, and southeast Iowa. Large areas of Iowa actually have very few hogs. But the total numbers are high. Iowa's area is only 1.5 percent of the U.S. total, but our state is home to 34 percent of the country's hogs—25 million in 2020—and although the population of Iowa beef cattle actually declined about 50 percent from 1980 to 1990, it has remained fairly stable since then, numbering about 900,000 in 2021.[9] But many cattle no longer spend much time grazing on pastures, having been concentrated instead into feedlots or covered but open buildings where their manure accumulates, presenting the same sort of environmental challenges as confined hog production. The population of egg-laying chickens has flown higher and faster than even that of pigs. In 1997, Iowa had 21.5 million layers; fast-forward twenty years, and Iowa was home to 56.6 million laying chickens. By 2020, an astounding 95 percent of all Iowa laying chickens were part of operations that housed 100,000 or more birds.[10]

The transition from diverse multispecies farms to farms specializing in the intense production of corn and soybeans, with a subset of the latter raising concentrated livestock, has produced both efficiencies of scale and negative environmental and sociological consequences, most noticeably water pollution. All these animals produce a lot of waste, and manure is a good fertilizer for our corn crops. Fertilizing with manure generated by modern livestock confinements, however, is a much more complicated and management-intense process. First, it's expensive to haul manure. On a pound-per-pound basis, commercial fertilizers are more nutrient-dense than manure, because manure is mostly water. Water is heavy, and it takes a lot of energy to haul it, so it doesn't make economic sense to haul manure more than about five miles. Beyond that, the farmer may as well buy commercial fertilizers. Second, exactly how much nitrogen is in the manure and how much will be available to the crops can be highly variable and difficult to quantify. For this reason, many farmers use manure to supplement a regimen of commercial fertilization or vice versa. Research has established that where livestock are concentrated and their wastes are incorporated into the fertilization scheme, stream nutrient levels are higher and the water is thus more polluted.

The amount of corn needed for animal feed has not changed much since 1980. During the same period, corn exports have been relatively stable, notwithstanding a modest increase in recent years. Corn yields, however, keep going up and up and up and have increased from about 100 bushels per acre in 1980 to about 175 today. All that corn had to go somewhere, and that somewhere was into our cars.

Although Iowans have put gasoline blended with ethanol in a 90:10 ratio into their gas tanks since about 1980, the widespread use of ethanol as a liquid fuel did not take off until the Energy Policy Act of 2005 expanded the amount of biofuel—any fuel derived from plant biomass—required to be mixed with gasoline.[11] In 2020, the U.S. Environmental Protection Agency required that liquid fuels sold in the U.S. contain in total about 20 billion gallons of biofuels, and this amount was slated to increase further. Soybeans are also made into renewable fuel—biodiesel, biomass-derived oils, or blends of diesel fuel and biomass oils—and the EPA required that 2.43 billion gallons of that stock be used in 2020.[12] These required ratios are part of what we commonly call the Renewable Fuel Standard. In 2020, more than 50 percent of Iowa's corn and about 20 percent of our land area were committed to ethanol production.[13]

There's been a mountain of peer-reviewed literature on the environmental pros and cons of crop-derived fuels, and it is safe to say that they modestly reduce greenhouse gas emissions compared to petroleum. Whether the environmental trade-offs linked to the intensified land use and degraded water quality associated with corn production are worth it and how they compare to the environmental costs of fossil fuel extraction have been left to politics. Policy seems to be driven, however, by farm-state zeal to continue doing what we have always done best: produce corn. It's Iowa's birthright, and our state has acted as if we should produce as much corn as we can, and let the rest of the world figure out what to do with it. But those days may be numbered. As electric cars seem poised to capture much of the vehicle market, reduced demand for liquid fuels in general and ethanol in particular looms on the horizon. It will be interesting to see how Iowa and other Corn Belt states respond to this and other energy trends.

The diverse multicrop farms of the pre–WWII era have been replaced in Iowa by farms dominated by two species—corn and soybeans—with livestock being concentrated on a relatively small percentage of farms. Such specialization reduced the need for human labor, enabling successful farmers to expand their operations at the expense of their less successful neighbors. The transition to this intense, all-cash-crops-all-the-time system has been continuous but not gradual. When I drive across the Iowa countryside now, I'm astonished by how clean the landscape and our farms look. Neat rows of corn and soybeans, nary a weed in sight, are bordered by mowed ditches that resemble suburban front lawns. Animals no longer linger around the well-painted barns; they're confined to a long metal building on the hill off in the distance. The whitewashed foursquare farmhouses are being replaced by brick McMansions. And long gone is my childhood image of hardscrabble individualists scratching out a living in the heart of North America. They've been replaced by modern businesspeople assisted by modern technologies. Such is the intense production system that is today's Iowa.

It's important to recognize that very few people in 1880 or even 1980 were making decisions designed with Iowa Agriculture Version 2022 in mind. Rather, decisions were being based on the needs of the day. Reconciling agriculture with our environmental objectives of the future will require strategic thinking that articulates environmental goals and makes decisions with those goals, not just the number of bushels, in mind.

NOTES

1. J. M. Gronberg and N. E. Spahr, "County-Level Estimates of Nitrogen and Phosphorus from Commercial Fertilizer for the Conterminous United States, 1987–2006" (Washington, D.C.: U.S. Geological Survey, 2012), https://pubs.usgs.gov/sir/2012/5207.

2. "Quick Stats" (Washington, D.C.: USDA–National Agricultural Statistics Service, 2021), https://quickstats.nass.usda.gov.

3. Dan Stork, Beulah Gocke, and Alex Martin, "The Golden Age of Pesticides" (York, Neb.: Wessels Living History Farm, 2007), https://livinghistoryfarm.org/farminginthe50s/pests_01.html.

4. Ibid.

5. G. P. Munkvold and R. L. Hellmich, "Genetically Modified Insect Resistant Corn: Implications for Disease Management," *APSnet Plant Pathology Online Feature* 15, 1999.

6. "Recent Trends in GE Adoption" (Washington, D.C.: USDA–Economic Research Service, 2020), https://www.ers.usda.gov/data-products/adoption-of -genetically-engineered-crops-in-the-us.

7. See K. L. Klarich, N. C. Pflug, E. M. DeWald, et al., "Occurrence·of Neonic- otinoid Insecticides in Finished Drinking Water and Fate during Drinking Water Treatment," *Environmental Science and Technology Letters* 4, no. 5 (2017): 168–173, and M. L. Hladik, D. W. Kolpin, and K. M. Kuivila, "Widespread Occurrence of Neonicotinoid Insecticides in Streams in a High Corn and Soybean Producing Region, USA," *Environmental Pollution* 193 (2014): 189–196.

8. "Quick Stats."

9. Ibid.

10. Ibid. And see the Iowa Department of Natural Resources' Animal Feeding Operation database at https://programs.iowadnr.gov/animalfeedingoperations.

11. K. Malmedal, B. Kroposki, and P. K. Sen, "Energy Policy Act of 2005 and Its Impact on Renewable Energy Applications in USA," IEEE Power Engineering Society General Meeting, Tampa, Fla., June 2007.

12. "Final Renewable Fuel Standards for 2020, and the Biomass-Based Diesel Volume for 2021" (Washington, D.C.: U.S. Environmental Protection Agency, 2019), https://www.epa.gov/renewable-fuel-standard-program/ final-renewable-fuel-standards-2020-and-biomass-based-diesel-volume.

13. "Corn Facts" (Johnston, Iowa: Iowa Corn Growers Association, 2019), https://www.iowacorn.org/media-page/corn-facts#:~:text=What%20is%20 it%20used%20for,percent%20of%20all%20American%20ethanol.

Farming My Values

Levi Lyle

I LIVE IN WASHINGTON COUNTY in southeast Iowa and farm corn and soybeans as well as niche fruit crops like honeyberries, tart cherries, and aronia berries. Along with my wife and our children, I sell our products directly to market and manage our farm as a U-pick. Our row crops consist of 600 acres of corn and soybeans. Sixty acres of the 600 are devoted to certified organic corn and beans and the berry crops.

Like many farm kids, after high school I left without a plan to return. More than ten years later, after I went to college and graduate school at the University of Northern Iowa and worked as a high school biology teacher, social worker, and college coach, the arrival of children gave my wife and me a new perspective on life. Family would become our guiding light, both the candle illuminating the way and the guidepost to measure all our activities.

Thus, when we were offered the opportunity to move back to the community where we both had been raised, we knew doing so was the right decision. Both our families still resided on farms there. I knew I wanted to farm. And we were fortunate to have support and encouragement from my father, who is still actively involved in the farm's day-to-day operation. Without these, I would have faced the barriers that discourage many young farmers from entering agriculture—high costs of farmland and limited access to it, large start-up investments, lack of experience, and market volatility—and I would have had difficulty getting started. Even with these aids, for a while I maintained an off-the-farm job while inspiration and effort paved the way toward full-time farming and organic agriculture.

From the start I knew I needed to align my farming practices with what I felt was right. My life was showing me that how we farm, the prevalence of cancer, and the state of our environment are threads of a single story about our rural communities. Previously, as a running back on the UNI football team, I had experienced the power of food as medicine. Both my journey to achieve optimal physical performance and my childhood memories of my father's diagnosis of cancer, which he successfully overcame, were at work within me.

I also remembered that when I was a child, in the 1980s, DDT had dramatically reduced bald eagle populations and the species was on the brink of extinction. In the years before moving back to the farm in 2010, I had only rarely seen bald eagles. After returning, I found populations had recovered, and eagles could be seen daily around the farm, sometimes even nesting high in old oak trees.

These realizations all supported my desire to farm organically, that is, to grow crops without synthetic pesticides or fertilizers in accordance with the National Organic Program standards. And I also wanted to maintain an intimate connection to the land like my father and grandfathers had done. For me, this has meant remaining small-scale and using farming practices that reflect nature's complex interconnections.

One extremely beneficial way I have done so combines practicing no-till and planting cover crops with the use of a device called a roller crimper that allows farmers to reduce or eliminate herbicide use while improving soil health. No-till is the conservation practice of planting crops without disturbing the soil with tillage equipment. Cover crops, which are grown from fall until spring when the land would otherwise sit fallow, protect the soil from the erosion and nutrient loss that pollute our waterways. Cover crops are often used as part of no-till agriculture.

The roller crimper is an implement attached to my tractor that lays the cover crop down, creating a weed-suppressing mat. Five years ago, I began using the no-till practice of roller crimping rye on organic soybeans. I plant a rye crop in October that grows through the winter. When the rye reaches maturity in early June, it is pushed down and "crimped" by the roller crimper, which effectively kills the cover crop without severing it from contact with the ground. Once the rye has been rolled and crimped, I plant soybeans directly into it. I accomplish all this by installing both a front-mounted roller crimper and a rear-mounted planter on my tractor, which allows me to do the whole operation in a single pass.

The one-pass approach has been crucial to improving my farming, my soils, and my profitability in many ways. It cuts down on my labor, decreases the use of fuel, and greatly reduces the soil compaction caused when tractors make many passes over the same ground as farmers plant and later spray their crops. What's more, while at first I limited use of the roller crimper to my organic acres, I have since found that I can profit by using it on my more extensive conventionally farmed acres. Thus I have eliminated herbicide use across much of my entire soybean acreage.

Furthermore, with my cover crop remaining alive in the soil as long as possible, the row crops reap multiple benefits. In addition to the way that the cover crop mulch suppresses weeds, I am putting armor on the topsoil and simultaneously creating the conditions to feed more soil microbes. By using no-till, cover cropping, and roller crimping, I am protecting the soil from sunlight—which causes evaporation of water and gassing off of carbon—and boosting carbon sequestration in the prairie-generated soils. I like to think that my actions resemble something bison may have done, their hooves knocking down the plants they did not eat and creating a soil-covering mat not unlike what's produced by my roller crimper. Boosting carbon sequestration provides a valuable service to society by helping mitigate climate change.

Questions of yields and profitability weigh heavily on any farmer. I have been incredibly happy with the amount of money I am saving by roller crimping instead of using herbicides and by making just one pass when I plant. Using these regenerative methods is improving my profits while building healthier soils and helping me address climate change.

For me, farming is also about safeguarding my family's health. I used to worry when I came home that my family would be exposed to insecticide and herbicide residues on my clothing. Now that worry is gone. Knowing that my children, who range in age from five to thirteen, can safely participate in farm activities is greatly rewarding. And I have begun to see butterflies and bees return to my fields.

Each season of the year has work my children can assist with. This is primarily mowing as well as maintaining and harvesting the bushes where our berry crops grow. Harvests are staggered by design, which means there is something new to pick and enjoy each month of the summer: honeyberries ripen in early June; tart cherries ripen in early July; aronia berries ripen in late August.

While many farmers profitably make the transition to organic production, I have seen that profitability alone is not enough to sustain a farmer's motivations. To endure the many challenges, I fall back on my commitment to a community that can support more small producers, who in turn support more local businesses to service those producers. This could mean the difference between keeping your local school open or seeing it close. It means giving the next generation an opportunity to farm. I hope to be part of a shift from an extractive agricultural paradigm to one of regenerative economics that values the most important system of all—that of our human communities. I endeavor to create value with principles that will remain staples of sustainable rural life: care for the land and regenerative stewardship. It is these reasons, not just financial profits, that drive me to succeed.

CHAPTER 4

The Regenerative Agriculture Movement
A Vision for the Future

Lisa Schulte Moore

MY DEVELOPING FORESTRY career took an unexpected turn when I arrived in Iowa from the Great Lakes region in 2003. As a scientist who seeks to inform how we use, manage, and restore natural resources, I was fascinated to find the core challenge I had been working on in forestry—balancing the short-term economic needs of landowners and rural communities with sustaining natural resources in perpetuity—sharpened and intensified in Iowa's agricultural context. I was hooked.

I have now spent close to two decades in Iowa soaking up as much knowledge as I can about agriculture from other scientists, farmers, and anyone else willing to share information. I have conducted interdisciplinary research with colleagues at Iowa State University and beyond to create new knowledge and technology to show what's possible. I have worked with farmers and other stakeholders to understand what's plausible. I now know what sustainable Iowa agriculture should look like. While the path toward this vision will not be easy, a few simple steps can get us well along our way. It all starts by providing widespread support for the farmer-leaders working to regenerate our agricultural soils.

IOWA'S SOIL HEALTH PROBLEM

Iowa is one of the few places in the world where climate, soil, and human ingenuity have conspired to create agricultural abundance on a vast scale. The combination of these factors has enabled our state to lead the nation in the production of corn, pork, eggs, ethanol, and bioproducts and also to produce large quantities of soybeans, beef, and dairy. While we celebrate this abundance, the extent of production along with its associated landscape simplification has unintentionally led to negative outcomes for our soils, as has been outlined in the previous chapters in this section.

The fundamental problem is the way that our two main crops—corn and soybeans—are typically grown: singly in rows with bare soil in between. Planted in late April to early June, they are ideally harvested in September for soybeans or October for corn. These practices leave our world-renowned soils bare and vulnerable to erosion for the remainder of the year. As a result, soil degradation is widespread; in some areas, the extent of degradation is so large that soil classifications identified during the original soil surveys no longer apply.[1] The predominant corn and soybean cropping systems and the concentrated animal production systems that depend on them are vulnerable to losing carbon and nutrients to air and water. When lost from crop fields, carbon and nutrients become climate and water-quality problems.

Our current production systems—stimulated by human ingenuity to improve farm efficiency, safety, and profitability—also require few people to run them. The social fabric of farming communities thus erodes with population decline and the lack of new economic opportunities. There are fewer people left in rural areas to notice soil degradation or care for our soils. Many people, farmers and consumers alike, are now looking at regenerative agriculture—farming methods that rejuvenate soil health—as a way to strengthen both farms and rural communities.

WHAT IS SOIL HEALTH, AND WHY IS IT IMPORTANT?

Appreciation of soil is not new. An extensive soil conservation culture developed in the United States as a result of the Dust Bowl of the 1930s, when President Franklin Delano Roosevelt proclaimed, "The nation that destroys its soil, destroys itself." Thousands of years earlier, Plato lamented soil degradation in what is now Greece. Early cultures in the Amazon basin nurtured the agricultural productivity of typically nutrient-poor tropical soils by adding charcoal. While appreciation for soil has been long-standing, what is new is our fuller, deeper understanding of soil patterns and processes and the agricultural practices that contribute to soil health.

Today we appreciate the fact that healthy soils are made up of complex ecosystems with intricate structures that are teeming with life. Life underground, just like life aboveground, needs to be fed, watered, and protected from the elements. In recognition of this basic fact, the mantra of Practical Farmers of Iowa, a farmer-led nonprofit organization that equips farmers to build resilient farms and communities, is Don't Farm Naked. Keeping a soil healthy requires continuous cover, including continuous living-plant cover with roots in the ground. Plants provide a jacket that protects soil from exposure to heat, cold, wind, and driving rains. Healthy plants also form a soil's pantry: they consume only part of the energy they harness from the sun's rays through photosynthesis, leaving the leftovers to nourish soil bacteria, fungi, and animals.

Plant—or crop—diversity is also important. Just like people, soils do better with a diverse and balanced diet. Livestock in good numbers further support healthy soil: they help maintain plant diversity through grazing; they recycle nutrients and further diversify a soil's food source with their raw, composted, or digested manure; and they move around beneficial soil microbes, replenishing them in areas where they may have been lost. It's also important to leave a protective cover of crop residues following harvest and to minimize soil disturbance during all farming operations. Together, these practices form the five principles of soil health: maintain continuous living cover, diversify plantings, include livestock, protect the soil, and minimize soil disturbance.

The U.S. Department of Agriculture defines soil health as "the continued capacity of soil to function as a vital living ecosystem that sustains plants, animals, and humans."[2] We're learning more about what healthy soils can do to give back to farms and society every day. For example, healthy soils require less fertilizer, instead harnessing soil biology to fuel crop and livestock productivity and improve their nutritional value; sequester carbon from the atmosphere and store it as soil organic matter, helping us adapt to and mitigate climate change; act like a sponge during heavy rainfalls, holding water within the landscape and reducing flooding; filter nutrients and harmful bacteria from water, helping keep it clean for drinking and recreation; and provide habitat for the multitude of subterranean organisms that create soil biodiversity, including vertebrate and invertebrate animals, fungi, and bacteria.

The Nature Conservancy, one of the world's largest conservation organizations, sums it up this way: "Soil health is inextricably linked to broader conservation goals."[3] Farmers commonly employ one or more soil health practices within their cropping systems because, as my farmer colleague Gary Van Ryswyk puts it, "If you farm, you do not want to lose your soil."

Applying all five practices together is a big challenge but an exciting one that forms the core of the regenerative agriculture movement.

WHAT IS THE REGENERATIVE AGRICULTURE MOVEMENT?

The idea that soil can not only be *sustained* but also *rejuvenated* within a productive and profitable farming operation is core to the regenerative agriculture movement. While the concept is not new, its mainstreaming is. You can now find information about regenerative agriculture in widely accessible books, the Minnesota Public Radio podcast *Field Work*, and the film *Kiss the Ground*.[4] As these sources and others detail, reasons for the movement are diverse and sometimes profound.

There is no simple recipe for regenerative farming, and that's part of its allure. Farmers with farms of all sizes, from small to large, talk about how their efforts to become regenerative have made farming an interesting occupation for them again. They each need to determine the right mix of practices that work for their operation, whether it's fruit, vegetable, grass, or grain; dairy, beef, pork, or poultry; small or large; organic or not. They all need to figure out how to balance short-term productivity with building soils over the long term given the natural, financial, community, and other resources available to them. Most farmers using regenerative techniques approach it as a journey, with each new growing season providing an opportunity to learn more.

Regenerative farmers typically have complex operations that require more people than conventional crop farms, and they manage farms as landscapes rather than as individual fields. They pay close attention to their costs as much as their income and strive to replace chemical or mineral inputs purchased off the farm with biological ones they can generate using natural processes on their farms. They reduce risk by having a diversity of crops at different stages at any given time, and they incorporate livestock into their operations both for soil health and because livestock can use crops that can't be sold. They generate additional income from the sale of the animals or their meat, eggs, dairy, and associated products. Francis Thicke's essay, in section III, describes how his regenerative grazing system for dairy cattle cuts carbon dioxide emissions even as it supports him financially.

Seth Watkins—see his essay in this section—approaches regenerative agriculture by doing his best to farm in nature's image. Seth owns and operates Pinhook Farm in southwest Iowa; his primary enterprise is a grass-based cow-calf operation. After they are weaned from their mothers, Seth grazes his calves to about 800 pounds before placing them in a feedlot for finishing. He also raises corn, soybeans, and small grains, manages native prairie and forest on his property, and leases his land for deer and pheasant hunting. While he doesn't farm organically, Seth is judicious in his application of chemical fertilizers and pesticides, preferring to use the more natural tools of continuous living-plant cover, including legumes, to build soil health; he also uses grazing and fire to cycle nutrients and control pests. He employs prairie strips—patches of reconstructed native vegetation interlaced within croplands—which have been shown to dramatically reduce soil erosion, improve water quality, and provide wildlife habitat with effects on grain yield proportionate to the amount of land taken out of crop production.[5] The hunting leases help him pay for the additional costs associated with conservation on his farm, including cover crops, prairie strips, and farm ponds.

Kellie and AJ Blair now operate a diversified farm in central Iowa, but it wasn't always that way. Fifteen years ago, they raised corn using full-tillage soil management as feed for hogs raised for a conventional market. Driven to meet their long-term sustainability goals, over time they have transitioned to no-till or low-till cropping systems and longer crop rotations, and they have increased diversity by adding crops—soybeans, cover crops, oats, and alfalfa—and cattle. Their beef is processed by a small butchery in their community and direct-marketed mostly to local buyers. Their farm now generates multiple income streams for economic resilience while helping build soil and protect water quality. The cattle, in particular, were an important addition to their farm. They add value to cover crops by turning forage into beef through grazing. They build soil structure, fertility, and biological complexity with their manure.

Bryan and Lisa Sievers raise crops, feed cattle, and produce renewable energy on their eastern Iowa farm. Environmental stewardship is a family ethic for the Sieverses and their children. They consider the land's topography by farming on the contour and using no-till or strip-till farming methods. They also incorporate terraces, grassed waterways, and grassy field borders where needed to protect soil, water, and wildlife. In 2009, they wanted to expand their beef cattle feedlot to improve their finances, but they were concerned about the effects on soil health, their carbon footprint, and water quality. Their solution was to redesign their entire farm system around the concept of circularity, with the outputs of one component providing the inputs to another. Key to this effort was the addition of two biodigesters: large tanks in which manure and soiled bedding from their cattle operation are mixed with biomass from cover crops; microbial processes then convert these materials into biomethane gas, which is burned to produce energy. The material that remains following biodigestion forms a carbon- and nutrient-dense soil amendment that fertilizes their crops and boosts soil health.

The chapters and essays in this book offer additional examples of how farmers across Iowa are now learning to better manage resources to enhance both economic and environmental outcomes. Clearly there is no one cookie-cutter recipe, but regenerative farmers care deeply both about the future of their farms and about leaving Iowa's land, air, water, and wildlife better off. They see improving the environment as central to improving their prosperity. They act on these values by minimizing soil disturbance through never-, no-, or low-till soil management practices; managing for continuous soil cover by planting winter crops or cover crops; integrating more plant diversity into their farms by using multispecies cover crop mixes and longer crop rotations (for example, three to six years); placing low-yielding acres or areas particularly vulnerable to soil and nutrient loss into continuous perennial cover using native grassland, wetland, or woody species as appropriate—the use of native plant species is important because they are well adapted to Iowa's climate and soils, and our native wildlife is adapted to them—and, finally, raising livestock in addition to crops.

My vision for sustainable Iowa agriculture focuses on making these practices—which form the core of the regenerative agriculture movement—the norm rather than the exception. In my mind's eye, I see a future where farms of different sizes and emphases collaborate with one another to ensure that our soil stays covered, nutrients are cycled, and more water is absorbed and held. I see farms where livestock, especially cattle, have returned because they provide the economic reason for crop diversity, including winter, spring, and perennial crops; offer management flexibility; facilitate farm resilience; and support additional jobs and businesses on farms and in communities. I see bioenergy production as a key part of the sustainability formula for the same reasons. And I see a future where farmers receive a fair price for their crops and livestock and are financially rewarded for producing ecosystem services of societal importance—for example, carbon sequestration, nutrient retention and water purification, flood control, and biodiversity preservation.

SCALING UP THE REGENERATIVE AGRICULTURE MOVEMENT

All farmers appreciate healthy soil, so why aren't they all using regenerative practices? Because regenerative farming is more complicated than the farming systems that currently dominate Iowa agriculture, it requires a change in support systems.

First, transitioning to regenerative practices involves building a supportive community. As with most people, farmers prefer to learn from others who are like them. For farmers looking to make changes, meeting with, seeing, and learning from other farmers are crucial parts of the process. Through field days, workshops, webinars, social media, and community-based events, organizations like Practical Farmers of Iowa have been encouraging farmers to become regenerative for over thirty years.

But a supportive farm community isn't enough to make these changes widespread. The second crucial piece of the transition puzzle calls for educating consumers. For many of us who live in the U.S. or another developed country, agricultural abundance is so ubiquitous that it's easy to forget food doesn't simply come from the grocery store. As a result, we too often take for granted the natural resources, livestock, and people required to provide us with our daily sustenance. But as farmer, writer, and activist Wendell Berry notes in his book *What Are People For?* "Eating is an agricultural act." We are all part of a cycle of life nourished by agriculture. We all need to do our part by making informed choices at the grocery store—smart choices not only about our own health but also about soil health and farm health.

The third crucial support element involves policies and programs that are better at balancing the short-term economic needs of landowners and rural communities with the necessity of sustaining natural resources in perpetuity. These are needed among national, state, and private actors. Many of the barriers to changing farm practices are systemic: they exist at multiple points along supply chains, within markets, and in government policies. Farmers and consumers can't make these changes on their own. They need help at every point along the supply chain. Through trial and error and with an eye toward continuous improvement, organizations are stepping up to assist. Businesses, universities, and governmental and nongovernmental organizations in Iowa and beyond are now facilitating this transition in the ways discussed in the next section.

Fourth, if we are to scale up the regenerative agriculture movement, we need people who are willing to put ego and tradition aside and dedicate themselves to honest conversations and an openness to change. Farmers, scientists, food retailers, and even chefs play crucial roles in educating eaters about what is possible and how much it costs. Eaters play a crucial role by choosing and, for those who are able, paying the higher cost of food that is grown according to their values. The whole process starts with being able to connect—farmers, eaters, and everyone in between—as people. We do this by listening, recognizing that we all require a safe and plentiful food system, and showing that we care for the people who produce our food as well as the soil resources that support us all.

REASONS TO HOPE

We have reasons to hope that Iowa's agricultural future will be more sustainable than today's. First, more than ever before, there's a broadening recognition of the need for improved soil health. Compared to recent generations, we have better scientific methods, data, and understandings of how soils work. We have more means to share and amplify our knowledge. And we have more ways through which farmers and consumers can connect with one another.

For example, it's hard to pick up a farm magazine today and not find a story about soil health. In 2014, the U.S. Department of Agriculture, which has enormous influence on what farmers produce, launched the far-reaching educational campaign Unlocking the Secrets of Soil that focused on building public awareness of the importance of soil health. In 2017, 76 percent of farmers indicated they were paying more attention to soil health than they previously had.[6] By 2021, businesses all along agricultural supply chains—from input providers like Land O'Lakes, equipment manufacturers like John Deere, producers like Smithfield Foods, aggregators like Cargill, food companies like General Mills and

Unilever, and retailers like Walmart—were making pledges around climate and soil health. Federal policies were also changing, making it easier and more cost effective for farmers to incorporate, for example, cover crops and prairie strips into their fields.

Second, agricultural markets are changing to reward the soil health that is central to combating climate change and improving water quality, and individuals, businesses, and governments are now willing to pay for these outcomes. Globally, new markets are rapidly unfolding around carbon reduction and removal. Nutrient markets—which focus on keeping nitrogen and phosphorus out of surface water—are also being developed. Providing well-supported, transparent, and stable structures for carbon and nutrient markets is crucial. Buyers want to pay for outcomes—clean air and water—not practices. Farmers will need to reconsider how they manage their entire operations to achieve these outcomes. Regenerative farmers are poised to take advantage of these new markets and to be compensated for their greater attentiveness to soil, air, water, and other natural resources. Well-designed policies in support of these markets can help rapidly expand the pool of regenerative farmers and penalize others who don't take care of the soil.

While I didn't expect to make a 90-degree career turn toward agriculture when I landed at Iowa State University, I'm so glad I did. It's an exciting time to be working in this space. Iowa hosts a cadre of innovative farmers—including those in this book—who are redesigning their farms to regenerate soil and protect the environment while they improve the financial aspect of their operations. They are willing to share their passion and knowledge with others in support of a regenerative agriculture movement. They can't do it on their own, however.

The first step toward greater agricultural sustainability involves widespread support for the farmer-leaders who are working to regenerate soil. This is actually happening: scientists, politicians, government bureaucrats, agribusiness professionals, commodity and consumer groups, and others are coming together to support farmers with soil health knowledge, policies, and markets. I'm excited and humbled to be part of these conversations. Regardless of your role, I ask you to do your part to help farmers move forward on soil health by learning about agricultural management, considering your food purchases, and advocating for better agricultural policies. Doing so will benefit farmers, consumers, and the planet.

NOTES

1. Kathleen Woida discusses how Iowa's soils have changed over time in *Iowa's Remarkable Soils: The Story of Our Most Vital Resource and How We Can Save It* (Iowa City: University of Iowa Press, 2021).

2. This definition of soil health can be found at https://nrcs.usda.gov/wps/portal/nrcs/main/soils/health.

3. See the heading on page 1 of the Nature Conservancy's "reThink Soil: A Roadmap for U.S. Soil Health," https://www.nature.org/content/dam/tnc/nature/en/documents/rethink-soil-external-paper-103116.pdf.

4. For example, see David R. Montgomery, *Dirt: The Erosion of Civilizations* (Berkeley: University of California Press, 2012) and *Growing a Revolution: Bringing Our Soil Back to Life* (New York: W. W. Norton, 2017), and Brian DeVore, *Wildly Successful Farming: Sustainability and the New Agricultural Land Ethic* (Madison: University of Wisconsin Press, 2018). The *Field Work* podcast discusses how conventional agriculture is working to become more sustainable: https://www.fieldworktalk.org. *Kiss the Ground*, released in 2020, is about the need for and potential of regenerative agriculture; see the Kiss the Ground Foundation at https://kisstheground.com.

5. For details about the science of supporting prairie strips as a conservation practice, see L. A. Schulte, J. B. Niemi, M. J. Helmers, et al., "Prairie Strips Improve Biodiversity and the Delivery of Multiple Ecosystem Services from Corn-Soybean Croplands," *Proceedings of the National Academy of Sciences* 114, no. 42 (2017): 11247–11252.

6. The Iowa Farm and Rural Life Poll is conducted annually by Iowa State University. The 2017 summary report containing information on Iowa farmers' perspectives on soil health can be found at https://store.extension.iastate.edu/product/15322. See page 6 for the information referenced here.

Section II

• • •

WATER

◆ ◆ ◆

MANY OF MY FONDEST MEMORIES INVOLVE WATER: paddling through the Boundary Waters, splashing in Lake Michigan, teaching our kids to swim, delighting when they ran outside into wild, windy downpours. Quietly kayaking through pond lilies as I watched the sun rise over a marsh.

If soil is the essential natural resource that's too easily ignored, then water is the resource we cannot ignore. From early morning's first refreshing mouthful to our nighttime shower, Earth's most essential fluid circulates through our daily lives and calls for our attention.

It's also key to human health and survival. Our body is almost two-thirds water, which transports nutrients, helps lubricate our joints, flushes our waste products, and assists with balancing our internal temperature. I've read that humans can live thirty to forty days without food but only three days without water. Water tends other organisms in similar ways, and water's quality and flow patterns shape habitat and determine whether native communities flourish or fail. Without water, nature as we know it would not exist.

However vital water is to life on Earth, its influence is shaped by circumstance. Water takes what it is given and returns life or death, blessing or curse. Feed water to living porous soil and you get prairie flowers and crystalline rivers. Feed it to dead compacted soil and you get floods and runoff thick with chocolate-brown sediment. Feed it to an overheated atmosphere and you get record rainfalls and monster storms.

Iowa's original expansive prairie soils and waterways formed a productive mutualism that brought out the best in both. Spring rains and meltwaters were absorbed into the prairie soil's voluminous air pockets. There some of the water fed dissolved nutrients to plant roots and soil microbes; the rest dribbled through earth that cleansed its trickling flows and guided them to a variety of distinctive aquatic communities. This infiltration hydrology ensured that the slow-moving water fed both aboveground and underground biodiversity.

Replacing Iowa's deep-rooted prairies with shallow-rooted crops has shifted water onto an entirely new course. Where biodiversity still abounds—and, to a lesser degree, wherever perennial plants dominate the landscape—precipitation still cycles into and through underground seeps and replenishes groundwater. But elsewhere much of it runs quickly over the surface of bare compacted soils, eroding topsoils as it races to streambeds that are continuously downcut by the runoff's power. These roiling waters often carry sediments, livestock manure, and synthetic chemicals—pollutants that diminish the biological diversity and environmental integrity of Iowa's rivers and aquatic communities. And, too often, flash floods spread waters beyond the streambeds.

Climate change magnifies these challenges as it dissolves Iowa's formerly predictable weather patterns by increasing annual precipitation and generating larger downpours. Record floods are on the rise, degrading floodplains that are some of Iowa's last remaining natural habitats. And Iowa's water problems are spreading far beyond our borders: nitrogen fertilizers washing down the Mississippi River exacerbate the growing Dead Zone in the Gulf of Mexico. In all these situations, water's extremes remain the obvious manifestation of climate, soil, and biodiversity problems that may be less visible.

Understanding Iowa's hydrologic flip-flop from infiltration to surface flow is essential for comprehending today's water problems. It explains the importance of returning diverse perennial plantings to Iowa's agricultural land so that water will once again flow into rather than over the earth. It supports the concept of reestablishing perennial plants, native biodiversity, and healthy soils to our working landscape for the benefit of both nature and agriculture.

We have already had some major successes tackling Iowa's water challenges. Chapter 5 talks about the benefits of taking care of northeast Iowa's trout streams and other local water initiatives. Chapter 6 reassures us that urban water contaminants have been largely cleaned up and that streamside conservation practices such as riparian buffers have helped reduce agricultural runoff. And chapter 7 explains how Iowa Flood Center research is increasing our understanding of flood processes, even as the center has significantly raised public awareness of flood problems and the need for more resilient landscapes. However, as with Iowa's other environmental problems, far more progress needs to be made.

This section begins with Mary Skopec's consideration of water as a recreational resource—indeed a critically important resource in our much-transformed state. Tying water to her own childhood awakening as a nature lover and her profession as a water scientist, she concedes that public perception of Iowa's water bodies has flipped from seeing them as "one of Iowa's most important economic and quality-of-life assets . . . into a hazard." But she argues that while many of Iowa's lakes and our state's 70,000-plus miles of streams and rivers are seriously polluted, they could—and should—become environmental and recreational assets that attract and entertain people, and she points out that contact with nature increases human happiness and health. The Iowa Great Lakes region has demonstrated that cleaning up our polluted waters spawns multiple benefits from declining pollutants and greater water clarity to expanding communities, recreational opportunities, and regional economies. Investing state funds in cleaning up Iowa's waters could transform our state, she writes. "All the elements exist to create a new future."

The following essay by Brian Soenen describes Iowa Project AWARE, "an immersive journey that focuses on action, education, and adventure." This week-long annual river cleanup, created by the author's passion, "gets into your blood," says Soenen, who endorses similar nature-based volunteer opportunities for "a cleaner, healthier, and stronger Iowa." Read this essay and you too will be convinced of the need for similar events and more Brian Soenens here in Iowa.

The next chapter gets down to basics: water pollution. Keith Schilling and Christopher Jones explain that water quality is neither easily defined, nor is it static. For example, Iowa's originally exceptional waters were first sullied by urban sewage. Today such pollutants that originate from a defined source have largely been cleaned up, but those derived from diffuse sources—such as agricultural expanses—are difficult to quantify and monitor. These agricultural pollutants—nitrate, phosphorus, sediment, bacteria, and other low-level contaminants including pesticides—are Iowa's greatest water pollutants today. After discussing them and admonishing that care must be taken when tracing pollution trends, the authors conclude that "it is beyond debate . . . that water-quality conditions in Iowa should and could be better." And because "we know more about water quality than ever before, there are no more excuses to be made. . . . the path to better water quality is well lit and open. All we need to do is take it."

County health department director Brian Hanft then writes about how he addressed arsenic pollution in private rural wells. He tells how this eight-year effort, which eventually protected the health of millions of people, served as "the most rewarding environmental project of my career." He hopes that applying scientific research to other water problems will help us "make smart and logical water policy changes for the greatest good."

The next chapter, by Witold Krajewski, examines Iowa's egregious increase in flooding, which has created massive agricultural and infrastructure losses, caused much human suffering, and increased erosion and water pollution. Krajewski tallies how our transformed landscape both suffers from and contributes to flooding. But climate change is also a proven culprit. He then describes his reason for hope: the Iowa Flood Center, which was established in 2009 and which he directs. He expresses his pride in the fact that the center makes Iowa "a model for the nation with our proactive efforts to build flood resilience and awareness." The center carries out scientific research and freely provides Iowans with online inundation maps as well as measurements of stream levels and flood predictions. This Iowa Flood Information System, combined with an energetic educational outreach program, has increased science-based understanding and awareness of flood processes and imminent dangers.

Jim Furnish's essay tells the story of Pat Sippy and her family, who for decades have made conservation plantings on their hilly farm to help quell regional flooding. This family's dedication to working with nature for the greater good triggered Furnish's memories of his own efforts as a U.S. Forest Service administrator, when he helped push the Forest Service from being an extractive agency to one governed by sustainability principles.

Larry Weber's concluding vision for the future takes a bird's-eye view of our state and proposes a water-centered approach that fits land use to landform. Doing so would remove row crops and urban development from our most flood-prone valleys, instead converting them to recreational lands and habitat for native plants and diverse wildlife. Such lands would give rivers room to flood. We could similarly de-intensify our most fragile and erosion-prone landforms such as western Iowa's Loess Hills. Intensive farming, guided by regenerative agriculture practices, would continue where flatter land is best suited for such use. These changes could be directed by government policies, incentives, and regulations that prioritize the land's long-term resilience. Weber has seen this work well in the Iowa Watershed Approach, a demonstration program that he directed through the University of Iowa. His chapter, which also meshes well with both Lisa Schulte Moore's and Tom Rosburg's vision chapters, brings focus to addressing our water problems and returning biodiversity to agricultural lands, thereby creating multiple benefits that will improve the quality of life for all Iowans.

CHAPTER 5

Loving the Lakes

Water as a Recreational Asset

Mary P. Skopec

IOWA HAS ALWAYS been my home. In my early years, I was annoyed by that fact. I often wistfully imagined how much better life would be if I lived near the ocean or in the mountains. The wildness of those environments seemed infinitely preferable to the tame and tightly controlled landscapes of Iowa. The vast sameness of Iowa made me wonder why anyone would live here if given a choice. What was there to learn among the cornfields that we didn't already know? Where were the mystery and wonder that surely would be found elsewhere? But then, when it came time to attend college, I inexplicably stayed in Iowa. I secretly eyed other locations and told myself that I would leave the second I had my chance. Graduate school followed and still I stayed. Finally, when I accepted a job with the Iowa Department of Natural Resources, I accepted that I felt called to protect and improve Iowa's environment. Leaving Iowa would have been an easy choice, but staying to fight for a better environment had become imperative.

COMING HOME TO IOWA

Like many adults who choose to stay in Iowa, I was eventually and ever so slowly sucked into the quiet charms of the state. My mom spoke fondly of the greenness of Iowa, which she vastly preferred to the perennial brown of her native Nevada. The green was given to us, of course, by Iowa's generously abundant water. But during my childhood, I was ignorant about the Cedar River, which flowed through my hometown of Cedar Rapids.

However, my relationship to Iowa's water began to shift when I entered my teen years. My parents had purchased a cabin on the shores of Big Spirit Lake in Dickinson County. Traveling to the lake felt like going on a grand adventure in a faraway and exotic land. Fascinated by the giant expanse of water and its changing moods, I spent hours on the dock watching the lake. Spirit Lake is aptly named—it is mercurial and alive. Some days the water was calm, serene, and flat as a pane of glass. Other days the wind would whip the lake into armies of whitecaps advancing menacingly toward me. It was here that I learned to water-ski, sail, and fish. And here that my siblings and I caught so many bullheads that we packed the cabin freezer until it nearly burst. I swore I would never eat another bullhead again in my life. Perhaps the real reason I stayed in Iowa as a college student was this lake. Did I really need to leave Iowa to have nature? To experience wildness? To be part of something beautiful and awe-inspiring?

I witnessed these same feelings in others when, as a young professional in the Iowa DNR, I helped launch Project AWARE. As Brian Soenen details in his essay, Project AWARE has been a pivotal experience for many Iowans. By working together to remove trash from rivers, participants have found a new and profound love for our state's waterways. They have also learned that leaving Iowa to search for nature experiences elsewhere is not necessary and that paddling along an Iowa river fuels their desire for wonder and builds community.

Reflecting on these experiences, I am reminded of Richard Louv's book *Last Child in the Woods: Saving Our Children from Nature-Deficit Disorder*. Louv notes the importance of nature for children's mental, spiritual, and intellectual growth. Children who are denied time outside suffer from what he calls nature-deficit disorder, which manifests in depression, anxiety, loneliness, and obesity. Louv talks of the power of transformative experiences in nature—experiences that shape and guide our development. In his book *Vitamin N: The Essential Guide to a Nature-Rich Life*, he maps out ways for parents and children to get their nature fix and advocates for society to reengage with natural resources in meaningful ways. He argues convincingly that doing so is not a luxury, it is essential to humankind's future.

Clearly, my decision to become a natural resources professional and a water scientist was born in those youthful moments. When I was immersed in Iowa's water, observing natural processes, my curiosity was unleashed. I am the living example of someone who was fortunate to have a transformative experience in nature. But that transformation didn't happen overnight. It took years of allowing myself to become comfortable in nature and connect with it on a deeper, more emotional level.

Today much of Iowa's water invokes fear in the average Iowan rather than adoration. Headlines filled with scary stories about water contamination and diseases transmitted by mere contact with water have driven people away from our rivers and streams. This fear has turned one of Iowa's most important economic and quality-of-life assets, abundant water, into a hazard.

To examine this issue, let's consider the example of beach monitoring at Iowa lakes. The Iowa DNR began testing public beaches in 1999 at state parks largely because of pressure from the news media. Stories in the *Des Moines Register* warned readers that Iowa beaches were contaminated with the bacterium *Escherichia coli* (see Keith Schilling and Christopher Jones's chapter for a discussion of bacterial contamination of recreational waters). Bacteria in beach water indicated that fecal matter from animals or humans was lurking in it. Immediately the public split into two camps: those who would never swim in Iowa beach water and the blissfully unaware beach goers. Early testing revealed elevated levels of *E. coli* at some of the beaches. Results could be 10 to 1,000 times higher than the recommended levels for safe recreation. Some of the beach goers in the blissfully unaware group defected to the would-never-swim category.

I remember the dilemma we faced when informing the public about the presence of bacteria at the beaches. On the one hand, I wanted people to get their nature fix. Recreating at our state beaches is a low-cost, family-friendly activity. Spending time swimming and playing outside promotes healthy and active lifestyles and makes people happier. On the other hand, I wanted people to be informed about the potential health risks of contact with polluted water and to make appropriate decisions that kept them and their families safe. The challenge was communicating the nuances of risks at the same time that we were learning about them. Unfortunately, nuance is lost in a world dominated by thirty-second media stories and good information was overwhelmed by opinion.

While I was comfortable with characterizing and communicating the swimming risks associated with exposure to bacteria, I was less so when dealing with blue-green algae toxins. In a healthy ecosystem, algae growth is limited by the availability of nutrients such as nitrogen and phosphorus. When excessive amounts of nutrients enter the ecosystem, the natural controls on algae growth are removed and algae populations increase exponentially until they form large colonies that appear as clumps or blooms. In Iowa, blue-green algae have generally become the dominant algal type in nutrient-rich waters.[1] As a result, Iowans have come to expect to see pea soup green and scummy water in most of our water bodies. While livestock producers have known for generations not to let animals drink from green ponds, it wasn't until the mid-2000s that we began to understand the role of green water in making people sick.

Some blue-green algae have a special adaptation that allows them to produce toxins, which can harm the liver, kidneys, and nervous systems of animals. The four main toxins—microcystin, anatoxin, saxitoxin, and cylindrospermopsin—are among the most potent toxins known in nature.[2] To complicate the matter, not all blue-green algae produce toxins, and those that can may not always produce them depending on environmental conditions. In other words, not all green water is toxic.

In the summer of 2004, I received a phone call reporting dead geese at Carter Lake. After that call, my professional world was never again the same. While we had little previous experience with blue-green algae toxins, we had enough information to believe that they had caused the geese to die. Analysis of lake water samples revealed elevated levels of microcystin, and the DNR issued no-contact advisories for Carter Lake.[3] Initially, this seemed like an isolated situation. However, the following year a large blue-green algae bloom occurred at Big Creek Lake near Des Moines, which increased pressure by the media and the public to monitor toxin levels more aggressively.

Microcystin testing is now a regular component of beach monitoring in Iowa, and the DNR posts numerous no-swimming advisories each year. A consistent upward trend in both the number of overall advisories and the number of lakes with an advisory is occurring in Iowa and this increase is accelerating. A variety of factors account for this upward trend, including climate change. Blue-green algae favor higher water temperatures. Heavy spring rainfalls provide early-season pulses of nitrogen and phosphorus to opportunistic blue-green algae, while hot, stagnant water (especially during times of drought) provides ideal growing conditions.

Lessons learned from our nearly two decades of beach monitoring are extremely valuable. We have learned that beaches tend to fall into one of two risk groups: those with very few advisories and those vulnerable to consistently high *E. coli* or microcystin counts. I have a high level of confidence that swimming at certain beaches poses little to no risk to my health and that spending time at these beaches will be a fun outdoor activity. Likewise, I will probably never swim at other beaches because they have a high level of fecal contamination from geese or livestock excrement or are pea soup green and contain significant levels of toxins.

Ironically, some of these beaches could be significantly improved with a little money and a little extra management, but declining state funds for state parks has resulted in a vicious cycle. Fewer financial or staffing resources reduce the ability to adequately maintain a park or beach, which makes for a less pleasant experience for visitors and therefore fewer visitors overall. Fewer visitors will be seen as justifying a reduction in expenditures at the park or beach. I find this situation truly frustrating. If we could invest more in our natural resources, the benefits would be considerable, and they would compound over time.

The economic drag caused by unpleasant and toxic blooms can be seen in the decline of attendance at problem beaches. Conversely, the lack of such blooms is increasing the recreational pressure around West Lake Okoboji. Property values around the Iowa Great Lakes are surging and overcrowding has become a topic of coffee shop conversation. At a time when most rural counties are losing population, Dickinson County is one of the few experiencing population growth.[4] I witnessed this dichotomy firsthand when I moved from southeast Iowa to Okoboji in 2016 to become the director at Iowa Lakeside Laboratory.

Decades of water-quality and landscape improvement investments in the Iowa Great Lakes have succeeded in reducing nutrients and increasing water clarity. Iowa Lakeside Laboratory's Cooperative Lakes Area Monitoring Project, CLAMP, is the longest-running lake-monitoring program in the state. Data from CLAMP show a doubling of water clarity in West and East Okoboji Lakes and significant reductions in phosphorus during the past twenty years.[5] Noxious algae blooms appear to be decreasing and aquatic vegetation is taking its place. Best of all, the Iowa Great Lakes fishery is healthy and thriving. Boat ramps are filled to capacity nearly every day and sales of water toys, paddleboards, and kayaks are surging.

When I worked for the DNR, people would often tell me that our state beaches lacked visitors because recreational preferences had changed—with interest shifting from lakes to swimming pools—yet I knew there had to be more to the story. The Iowa Great Lakes demonstrate the truth behind the trends. People crave contact with our natural resources, but they want high-quality resources, not brown, green, or foul-smelling water. As a saying from a famous movie goes, "If you build it, they will come." We need to reverse this saying. I firmly believe that when it comes to improving our water quality, if we can build demand for high-quality, nature-based recreation *in Iowa*, we will create demand for high-quality water.

A NEW FUTURE FOR RECREATION IN IOWA

It's clear that recreational use is an obvious platform for making headway in our battle to improve water quality. As Florence Williams writes in *The Nature Fix: Why Nature Makes Us Happier, Healthier, and More Creative*, people are substantially happier in natural environments than in urban environments. While we could argue about whether Iowa's landscape is really natural, our rivers, streams, lakes, and wetlands do retain a level of the wildness and wonder that humans need. Rather than arguing about milligrams per liter of this contaminant or that compound, what if we committed to revitalizing nature in and along our water bodies across the state? In the Iowa Great Lakes region, we rarely speak of phosphorus or nitrate. But regardless of political affiliation, nearly everyone agrees that we want to protect the lakes.

The restoration and construction of dozens of wetlands have resulted in new habitat for waterfowl and other wetland species. Nests of trumpeter swans have returned to the Iowa Great Lakes. Permanent conservation easements for prairie ecosystems have similarly protected upland ecosystems. Delighted children can see salamanders, mink, and other animals that used to be common but have become much less so in Iowa during the last century. Moreover, attention to the landscape's opportunities has also multiplied non-water-based recreational activities; investments in hiking and biking trails, for example, have added hundreds of miles to our state's recreational portfolio.

I wonder what the same care and attention could do for the many water bodies in our state that are largely ignored. Could the revitalization of rural southwest Iowa be spurred by a crystal-clear Green Valley Lake? In a state with so few public lands available for nature-based recreation, our water bodies are a critical piece of the puzzle of how we create transformative nature experiences for Iowans. Lakes are an obvious target for protection and improvement, but Iowa also boasts more than 70,000 miles of rivers and streams. Imagine the possibilities if we invested in all those resources. Decades of work on cold-water streams in northeast Iowa reveal the possibilities. Careful restoration work on these habitats has already paid dividends, with natural reproduction in trout streams increasing from six streams in the 1980s to seventy-three in 2017.[6] Estimates are that cold-water streams bring more than $1.6 billion to the driftless region of Iowa, Wisconsin, and Minnesota each year.[7]

Rivers are a place for biological diversity and a refuge for much of Iowa's wildlife. As James Pease describes in chapter 15, rivers and adjacent riparian corridors link natural landscapes and animal habitats and provide critical ecosystem services, such as filtering water, to the broader surrounding landscape. These natural corridors also provide abundant nature-based recreational experiences. Birding enthusiasts flock (pun intended) to river corridors to observe a variety of species. Here again Iowa's rivers could provide the key to instilling a sense of wonder and pride in our state's natural heritage.

Des Moines has already started to embrace this philosophy. Spurred by the success of low-head dam removal in Manchester and Elkader, Des Moines has envisioned a bold new plan to reconnect the city with its rivers. Dam modification, white-water paddling, trails, and green spaces will draw people back to the water and to Iowa.[8] The potential economic boon for Des Moines is thrilling. In a postpandemic world where job location is flexible and quality of life is paramount, what if Iowa's youth chose to stay in Des Moines (or Creston or Algona)? What if well-educated young people and new businesses lured by quality-of-life possibilities decided to locate here *because* of our water resources? What if we could finally flip the script back to one where Iowa is *the* place to be due to our incredible natural resources? I think that day is completely within the realm of possibility. All the elements exist to create a new future. Are we willing to embrace it, or do we just move away? I for one am here to stay.

NOTES

1. C. T. Filstrup, A. J. Heathcote, D. L. Kendall, et al., "Phytoplankton Taxonomic Compositional Shifts across Nutrient and Light Gradients in Temperate Lakes," *Inland Waters* 6 (2016): 234–249.

2. I. Chorus, ed., *Cyanotoxins: Occurrence, Causes, Consequences* (Berlin: Springer, 2012).

3. Iowa Department of Natural Resources, "Cyanobacteria in Iowa's Waters," January 2005, https://www.iihr.uiowa.edu/igs/publications/uploads/wfs-2005-05.pdf.

4. World Population Review, "Population of Counties in Iowa," 2021, https://worldpopulationreview.com/us-counties/states/ia.

5. Iowa Lakeside Laboratory, "Cooperative Lakes Area Monitoring Project (CLAMP)," clamp1909.blogspot.com.

6. Iowa Department of Natural Resources, "2016 Trout Angler Survey," Trout Angler Survey.pdf (iowadnr.gov).

7. Trout Unlimited, "Celebrating the Economic Impact of a Priceless Jewel," Economic Impact Summary of Trout Angling in the Driftless Area resized.pdf (tu.org).

8. Des Moines Area MPO, "Water Trails and Greenways Master Plan," https://dmampo.org/water-trails.

Creating Iowa Project AWARE

Brian Soenen

IT WAS A WATERSHED moment that I'll never forget. At the mere thought of it, I still get emotional. Walking into a natural resources volunteer conference a few decades ago, I asked the registrar about the keynote speaker. Barely glancing up, she mumbled, "Some guy who picks up garbage out of rivers." I walked into the auditorium and slumped into my chair, planning to zone out. But the minute Chad began to speak, I sat up and listened with rapt attention. This guy was much more than an aquatic garbageman. He was changing the world. And I wanted to be part of his actions.

When I first met Chad Pregracke, I was twenty-four years old and had just been hired as the coordinator of a volunteer water-quality monitoring program for the Iowa Department of Natural Resources. My job was, in its simplest form, to teach volunteers how to study water and the critters who live in it. After hearing Chad speak, I decided that picking up river garbage would also be a good thing to do.

Chad and the history of his organization are legendary. Since hatching Living Lands and Waters to clean up the Mississippi River in 1998, Chad has removed over 10 million pounds of trash from the Mississippi and its tributaries, grown and planted almost 1.5 million river-bottom trees, and involved tens of thousands of volunteers in his projects.

In 2002, the first time I heard Chad speak, each of his words made me more eager to become part of a solution to any number of the problems that our world faces. Had I not been newly married and just starting my career, I would have followed Chad back to his Mississippi barge. Instead, in the weeks and months that followed, I relived his presentation, pondered why it had made me so excited, and considered what more I could do to follow his lead.

The idea for Iowa Project AWARE took root at a routine staff meeting just two months later. I can't tell you what was on the agenda that day, but when we turned to volunteer recruitment, I had my eureka moment. I asked one simple question: "Could we do a river cleanup?" My life and the lives of countless other volunteers were changed forever when my boss, Mary Skopec, the Iowa DNR's water-monitoring section supervisor, answered, "Sure, what do you have in mind?"

My rationale was simple. My job was to engage volunteers in water-quality monitoring. Iowa has nearly 72,000 miles of rivers and streams, and while I hadn't seen them all, I'd never been to one without seeing trash. I had also coordinated dozens of water-quality training sessions, and I knew that when you talked about data, people fell asleep. In contrast, when you gave them a net and put them in a stream to find bugs, they came alive. My conclusion: the best way to help people care about water quality is to get them into the water. A river cleanup was a perfect way to get people involved.

I couldn't abandon my life to go live on Chad's boat and pick up trash, but I could organize my own river cleanup. And although I had never participated in a cleanup before, and I had no idea how to put such an event together, I knew from the start that organizing an Iowa-based river cleanup could be epic.

Iowa Project AWARE got its name from what I wanted it to be: A Watershed Awareness River Expedition. Not just a cleanup but an immersive journey that focuses on action, education, and adventure. During the event, participants paddle canoes searching for river and riverbank trash by day and camp in local campgrounds and communities by night. Throughout the week, they also attend educational programs emphasizing local history, culture, and nature.

An annual event, Iowa Project AWARE moves around the state to a new river each year, which not only makes it accessible to all Iowans at some point but also provides opportunities for repeat volunteers to experience the beauty and diversity found throughout our state. With canoes provided by Iowa Project AWARE, the event is welcoming for all.

Since its inception in 2003, Iowa Project AWARE has amassed some impressive statistics. As of 2021, nearly 3,000 volunteers from across the country have cleaned up over 1,260 river miles, removing more than 444 tons of trash, 77 percent of which has been recycled. There is no such thing as a typical volunteer—they range in age from toddlers to eighty-five. Their occupations—from farmers to lawyers, plumbers to social workers, school cafeteria workers to engineers—are as varied as their ages. Their mission—to clean up Iowa's rivers—is the common link that bonds this diverse group in very special ways.

Picking up garbage from a muddy river bottom in the middle of July is far from fun. For all practical purposes, it's miserable. Despite this, river cleanup volunteers are the first to admit that Iowa Project AWARE is one of the most fun, meaningful, and memorable experiences of their lifetimes. Somehow wretched conditions mixed with community, fellowship, and a focus on our state's natural, cultural, geological, and archaeological resources form a magical combination.

And the beautiful thing is that the experience is contagious. Over the past two decades, there has been a surge of local cleanups across the state, creating what some have termed a cleanup culture. Not content with just attending Iowa Project AWARE, many volunteers seek out similar opportunities throughout the year. Whether they participate in river cleanups, neighborhood garbage grabs, and natural resources restoration efforts or simply decide to make more environmentally friendly choices, Iowa Project AWARE volunteers tend to be leaders in their communities, motivating and inspiring others through their actions.

Picking up trash, of course, won't solve Iowa's water-quality problems. But it does get people involved. It brings people together in a way that encourages teamwork, builds camaraderie, and empowers meaningful change. River cleanups are like a gateway drug to cooperative environmental activism. They're a common rallying point that can unite individuals with differing viewpoints, and they help Iowans connect with their rivers, understand their watersheds, and make a difference in their communities. There's something about river cleanups that gets into your blood—something that, if enough people experienced it, could lead to a cleaner, healthier, and stronger Iowa.

I'll never forget the first Iowa Project AWARE planning meeting in 2003, when everyone I spoke with anticipated barriers and emphasized the reasons why we could not do this. I always responded with the same question: "So, does that mean we shouldn't do a river cleanup?" Not once did anyone answer, "Yes, let's give it up." Instead, my question focused the conversation on looking at what we could do rather than what we couldn't do. That positive mentality is exactly why Iowa Project AWARE has succeeded.

It is so easy to get frustrated, disappointed, and discouraged about environmental issues. There are so many things that are bad and getting worse. Despite this, there is so much good on this planet. So many reasons for hope and optimism. Even if it feels like there are a million things you can't do, there's always at least one thing you can do. Start with that. And don't forget to work together, because the greatest resource we have is each other. One person can inspire change, but it takes a community to make something happen.

I don't expect our rivers to be trash-free anytime soon, certainly not in my lifetime, but maybe some day it will happen. One piece of garbage at a time.

CHAPTER 6

Tracing the Trends

Improving Iowa's Water Quality

Keith E. Schilling and Christopher S. Jones

A RIVER BROUGHT US TOGETHER. In 2009, Chris was the laboratory supervisor at the Des Moines Water Works and Keith was a research geologist at the Iowa Geological Survey. We both focused on the Raccoon River—more specifically, on its water-quality impairment due to excessive nitrate and bacteria. These contaminants were affecting the river's use for drinking water and recreation. Our job was to help develop a plan to address this problem. This was a daunting task at the time, and it remains daunting today; water-quality conditions in Iowa's rivers and streams are one thing, a consensus on solutions for improving water quality is quite another. In this chapter, we share our understanding of water-quality issues in Iowa and then consider opportunities and challenges for the future.

WHAT DO WE MEAN BY WATER QUALITY?

When we fished Iowa streams as boys, it was common for each of us to see foam on the water and instinctively conclude that this was a sign of bad water quality. Several years later, foam observed on clear mountain streams in Montana and the rocky shores of Lake Superior left us both wondering, Was foam a good or a bad sign? The answer to this and related questions is not always straightforward.

Water quality is a function of temperature and of anything and everything that water dissolves or transports as it travels over and through the land and flows into streams, lakes, oceans, and aquifers. Some might also include the assemblage of species that a water body supports, but these are tightly linked to the chemical and physical attributes of water along with the movement of water relative to the land. A site's geology (what the water is traveling over or through), land use (such as agriculture or urban developments), precipitation (rainfall intensity, floods, droughts), and time (of day, season, etc.) all help determine its water quality. There are also feedback loops between water quality and living things. With all these factors, it can be difficult to make objective judgments about water quality being good, medium, or poor using just a simple list of dissolved or suspended materials.

What then is pollution? Pollution is the introduction of contaminants such as chemicals, heat, noise, trash, light, and microorganisms that cause adverse changes in the natural environment. One species' pollution might be another's food or habitat! Similarly, other species and natural processes can degrade water for human uses. No one should drink water from a stream teeming with beavers or flowing through geological deposits of lead or arsenic, but the water might be safe for trout or crayfish. Water quality in a lake or stream might best be described by how closely it resembles water thought be relatively unaffected by human civilization.

THE HISTORY OF WATER QUALITY IN IOWA

Just like the other historical environmental changes described in this book, water quality is not static. It can change markedly over time, especially when people are involved. How has Iowa's water quality changed since the 1830s?

Historic biological surveys indicate that prior to Euro-American settlement, Iowa had exceptional water quality. Many early reports describe surface water in streams as "clear," "pure," and "excellent." One report describes it this way: Prairie streams' "beginnings can be traced back to the swales and marshy meadows of the Iowan drift plain. Out from those boggy sloughs the water slowly filters forming perennial springs. These unfailing fountains feed the larger streams with a constant supply of clear, pure water."[1] Sounds pretty nice, doesn't it?

As the population grew, so did concerns about Iowa's water resources being polluted by people and cities. By 1873, Iowa had passed a pollution law forbidding the disposal of dead animals, night soil, or garbage into any river, spring, cistern, reservoir, stream, or pond. Twenty years later, biologist Seth Meek remarked on the poor quality of Iowa's rivers, noting that "rivers are becoming, to some extent, the sewers for the large cities, [which] is a probable cause for the diminution of some of the food fishes" such as pickerel, bass, or catfish.[2]

About that time, although farmers complained that city waters were sickening their livestock, agriculture had already initiated practices that would change our water quality forever. The quest to drain Iowa's land had begun. Beginning in the late 1800s to about 1920, vast networks of underground pipes were installed (often by hand) and connected to drainage ditches dug by steam shovels to dry out the countless wetlands that dotted north-central Iowa's landscape. The early clay pipes—tiles— were laid in loosely aligned sections to allow soil water to seep in, lowering the water table and allowing cultivation of the annual crops that displaced wetland and prairie perennials. To appreciate the scale of this endeavor, Fred Beckman at Iowa State College in 1913 remarked that the cost of land drainage work in Iowa exceeded the cost of digging the Panama Canal![3] In addition, streams and rivers were straightened to hasten water's flow and to square up fields for easier cropping. This transformation of Iowa's wetland and stream hydrology was inseparable from its water quality, as we would later discover. Iowa's streams became muddier and more subject to flash flooding and this, along with urban pollution, caused water quality to reach its lowest point in the 1920s and 1930s.

Conditions began to improve from the 1930s to the 1950s with the emergence of wastewater treatment for major cities and the adoption of new soil conservation practices on farms (see chapter 2). In the 1960s, water-quality concerns were increasingly highlighted by national media and publications such as Rachel Carson's book *Silent Spring*. Finally, in 1972, the U.S. Congress passed the Clean Water Act, which established new standards and expectations for water quality. The law sought to "restore and maintain the chemical, physical, and biological integrity of the waters of the United States," and it fostered a new round of wastewater treatment plant construction and reduced pollution discharge from factories and cities. It required point-source dischargers to obtain discharge permits, monitor the water being discharged, and remove or remediate harmful levels of pollutants like ammonia, heavy metals, pH, and salts, which are acutely toxic to aquatic life. The law has tremendously improved the nation's water quality. For example, the number of U.S. waters categorized as unfishable was cut almost in half between 1972 and 1996.[4]

However, the Clean Water Act did not place similar limits or controls on nonpoint-source pollution, that is, pollutants that enter a stream, lake, or aquifer from a multitude of locations. Unlike discharges from the end of a pipe, nonpoint sources are difficult to quantify and monitor. In Iowa, they are overwhelmingly linked to agricultural pollutants. Since almost all of Iowa's workable land is committed to row crop and animal agriculture, including concentrated animal feeding operations, nonpoint-source pollution dominates the state's water-quality conditions.

It is interesting to note the shift in blame regarding water quality from agricultural producers complaining about city pollution in the early 1900s to city dwellers now complaining about poor water quality emanating from rural areas. The transition from the dominance of point sources to nonpoint sources has been a huge change for Iowa, and with this change our most common pollutants are now traced to agriculture: nitrate, phosphorus, sediment, bacteria, and other minor contaminants.

COMMON IOWA POLLUTANTS: NITRATE, PHOSPHORUS AND SEDIMENT, BACTERIA

The element nitrogen (N) is essential for all life and a key component of proteins and DNA. It's also the main component (78 percent) of Earth's atmosphere, existing as dinitrogen gas (N_2), which cannot be used by most life-forms. So where does life get its nitrogen? Until about a century ago, most nitrogen available to living organisms was produced by nitrogen-fixing bacteria in the soil and root nodules of legumes. These green manures were supplemented with animal manure to provide crops with crucial nitrogen.

Nitrogen availability was a huge limitation to crop production prior to World War II, after which the development and distribution of synthetic fertilizers (see chapter 3) increased the supply for farming. This revolutionized agriculture and helped farmers multiply their production of grain and other food crops. Chemical fertilizers also enabled livestock production to be separated from crop production, something that has had profound water-quality consequences in Iowa and elsewhere. Manure has become super-abundant in areas where livestock are housed in concentrated animal feeding operations, creating management issues for farmers and inviting the overapplication of cheap and plentiful nutrients to cropland.

Today Iowa farmers fertilize corn with about 150 to 200 pounds per acre of synthetic nitrogen. Chemical fertilizers are often supplemented with animal manure from concentrated animal feeding operations, driving the actual fertilizer applications much higher. These operations may house thousands or tens of thousands of hogs, cattle, or poultry in closely packed conditions. In addition to the way that their manure presents a chronic overabundance of soil nutrients, animal wastes can wash into streams and rivers directly from these facilities or after they are spread on cropland, creating acute pollution episodes such as fish kills.

Only rarely is commercial nitrogen fertilizer spread as nitrate, but the applied forms of ammonia and urea are quickly converted to nitrate in the environment through bacteria-mediated oxidation. Nitrate is readily soluble in water and thus can easily escape a farm field before crops can use it. Average nitrate concentrations in our streams have increased from around 1 part per million in 1900 to 6 to 8 parts per million in 2018.[5]

Once nitrate gets into streams, lakes, and aquifers, it can wreak havoc by fertilizing harmful algal blooms that degrade the quality of water for desirable species. Nitrate is also a drinking-water contaminant that is toxic to infants and possibly a cancer risk for adults. About sixty public water supplies in Iowa remove nitrate so that the community's drinking water will be safe, and about a third of Iowa's public water supplies are considered vulnerable to nitrate contamination.[6] Thousands of private wells in Iowa are also contaminated with nitrate.

Finally, nitrate from Iowa is a strong driver of the Gulf of Mexico's Dead Zone. Iowa streams carry nitrate that ultimately ends up in the Mississippi River, which drains into the gulf. This high-nutrient water feeds marine algae, causing them to explosively multiply. As they die, their decaying bodies consume oxygen and make conditions along the Louisiana and Mississippi coasts unsuitable for shrimp, fish, and other aquatic organisms. This has a severe economic impact on the commercial fisheries of the region. In 2018, Iowa contributed about 29 percent of the nitrogen load that reached the gulf via the Mississippi River.[7]

Excessive sediment in our rivers is another major source of water pollution, filling wetlands, ponds, and reservoirs while decreasing water clarity and interfering with the growth and reproduction of fish and other aquatic life (see chapter 2). Sediment is derived mainly from the erosion of upland agricultural fields, streambeds, and streambanks.

Suspended sediment is also the primary carrier of the nutrient phosphorus, which attaches to soil particles. Phosphorus is transported to streams wherever sediment erosion is a problem, and thus more sediment-bound phosphorus washes down western Iowa's steeply sloping Loess Hills and the rolling hills of southern Iowa than elsewhere. However, there is also a dissolved form of phosphorus that contributes to stream loads, and this form is more common where row crop lands are intensively tiled and receive large amounts of manure in, for example, north-central Iowa.

Although phosphorus is naturally present in Iowa's soils, it's applied as fertilizer to row crops. Both the particulate and the dissolved forms of phosphorus work with nitrate to stimulate excessive phytoplankton and algae growth in water bodies and to contribute to oxygen-depleted aquatic dead zones. In 2020, Iowa streams contributed about 15 percent of the phosphorus discharged into the Gulf of Mexico from the Mississippi River.[8] Microorganisms, which can exist virtually anywhere from polar ice caps to geothermal hot springs to the deepest ocean bottoms and the highest mountaintops, are another common pollutant in Iowa. Bacteria that cause disease in humans are called pathogens. Fortunately, these are relatively scarce compared to the estimated trillion bacteria species found in the environment.[9] However, pathogens, which Mary Skopec also discusses in chapter 5, can concern us when we play, swim, or kayak in an Iowa lake or stream.

Because 1,400 bacteria have been identified as pathogens, testing for individual species would be expensive and time-consuming, making this type of monitoring impractical.[10] Thus, we look for other bacteria that indicate when pathogens could be present. The bacterium *Escherichia coli* is one such indicator. Because *E. coli* exists within the intestinal tract of vertebrates, its presence in a water body indicates the possible presence of fecal material. Testing for *E. coli* is easy and inexpensive.

Although some strains of *E. coli* can be pathogenic, most are not. They concern us, however, because their presence increases the likelihood that pathogens such as *Salmonella, Campylobacter,* and *Klebsiella* bacteria as well as *Cryptosporidium* and *Giardia,* which are parasites, are also present. The presence of *E. coli* can also correlate with pathogenic viruses. Conventional *E. coli* monitoring does not distinguish among potential sources, and so *E. coli* data should be viewed as an assessment of risk and not necessarily as a statement of certainty about the presence of pathogens. In most Iowa watersheds, the overwhelming source of bacteria is manure from swine, cattle, and poultry. For example, in the

Raccoon River, 99.9 percent of the bacteria produced in the watershed are derived from these three sources.[11] Monitoring data from Iowa lakes and streams indicate that in 2020, many of these were impaired because of acute and chronic levels of bacteria, posing a risk mainly through recreational contact. About two-thirds of our lakes and 61 percent of our streams are considered impaired for their designated use, and the most common impairment is for indicator bacteria like *E. coli*.[12] Iowa's best streams in terms of clarity tend to have lower *E. coli* numbers, while muddy streams often carry large numbers of these bacteria.

Additional pollutants present local and regional concerns in Iowa. Agricultural pesticides applied to corn and soybeans, such as atrazine and glyphosate (also known as Roundup), are often found in Iowa's rivers and streams in extremely small concentrations. While nitrate and phosphorus are measured in parts per million, pesticides are measured in parts per billion, a value 1,000 times lower. However, these contaminants can affect health, recreational water use, and ecosystems at low levels, and their occurrence in drinking water is highly regulated. Their presence in rivers and streams is most often associated with spring runoff soon after they have been applied on croplands.

Urban contaminants are often associated with infrastructure such as roads and parking lots. Winter applications of road salt can produce high concentrations of chloride in municipal surface-water and groundwater supplies. Runoff from parking lots and rooftops can deliver oils, grease, and metals such as nickel and lead to streams, though often at fairly low levels. Although wastewater treatment plants have greatly reduced many urban pollutants, new research is showing that these facilities cannot remove everything we flush down the drain. With sophisticated laboratory equipment, scientists are now able to detect many types of contaminants in treatment plant discharges at parts per trillion concentrations, including caffeine, steroids, prescription drugs, and even hormones. Likewise, low concentrations of animal growth hormones and antibiotics are detectable in rivers draining areas with concentrated animal feeding operations. More is being learned about the health and ecosystem effects of these emerging contaminants.

In today's rapid-fire world, news and social media outlets quickly pounce on word of the latest manure spill or water-quality violation, intimating that Iowa's water quality is getting worse. But is it? To answer this question, we need data to assess trends, but trends can be misleading. If you say water quality is getting worse, are you comparing conditions today to last week, last year, ten years ago, or even a hundred years ago? It would be safe to say that Iowa's water quality was better prior to Euro-American settlement, but even at that relatively pristine time soils eroded and organic nitrogen moved through the ecosystem. Over the last few decades, trends have become more ambiguous. Pollutants flow from wastewater treatment plants at far lower concentrations today than fifty years ago, and this represents a tremendous improvement. No longer do we have raw waste or toxic ammonia concentrations discharged into our streams.

On the other hand, despite an increase in streamside conservation measures such as riparian buffers, filter strips, and saturated buffers, we could argue that nonpoint-source pollution is worse than ever. Iowans farm more row crops, apply more fertilizer and manure, and have more artificial drainage than ever before. But care must still be taken to decipher water-quality trends from weather-dominated year-to-year variabilities. Also, the same monitoring record can show both increasing and decreasing trends, depending on the start and stop dates. Thus, caution is warranted when considering trends. It is beyond debate, however, that water-quality conditions in Iowa should and could be better.

OBSTACLES AND CHALLENGES FOR IMPROVEMENT

While folks can debate current trends, one thing is certain: everyone is far more aware of water quality than ever before. We now better understand the causes of poor water quality and the consequences of poor land management. We're able to monitor water conditions in real time. We also better communicate these issues to the public through web portals and social media.

In the past, decisions about our environment were often made without understanding ecology, hydrology, and future water-quality consequences for Iowa. We can examine historical land-use decisions through this lens. Today, since we know more about water quality than ever before, there are no more excuses to be made. We *know* what needs to be done. So now the question is, Do we have the will to do it?

In preparation for writing this chapter, we revisited the Raccoon River Water Quality Master Plan and the report published in 2011. The 2009 planning meeting was ambitious, bringing in science experts from across the state with the goal of identifying which agricultural practices "hold the most promise to restore and maintain an environmentally and economically sustainable watershed." Potential water-quality benefits of many practices were tested using a watershed model, and the results demonstrated that a mix of nutrient management and alternative cropping systems would obtain the greatest benefits.[13] The most effective practices included reductions in the application of fertilizer and manure as well as an increase in perennial land cover using grazed pastures and diversified crop rotation. Other practices not simulated at the time but known to work include cover crops, riparian buffers, and constructed wetlands. By the meeting's conclusion, we had a plan for improving water quality in the Raccoon River.

Do you know what happened in the decade that followed? Not much at all. Few of the master plan's proposed recommendations were implemented in any meaningful way.

This, in a nutshell, indicates the challenges we all face when trying to improve Iowa's water quality. The science is actually pretty simple and the proposed solutions are not complicated. So we are left to wonder, Do we have sufficient societal will to make the changes needed to improve water quality? Because so much economic activity in Iowa depends on the status quo, changes of this sort will be very challenging. But the path to better water quality is well lit and open. All we need to do is take it.

NOTES

1. T. E. Savage, *Geology of Benton County* (Iowa City: Iowa Geological Survey, 1905).

2. "Quality of Surface Waters of Iowa, 1886–1954" (Iowa City: Iowa Geological Survey, 1955), *Water Supply Bulletin* no. 5.

3. Frederick Beckman, quoted in the *New York Times*, September 22, 1913.

4. D. A. Keiser and J. S. Shapiro, "Consequences of the Clean Water Act and the Demand for Water Quality," *Quarterly Journal of Economics* 134, no. 1 (2019): 349–396.

5. C. S. Jones, K. E. Schilling, I. M. Simpson, et al., "Iowa Stream Nitrate, Discharge and Precipitation: 30-Year Perspective," *Environmental Management* 62, no. 4 (2018): 709–720.

6. R. R. Jones, P. J. Weyer, C. T. DellaValle, et al., "Nitrate from Drinking Water and Diet and Bladder Cancer among Postmenopausal Women in Iowa," *Environmental Health Perspectives* 124, no. 11 (2016): 1751–1758.

7. C. S. Jones, J. K. Nielsen, K. E. Schilling, et al., "Iowa Stream Nitrate and the Gulf of Mexico," *PloS ONE* 13, no. 4 (2018): e0195930.

8. K. E. Schilling, M. T. Streeter, A. Seeman, et al., "Total Phosphorus Export from Iowa Agricultural Watersheds: Quantifying the Scope and Scale of a Regional Condition," *Journal of Hydrology* 581 (2020): 124397.

9. "Microbiology by Numbers," *Nature Reviews Microbiology* 9 (2011), https://doi.org/10.1038/nrmicro2644.

10. Ibid.

11. K. E. Schilling and C. F. Wolter, "Nitrate Load Reduction Strategies for the Raccoon and Des Moines Rivers," 2008, https://dr.lib.iastate.edu/handle/20.500.12876/53523.

12. Iowa Department of Natural Resources, "Monitoring Impaired Waters," https://www.iowadnr.gov/environmental-protection/water-quality/water-monitoring/impaired-waters.

13. Iowa Department of Natural Resources, "Raccoon River Water Quality Master Plan," 2011, https://www.iowadnr.gov/Portals/idnr/uploads/water/watershed/files/raccoonmasterwmp13.PDF.

Arsenic in the Well

Brian Hanft

IN 2002, I JOINED THE Cerro Gordo County Department of Public Health as the environmental health service manager to oversee the county's environmental inspection services—restaurant food safety, swimming pools and spas, surface-water and groundwater protection, and the like. Shortly after my arrival, the Iowa Geological Survey contacted me to talk about several county water samples with high arsenic concentrations. Most notably, one sample had Iowa's highest recorded arsenic concentration: 567 parts per billion. The geologist had a theory and wanted to know if my team and I could help him investigate it further. I had no idea that his request would become the start of an eight-year multifaceted project resulting in local, state, and national policy enhancements that would affect millions of people and serve as the most rewarding environmental project of my career.

Cerro Gordo County, in north-central Iowa, had a population of 43,127 as of 2020 with nearly a third of these residents getting their drinking water from private wells. Most of the county's estimated 3,200 private drinking-water wells precede record keeping, which started in 1989. Most are more than fifty years old, have received little or no maintenance beyond pump replacement, and have never been tested for water quality, even though Iowa's unique Grants to Counties program tests wells for free.

Annually, Cerro Gordo Public Health tests between 200 and 300 wells for nitrate, coliform bacteria, and fecal bacteria. Results from these tests are provided to the well owners without concern for enforcement or repercussions. This nonenforcement policy has been well received by participants, and it was an important feature of our project, which would require access to private wells and the trust of well owners.

Our department's arsenic studies began in 2003, when we conducted a small study showing that arsenic was naturally found in pyrite and that some of our subsurface ground layers have pyrite in them. We were not sure how the arsenic was leaching from the pyrite into the groundwater. In 2001, the Environmental Protection Agency had adjusted the maximum contaminant level for arsenic from 50 to 10 parts per billion—approximately 10 drops of water in an Olympic-sized swimming pool. Immediately, many wells previously considered safe became unsafe. I realized that hundreds of our county families might unknowingly be drinking contaminated water. In 2007, we rewrote our well ordinance to include a fifty-six-square-mile arsenic zone that had wells testing over 10 parts per billion. All new and reconstructed wells in this zone were required to have an arsenic test and to follow new drilling and casing guidelines. I was pleased that we were implementing some controls.

In 2008, the State Hygienic Laboratory at the University of Iowa requested our well-drilling data for its own arsenic study. Its assessment of nearly 750 county wells supported the Iowa Geological Survey's theory. Also, a group of experts from academia, government, and business met to discuss the issue of arsenic in groundwater in preparation for submitting possible future arsenic-related grants. That possibility materialized in 2009, when the Centers for Disease Control and Prevention announced a grant program for groundwater-quality projects. Our county received one of these grants in June 2010, which finally provided adequate funds for in-depth studies of our local wells.

Over the following five years, we studied 68 wells. Our primary goals were to determine how arsenic enters our water supply and to help rural well owners avoid this entrance. We also wanted to take a broader look at arsenic contamination and its prevention. In the first year of the grant, we identified 110 suitable wells. More than 70 of their owners responded to an inquiry letter, a response rate that is almost unheard of in academic research. I believe this high response rate resulted from the trust built within the rural community through our Grants to Counties program. In years two through four of the grant, we sampled wells twice a year, studied rock chip samples from new wells, analyzed water and rock chip samples, and shared our study results with well owners. I was amazed to watch our project evolve, with one set of conclusions providing clarity for our next steps. During this period, we discovered that arsenic contamination was a problem throughout our entire county, not just in isolated areas. In year five, we pulled our information together and prepared a final report that gave clear reasons for ordinance updates that would expand our well-drilling requirements from two small arsenic zones to the entire county.

The results of our survey defined the chemistry of how arsenic was entering rural water supplies. We also made policy changes concerning the depth of new wells and their exposure to existing shallower wells. Because of our local policy changes, the Iowa Department of Public Health revised its Grants to Counties rules to allow Iowans to test for arsenic at no additional cost. Furthermore, Cerro Gordo Public Health joined an EPA work group that wrote a report for Congress regarding potential rule changes for small public water systems and arsenic contamination.

In my more than twenty-seven years of local public health experience, this project remains my proudest professional accomplishment because so many environmental health professionals and scientists worked together to achieve broad community benefits that stretched far beyond county and state borders. Many counties in Iowa and around the country are dealing with arsenic in their public and private water supplies, and our research offered solutions for both removal and prevention.

I am incredibly proud of this project for so many reasons. First, it demonstrated that local public health agencies have so much to offer the scientific community. Second, its collaborative partnerships were instrumental in achieving the kind of success that greatly improves public health. In addition to my colleagues Sophia Walsh and Dan Ries, our partners included the Iowa Department of Natural Resources, the State Hygienic Laboratory, IIHR–Hydroscience and Engineering at the University of Iowa, the Shawver Well Company, the University of Iowa's Center for Health Effects of Environmental Contamination, and the Iowa Geological Survey. Private well owners Jack and Sandy Davis, whose well had over 70 parts per billion of arsenic, wrote a letter explaining how Sandy had suffered physically from drinking its water over the long term. I was honored to work with these agencies and individuals without regard for who got credit for our success.

The interventions from this project reached well beyond what we had thought possible. The published report for our project helped drive the movement to change water-testing and well-drilling regulations and laws throughout Iowa. Data are still being collected statewide that should give important water-quality results for hundreds of thousands of Iowans. Cerro Gordo Public Health not only completed our project but also set the bar high for other agencies to duplicate our success. For me, it was a great honor to be in the forefront of public health advancements.

This project showed that by identifying a problem, using scientific research to study it and determine solutions, and working with others to enact a range of solutions—in other words, when scientists, policy makers, and members of the public join hands—we can successfully address Iowa's water pollution. My hope is that this story engages others to use these powerful tools to attack other forms of our state's water-quality problems and to make smart and logical water policy changes for the greatest good.

It is safe to say that my colleagues and I made a difference. In the years since our project was completed, hundreds of wells have been drilled using our latest information and only a fraction have had any identifiable arsenic. However, there are still many unanswered questions. For example, how does arsenic affect people of varying sizes—kids versus adults—at concentrations below the maximum contaminant level? In time, I trust that the data we collected will be used to tell, as radio broadcaster Paul Harvey used to say, "the rest of the story."

CHAPTER 7

Rising Rivers, Raising Resilience

Flooding in Iowa

Witold F. Krajewski

FOR ME, IOWA'S JUNE 2008 flood was a time of intense frustration. I had been traveling on business and returned to Iowa City for just one day before I was scheduled to fly out again. As I walked across the bridge over the swollen Iowa River toward my home institute, IIHR–Hydroscience and Engineering, I saw several staff members who worked in the front office carrying sandbags to protect the building, which is situated by design almost in the river.

At that moment, the seriousness of the situation hit me. I could not leave—I had to help. But even as an expert in hydrology and precipitation, I could do little more than join the sandbag crew. I tried to do my part—I brought my truck and helped deliver sandbags to wherever they were needed.

It was so painful to watch my community suffer. I wanted to do more.

FLOODING IS GETTING WORSE IN IOWA

I didn't realize at that moment how profoundly this flood would affect my personal and professional lives. As a civil and environmental engineering professor at the University of Iowa and now director of the IIHR-based Iowa Flood Center, I work more at a computer than with people. But this experience helped me understand and empathize with the Iowans who have endured the flooding of their homes, businesses, and communities. Seeing my professional home swallowed up by muddy brown floodwaters made it clear that floods don't just damage property—floods destroy and take lives. In 2019 alone, ninety-two people died as the result of flooding in the United States.[1]

The last thirty years have left many Iowans perplexed and sometimes angry. A 100-year flood, as it is widely understood, should happen about once every hundred years. And a 500-year flood, such as the one we experienced in 1993—well, we should never see such an event again in our lifetimes, correct?

Actually, no. These terms describe the statistical probability of floods; they are not a prescription for how often they will occur. A 100-year flood, for instance, has a 1 percent probability of occurrence in any given year. For homeowners, this means a 26 percent chance of being flooded at some point during their thirty-year mortgage. It's not impossible for a 100-year flood to occur in back-to-back years. A 500-year flood, which has a 0.2 percent chance of annual occurrence, can and likely did occur twice in less than twenty years here in Iowa—in 1993 and 2008.

But it's understandable that when two seemingly once-in-a-lifetime floods occurred in just fifteen years, Iowans felt defeated and confused. Even the casual observer cannot help but recognize that floods are happening more often in our state.

In recent decades, Iowans in some parts of the state have watched floodwaters swallow up their communities; this happened in 1993, 2001, 2002, 2004, 2007, 2008, 2010, 2011, 2013, and every year since until 2021, the year this book was written. Collectively, these events have brought massive economic losses of billions of dollars, displaced people from their homes, destroyed important infrastructure, and taken lives.

A 2015 scientific study tells us that the Midwest has endured more frequent floods in recent years. Analysis of U.S. Geological Survey stream gauge data collected between 1962 and 2011 in fourteen midwestern states revealed that flooding occurred more frequently over the latter period of the record. Thirty-four percent of the sites saw an increase in flood events, while only 9 percent experienced a decrease.[2]

My Iowa Flood Center colleague Antonio Arena analyzed presidential disaster declaration data collected by the Federal Emergency Management Agency for thirty years. From 1989 through 2019, Iowa counties received more than a thousand such declarations. That makes Iowa fourth nationally for flood-related presidential disaster declarations—more than almost any other noncoastal state. Some counties in the northeast part of Iowa endured some twenty flood events of this magnitude—more than one every other year, on average. The property and crop damage associated with these disasters totaled more than $20 billion statewide.[3]

Flooding is not just expensive and bad for property and infrastructure. It also harms the natural environment and the ecosystems upon which we rely. This harm can be difficult to quantify, but it is no less serious. For example, consider changes in the forest coverage of islands in the Mississippi River along Iowa's eastern border. With the increase in the frequency and magnitude of flooding that accompanied the 1930s construction of the Mississippi's nine-foot channel, once-diverse island and floodplain forests have given way to expanses of just one tree species. These simplified forests, in turn, have reduced the habitat for diverse animal residents.

Water quality takes a serious hit from flooding. Flood-related runoff from farm fields often carries with it excess nutrients, primarily nitrate from agricultural fertilizers and the application of manure to fields. Urban and industrial toxins, too, are swept up in floodwaters, contributing to a toxic stew of contaminants that finds its way into surface-water and groundwater supplies. These pollutants affect water quality and drinking-water supplies, recreation, tourism, and biodiversity. A larger-than-normal pulse of nutrients and other pollutants in flood runoff races down Iowa's rivers and streams to the Mississippi River and beyond, contributing to the Dead Zone in the Gulf of Mexico, an area the size of New Jersey where no aquatic life can survive.

Flooding also causes streambanks and gullies to erode, carrying away valuable topsoil and depositing sediments on agricultural fields. Floodwaters inundate local landscapes, killing or displacing wildlife and contaminating their habitat.

THE CLIMATE CONNECTION

It's common wisdom that weather does not equal climate, and scientists are almost always reluctant to ascribe any single weather phenomenon directly to a warming climate.

The facts are clear, however: since 1900, the annual average Iowa temperature has risen about 1°F. This warmer air can carry more moisture, which brings with it increased precipitation. The spring and early summer flood season—April through June—has been particularly wet in recent years, more than 40 percent above average since 2008. Precipitation across the Midwest also tends to fall in fewer but more intense extreme rainfall events.[4]

A recent study connected climate change with Iowa's more frequent flooding.[5] This research shows that the rising levels of greenhouse gas concentrations associated with burning fossil fuels are producing an upsurge in the frequency of a particular weather type—the Midwest Water Hose—that has been linked to flooding. This weather type is characterized by moisture-laden air that is transported from the Gulf of Mexico to the Midwest, where it becomes precipitation. In the first five months of 2019, the Midwest Water Hose contributed more than 70 percent of the region's total precipitation. The weather pattern associated with it is akin to what happens with atmospheric rivers—relatively long and narrow atmospheric regions, like rivers in the sky, that transport most of Earth's water vapor outside of the tropics. Atmospheric rivers can be staggeringly strong. For instance, the atmospheric rivers that led to eastern Iowa's 2008 flood carried within them 110 times as much flow as the Mississippi River at St. Louis.[6]

Iowa's flood season was especially bad in 2019. The Mississippi and Missouri Rivers that form our state's eastern and western borders both rose to major flood stage, causing levees to breach and producing widespread flooding. Small towns such as Hamburg and Pacific Junction were inundated in murky floodwaters for weeks, devastating homes and businesses. Larger cities such as Davenport also experienced catastrophic flooding. The Midwest Water Hose, which has been occurring more frequently in the last forty years, delivered much of the precipitation punch behind this flooding.

Modeling results showed that natural climate variations alone could not explain the more frequent occurrence of the Midwest Water Hose. When the rising greenhouse gas concentrations caused by human activity were accounted for, however, the results reproduced the observed increase in the occurrence of this weather type quite well.[7] This research provides strong evidence that climate change has made flooding more likely. This type of flooding is expected to become more common in the Midwest if we do not take immediate actions to cut greenhouse gas emissions.

Climate change is just one factor contributing to Iowa's increased incidence of flooding. Landscape transformation is another. Before the first plow turned over Iowa's lush grasslands, the deep-rooted tallgrass prairie stabilized Iowa's thick black topsoil, which absorbed and held large amounts of rainfall so that it coursed slowly through the soil. Roots and soil together acted like a sponge, slowing runoff.

Today Iowa's watersheds have lost a great deal of their natural resilience. The state's topsoils, thinner and less rich in organic matter, can absorb far less precipitation, allowing much of our rainfall to flow rapidly over the land's surface into drainageways. In addition, today's more frequent extreme rainfall events exacerbate peak water flows. And tiled fields and straightened waterways move water more quickly. The more voluminous and accelerated flows heighten the risk of flooding, especially flash flooding.

One additional factor increases our awareness of floods and their costly damages. Many Iowa cities are located alongside major rivers, with significant building and infrastructure in the floodplains. In rural locations, many floodplains are croplands. Both these uses raise the price tag of flood disasters. As Larry Weber and James Pease promote in chapters 8 and 15, converting floodplains that flood regularly to recreational lands or nature preserves and perhaps converting rural floodplains to pasturelands or other forms of perennial cover would give our rivers more room to flood. This in turn would reduce damage to human-made structures and intensively farmed lands. Converted floodplains would also increase habitat for wildlife and native plants, thus supporting biodiversity, which in turn could help limit flooding in future years.

THERE IS HOPE

It might seem that Iowa is doomed to even more flooding in the future. But Iowans have not been sitting back waiting for more floods to occur. We have made our state a model for the nation with our proactive efforts to build flood resilience and awareness.

At the behest of a few key Iowa legislators, I proposed the creation of the state-funded Iowa Flood Center at the University of Iowa, which was signed into law in 2009. I am proud of the significant progress we have made toward a more flood-resilient Iowa. I believe that the Iowa Flood Center has proven to be one of the best investments the state has made related to flood preparedness. As the nation's first and only academic center devoted to the study of floods, we provide Iowans with accurate scientific information to help them better understand and reduce their flood risks through improved flood monitoring and prediction capabilities. The Iowa Flood Center was not created to replace state or federal agencies, such as the U.S. Army Corps of Engineers or the Iowa Department of Natural Resources, but rather to augment their efforts. For example, several government agencies provide a large amount of data that are critical to the functioning of our online information platforms, and we are grateful for the partnerships we share with them. By collaborating with these agencies as well as with communities, individuals, and decision makers, the Iowa Flood Center is bringing engineering and scientific expertise to flood-related issues.

One of the center's most innovative and effective projects is the Iowa Flood Information System, IFIS. This system gives Iowans easy online access to information about rainfall, river and stream levels (monitored by our own network of some 300 stream-stage sensors), flood predictions, and flood inundation maps for forty communities (with more to come) that show what a predicted flood stage will mean for homes, businesses, and schools. It puts information directly into the hands of the people who need it—emergency managers, public safety personnel, and the general public. With this information, Iowans can make better decisions about protecting their property, their families, and their livelihoods.[8]

Before the Iowa Flood Center launched IFIS, it was difficult for Iowans to know how forecasted floods would affect them. The easy-to-understand information now freely available through IFIS provides the necessary context to support good flood-related decision making at all levels from government agencies to individual citizens. The Iowa Flood Center's energetic outreach program, which reaches thousands of Iowans statewide every year through media reports, STEM festivals, other K–12 educational events, and other projects, has raised flood awareness among all Iowans. This rise in public awareness and understanding of flooding is one of the center's greatest achievements because it lays the groundwork for flood-related actions.

This enhanced awareness and understanding can lead to other positive outcomes—for instance, new floodplain ordinances in Iowa City and Cedar Falls. In 2010, both communities adopted the 500-year floodplain as the standard floodplain, requiring that all new or substantially modified structures be one foot above the 500-year flood elevation.

Iowa Flood Center researchers have put their ingenuity, vision, and energy to work for Iowans, setting a high standard for service to the public. Sometimes people ask me if the center can prevent floods. And my answer, kind of jokingly, is not yet, but we are working on it! This is the next phase: what can we do to really mitigate flood damage—and not only the damage but also the floods themselves—to make them smaller and more manageable? This is perhaps our most difficult challenge.

But now, thanks to the Iowa Watershed Approach that Larry Weber describes in chapter 8, we are really making progress on this. The Iowa Watershed Approach is a statewide watershed improvement program designed to slow down the movement of water through the landscape by strategically building farm ponds, wetlands, and other conservation practices in watersheds. Researchers hope to restore some of Iowa's natural resiliency to heavy rainfall while improving water quality, adding natural beauty to the landscape, creating wildlife habitat, and restoring ecosystem services.

The Iowa Flood Center is also working to reduce flood damage in the future by educating the next generation of flood professionals and researchers—the students who go through our program and gain hands-on training and expertise in hydrology and other areas of study. They enter the workforce prepared to help solve complex water-related problems in the future in Iowa and around the world.

I am proud of what the Iowa Flood Center has achieved. Thanks to the center, Iowa is more flood-resilient, as evidenced by the minimal damage caused by the 2016 flood in Cedar Rapids, with its second-highest flood crest after 2008. However, I am also humbled because I understand the immense scope of the work still to be done. When I remember how profoundly discouraged I felt in 2008 as my campus disappeared into a murky soup, I am now equally grateful for the opportunities I have to make a difference. Most of all, as Iowans, my colleagues and I are honored to serve the people of this state.

NOTES

1. National Weather Service, "Summary of Natural Hazard Statistics for 2019 in the United States, Flood," https://www.weather.gov/media/hazstat/sum19.pdf.

2. I. Mallakpour and G. Villarini, "The Changing Nature of Flooding across the Central United States," *Nature Climate Change* 5 (2015): 250–254.

3. Antonio Arenas, personal communication, October 27, 2021.

4. NOAA National Centers for Environmental Information, "IOWA State Summaries 2019," https://statesummaries.ncics.org/chapter/ia.

5. Wei Zhang and Gabriele Villarini, "Greenhouse Gases Drove the Increasing Trends in Spring Precipitation across the Central USA," *Philosophical Transactions of the Royal Society A: Mathematical, Physical and Engineering Sciences*, March 2021, https://royalsocietypublishing.org/doi/10.1098/rsta.2019.0553.

6. D. A. Lavers and G. Villarini, "Atmospheric Rivers and Flooding over the Central United States," *Journal of Climate* 26, no. 20 (2013): 7829–7836.

7. Zhang and Villarini, "Greenhouse Gases."

8. W. F. Krajewski, D. Ceynar, I. Demir, et al., "Real-Time Flood Forecasting and Information System for the State of Iowa," *Bulletin of the American Meteorological Society* 98, no. 3 (2017): 539–554.

Conserving the Family Farm

Jim Furnish

MEET PAT SIPPY. She came to a fork in the road and decided to take a different path. I can understand. Pat and I both made that decision some time ago. She's a rural landowner and retired U.S. Department of Agriculture employee and I'm a retired forester. We both confronted entrenched systems that eventually led each of us to find ways to help make landscapes more sustainable.

Pat and her brother Burne manage about 300 acres of family farm property in the upper headwaters of Clear Creek, which flows into the Iowa River just above Iowa City. The farm—rolling hills with fertile soils—was originally purchased by Pat's grandmother in the late 1930s after her husband died; she and her children managed it as cropland and pasture. Pat's parents later shifted the farm to a cow-calf operation and started to establish conservation plantings, and then Pat and Burne gradually took over the farm's management. Pat can't remember a time when she was not "on the farm," she says.

Soft-spoken but strong-willed and purposeful, Pat and her brother began years ago to look at her land not with dollar signs but with soul. Pat knew changes were in order.

Persistent flooding of Clear Creek makes big trouble downstream for businesses and residents alike where it flows through Coralville. Pat and her family worked for decades to transform how her farm behaves when the hard rains come. The advent of the federal government's Conservation Reserve Program in 1985 meant the family could afford to move from costly and labor-intensive livestock farming toward greener conservation.

Pat's father first planted walnut trees about forty years ago, "throwing away" perfectly good farmland for conservation purposes. He also converted corn to pasture grass, which eventually was replanted as diverse tallgrass prairie that Pat burns frequently to maintain native plant diversity and vigor. Then, in 2018, Pat heard a pitch to area farmers and signed on to the Iowa Watershed Approach, a program led by the Iowa Flood Center at the University of Iowa. The program was funded by a multi-million-dollar federal grant that gets farmers working together to reduce flooding and improve water quality.

When rain falls, every square inch of land is fed, and streams—like veins carrying blood—are a remarkably accurate indicator of land health. Muddy water gushes into streams during extreme rainfalls speaking an undeniable truth, as does a healthy landscape that yields more measured, clear, and clean runoff. Land-use decisions and climate change are reshaping water systems and even little Clear Creek speaks loudly of its distress.

Continued flooding made Pat determined to transform the one-time cow-calf operation with conservation plantings and ponds, creating a headwaters sponge. She says the effect of all this work is to retain enough water to cover nearly fourteen football fields with water about one foot deep. Several of her neighbors also participate in the Iowa Watershed Approach, in total affecting 10 percent of the Clear Creek watershed.

To casual observers driving past Pat's farm, nothing dramatic appears —just more green stuff. The patch of woods her family planted almost forty years before stands out among all the neighboring croplands but offers no hint of the years of dedicated effort to keep those little tree seedlings alive. The restored prairie's display of six-foot-tall big bluestem evidences something different. Birds are just birds to most folk, but Pat speaks lovingly of the return of bobolinks.

Like Pat, I have Iowa roots. Frequent childhood trips to the American West with my dad, a geologist, led to an Iowa State forestry education and a thirty-five-year career with the U.S. Forest Service. From coast to coast I worked my way up from a dirt forester to become deputy chief. Now I'm home to stay after returning to Iowa City in 2018.

I see similarities between Pat's battles with Big Ag and my battles within the Forest Service, which stewards 9 percent of all U.S. lands. Facing strong demand for housing products after World War II, the Forest Service shifted gears to supply lumber and plywood by aggressively logging remote native forests. The agency applied an industrial mindset to living forests, treating them as machines that produced wood. Until the Big Comeuppance, that is—the spotted owl crisis of the 1990s that brought the agency to its knees. Environmental groups successfully sued the Forest Service, forcing it to rethink its approach to forest management. As for me, I sensed that the forest ached to be so much more than a grandiose tree farm. And I worked toward broadening the agency's vision and restoring much of what had been lost.

The Forest Service finally confronted the ruinous consequences of managing land primarily to extract timber. Not working *with* nature came at the expense of many important environmental services like clean water, healthy fish and wildlife habitat, and carbon storage, as we now know all too well. The agency has since been transforming itself into an ecosystem management agency using a values-driven approach, supported by best scientific practices, which seeks to optimize its environmental and social assets as well as its timber production. It had to acknowledge and incorporate a broader value system, a more expansive view. Progress is slow, maybe too slow, but sure.

I returned home to find Iowa's farm country transformed, not for the better. I'm disturbed by what I no longer see—the natural diversity that went along with smaller family farms, wooded bottomlands, fencerows, and livestock in pastures—sights common when I was a child. Many scientists sound the alarm about Iowa's agricultural practices. Increased flooding, poor water quality, and soil degradation and loss provide perhaps the most apparent and easily measured examples of our problems. But if transforming a monolithic federal agency is possible, why not the traditional commercial crop dogma of agriculture? Naturally, after hearing about Pat's work, I just had to learn why and how she changed her farm.

Pat and her farm represent a truism crucial to our quality of life in Iowa and to life in general. We need an ecosystem management approach to our agricultural policies and programs because farmlands do so much more than grow crops. They provide services that are vitally needed to safeguard the quality of life and life itself for humans and other species. True, this is happening now on some lands and among some farmers, for example, among members of Practical Farmers of Iowa and SILT, the Sustainable Iowa Land Trust, but we need much more. Our richest and least vulnerable lands may always be used more intensively, but we need to address floodplains, fragile slopes, and native remnants in a different manner and elevate the value of biological diversity in farming practices wherever possible.

Pat now sees the product of her passion. "I imagine what Iowa used to be like, and I feel good about what we've done here. I know it's not the same as it ever was, but this farm hints at the Iowa of old." She knows that the old days are gone for good. Yet she is resolute and fully committed to transforming her farm, both its purpose and its appearance. Hers is a quiet pursuit, gratifying to her soul. For me, knowing a kindred steward of the land gives me an upwelling of hope and encouragement for the long pull ahead. I ask myself, If a major shift in land use can happen in our national forests, with all their vested interests, why can't it happen with agriculture and farm policy?

CHAPTER 8

Water-Centered Land Management

A Vision for the Future

Larry Weber

EVERY DAY AS A BOY I would walk out through farm fields in the late afternoon to bring in our herd of dairy cows. Spring, summer, and fall, this was one of my chores on the farm.

And if I'm being honest, I almost always managed to sneak in a little fun.

A shallow creek flowed through the pasture where the cattle grazed; it drew me like a flower draws a bee. Year-round the creek, whose personality changed with each season, was my favorite place to play. I remember crouching on the sand and gravel bars, watching minnows and water bugs flit through the clear water. Frogs, minnows, muskrats, great blue herons, and more—the diversity of the creatures I saw fascinated me. I could have spent hours at the creek on those late afternoon walks if I hadn't known I was expected home with the cows promptly at milking time.

I loved observing how the water moved through the creek bed, building and rearranging the sandbars in an endless process. At the creek, I learned the basics of river hydraulics, the field that would eventually be the foundation of my professional career. My fascination with this area of study carried me to the University of Iowa, where I am now a professor of civil and environmental engineering. In this role, I teach and conduct research in water resources engineering, ecosystem restoration, flood mitigation, and water quality.

A BOYHOOD ON THE FARM

Our small family farm near Dyersville in northeast Iowa gave us everything we needed but little more. We weren't rich, but we were always well fed.

Before organic, locally sourced, and non-GMO food became trendy, our food was all of these. In summer, we feasted on garden produce—tomatoes and melons so fresh they were still warm from the sun. During the cold months, we ate our home-canned and frozen bounty from last year's garden. We raised the chickens (about 500 of them most years) that fed our extended family; someone else grew sweet corn; yet another family raised beef; and others contributed in their own ways. We used what we had and sold the surplus; profit was not the driver. Economy of scale and specialization had not yet taken over agribusiness decisions on our family farm.

Hard work filled our days. Farming was both a struggle and a source of pride for my family. We were part of a community of family and friends who supported one another. Although our farm was small—only 128 acres—it was a diverse combination of pasture, timber, and a four-crop rotation of small grains, alfalfa, corn, and soybeans.

Despite the rose-colored glasses of my memory, I recognize that ours wasn't a perfect world. The flawed farming practices of the day included deep fall plowing, inevitably followed in wintertime by the all-too-common black snowdrifts caused by windblown soil erosion. Farmers in those days judiciously applied land improvement practices, specifically tiling, to dry out the wet spots in the bottomlands—another practice with unintended environmental consequences (many of the nuisance wet spots from the 1970s are the much-valued wetlands that I work to restore today!). Cattle and hogs spent their days in the open feedlots, pastures, woodlands, and creeks that are prevalent throughout northeast Iowa, degrading the woodlands and polluting the streams. On the plus side, fencerows were part of every farm, offering wildlife a refuge of native grasses and woody plants.

Rainfall, in the right amount and at the right time, was as essential to our farming operation as the soil itself. In those years before climate change, we largely enjoyed the sweet spot of Iowa precipitation—not too much and not too little, falling in gentle showers and occasionally in more dramatic fashion as thunderstorms raced across the landscape. Flooding was infrequent, and so were droughts; for the most part, Mother Nature provided the rainfall we needed.

I don't think we fully appreciated just how fortunate we were. And then it all began to change.

Farming in Iowa has been transformed since my boyhood in the 1970s. The farm crisis of the 1980s led to fewer and larger farms and a more corporate approach to agriculture. Too often, conservation has taken a back seat to the seeming progress of industrialized agriculture. Modern farming has its pros and cons. On the plus side, soil conservation practices such as no-till farming have reduced erosion; we now see fewer black snowdrifts on winter days. Agricultural practices such as cover crops have also improved soil health where they're implemented.

But the modernization and intensification of agriculture have also brought serious consequences. In the frenzy to plant more corn during the ethanol boom, farmers plowed under the fencerow habitat that had sustained native plants and wildlife and safeguarded water's flow for generations. Excessive use of chemical fertilizers is now pervasive, polluting waterways and leading to toxic algae blooms. Cattle, hogs, and poultry grown in concentrated animal feeding operations have resulted in a glut of animal manure being applied to our land twice a year in increasing doses, leading to the undeniable degradation of water quality across the state. And agriculture as it is practiced today has serious impacts on water runoff. Water races across the tiled landscape, carrying with it the excess nitrate spread on our farm fields in search of higher yields, increasing downstream flooding, and further degrading our water quality.

Climate change has aggravated many of these problems. Warmer surface waters exacerbate algal growth, which can make our lakes and streams unsafe for recreation and close Iowa beaches. Climbing temperatures also mean more moisture in the atmosphere, leading to more frequent extreme rainfall events. These, in turn, bring increased flooding to Iowa along with heavy economic losses such as those from recent repeated floods. In eastern Iowa, a 500-year flood in 1993 was followed by one in 2008, just fifteen years later, and historic Missouri River floods occurred in 2011 and 2019, only eight years apart.

Flooding worsens soil erosion and washes out nitrate applied as commercial fertilizer and livestock manure from the landscape. In fact, during a period when Iowa was supposed to have reduced the nitrate load leaving the state, that load has doubled and there is no end to the increasing nitrate load visible on the horizon.[1]

What I have described is a landscape badly out of balance.

I propose a new water-centered vision for Iowa. It's a vision in which water becomes a *commons*—something of great value that belongs to us all, a resource that we actively protect and manage for our collective good. By managing and protecting our water, we would begin to change the mindset of Iowans, encouraging everyone to safeguard and preserve all our natural resources. My vision includes allowing our floodplains— the usually flat areas of land next to a river that is prone to flooding—to remain natural, untilled, and undeveloped in both rural and urban land- scapes, thus giving rivers room to flood. These floodplains would also provide space for trails, parks, hunting, outdoor recreation, wildlife, and native plants as well as floodwaters when needed. My vision includes net- zero runoff for all future developments in all locations. This *can* be done if new construction includes ponds, wetlands, and other water-holding features to help mitigate future flooding. This vision would slow the flow of water across the landscape, allowing it to percolate through the soil as it did when Iowa was covered with prairies, filtering out pollutants and reducing downstream flooding.

It is a vision based on science that accurately accounts for management of the chemical, fertilizer, and manure inputs of modern agriculture. This vision would set statutory standards for environmental performance, including airborne and water-soluble contaminants. To make this vision a reality, we must achieve four key goals.

First, we need more conservation on private lands, resulting in flood reduction and improved water quality and biodiversity. This includes preservation of existing natural areas but also (and perhaps more impor- tantly) the statewide restoration and reconstruction of green or natural infrastructure in the form of wetlands, restored oxbows, floodplains re- connected to rivers and streams, and reconstructed native perennial grasslands and woodlands (see chapters 15 and 16).[2]

Second, we should reduce row crop production in the most recurrent floodplains—that is, the two-year floodplains that have a 50 percent chance of flooding each year—to provide room for rivers to spread out during flood events, thereby reducing flood damage and providing a biogeochemical engine that will boost biodiversity, store carbon, and process nutrients rather than polluting our water system with highly mobile agricultural chemicals.

Third, we need to increase biological and agricultural diversity across the landscape, transitioning from our nearly ubiquitous two-crop mono-culture to a system with greater prevalence of small grains, vegetables, fruits, nuts, and open grazing of livestock. Iowans and all people across the Midwest have a growing interest in locally sourced farm-to-table food programs. Biodiversity can be increased by reestablishing native perennial vegetation in riparian zones and restoring grasslands and native woodlands elsewhere wherever possible.

Fourth, we should work toward a de-intensification of agriculture on Io-wa's most vulnerable landforms. These would include the geologically and ecologically wondrous Loess Hills bordering the Missouri River and the driftless region in far northeast Iowa, as well as two-year floodplains and prairie potholes. Meanwhile, intensification of agriculture might continue on Iowa's most productive row crop lands, preferably following the tenets of regenerative agriculture that Lisa Schulte Moore outlines in chapter 4.

We can encourage and strengthen these proposed efforts by reevaluating current state and federal policies and viewing them within a holistic framework. Too often, policies have competing goals and, in many cases, they conflict with each other when it comes to seeing water as a commons for Iowa's residents. For example, the Renewable Fuel Standard and the federally subsidized crop insurance program encourage producers to farm a statewide total of 400,000 acres—about 1.5 percent of Iowa's total cropped acres—within Iowa's two-year floodplains. This is essentially tempting and rewarding farmers to take risks that harm the environment and exacerbate flooding.

Conversely, conservation programs such as the Emergency Wetlands Reserve Program and the Wetlands Reserve Program are vastly under-funded. In 2019, the Emergency Wetlands Reserve Program provided $36 million to Iowa to remove approximately 3,600 acres of row crop production from the floodplain. Success! But many more landowners would have participated if the funds had been there. Based on applications to this federally funded program, we could have removed 26,000 acres from production. This was a missed opportunity. That flood-prone land went right back into production. In this case, farmers wanted to do the right thing but needed public assistance to do it.

My vision is not a pipe dream. From 2016 to 2022, I led a project focused on building and implementing a new vision for Iowa: the Iowa Watershed Approach. As its leader, I saw how this approach could transform a watershed for the betterment of all. The project was a collaboration of many organizations and agencies statewide, including the Iowa Flood Center at the University of Iowa.

The Iowa Watershed Approach was a statewide watershed improvement demonstration program designed to slow down the flow of water through the landscape by strategically building farm ponds, wetlands, terraces, and grassed waterways and implementing perennial cover and other conservation practices throughout the watershed. In the process, we restored some of Iowa's natural resiliency to heavy rainfall while improving water quality, adding natural beauty to the landscape, creating wildlife habitat, preparing the land for intensifying climate change, and restoring ecosystem services.

Through this innovative program, the state received almost $100 million from a federal grant designated to support flood-related infrastructure improvements in three Iowa cities and across eight rural watersheds. A resilience component focused on the human cost of flooding. Funding for this initial six-year project, which was completed in September 2022, provided a template for future watershed programs in Iowa, around the Midwest, and across the country. The Iowa Watershed Approach has attracted interest from the neighboring states of Wisconsin, Illinois, Missouri, Kansas, Nebraska, and Minnesota. In August 2019, twenty people from North Carolina traveled to Iowa to learn more about it, as did thirty people from Texas in January 2020.

The program's systems-based approach began with the formation of a local governance body called a watershed management authority. It included development of a twenty-year watershed plan, engagement with volunteer landowners, implementation of conservation practices, and much more. Its collaborative approach brought together groups and constituents from across the state. It was about everybody coming in and lifting a little bit for the benefit of all.

In total, we constructed more than 800 farm ponds, wetlands, grade control structures, terraces, grassed waterways, and streambank stabilization projects. As we neared the end of the demonstration program, landowner interest far exceeded the funding available for conservation practices.

We know this works—we can see the evidence in the farm ponds and wetlands that have brought diversity and resilience to the watershed by reducing downstream flooding after heavy rains. When Iowans come together, we can make a systemic transformation to a more ethical and sustainable way of managing the ecosystem. The challenges at hand are first to develop a real, reliable, and renewable funding strategy to implement the Iowa Watershed Approach across the entire state and, second, to establish environmental performance standards on farms that participate in these publicly funded programs.

To address the first point: although $100 million might seem like significant funding (and in many ways it is!), I estimate that we need $5 billion for watershed improvement projects across our state for green or natural infrastructure to reduce flood damage during heavy rainfalls, then an additional $5 billion for green or natural infrastructure to improve water quality throughout the entire year. Although this total of $10 billion may seem insurmountable, if Iowa would invest $200 million a year over fifty years, we will have changed the way in which water, sediment, and agricultural pollutants come off our land, reducing flood damage during intense rainfalls and improving water quality year-round. The beneficial results of such a long-term program would start becoming evident within a few years.

Fortunately, a potential source of this funding already exists. In 2010, with support from 63 percent of Iowa voters, the state adopted Iowa's Water and Land Legacy. This program created the Natural Resources and Outdoor Recreation Trust Fund to support permanent, reliable, and substantial funding to improve water quality, protect soils, enhance wildlife habitat, and increase outdoor recreation throughout Iowa. To fund the trust, the Iowa legislature would have to raise Iowa's current state sales tax to add three-eighths of a cent to each dollar collected. This would garner enough income annually to fund the vast majority of my vision's projected needs. It has now been over ten years since voters overwhelmingly supported creating the trust to build a better future for all Iowans. Unfortunately, Iowa legislators have not yet had the courage to fund it.

To address the second point: we must establish basic environmental performance standards for all farm operators, especially those receiving state or federal cost-share funding for conservation programs. Put another way, we cannot work toward reducing flooding and improving water quality by simply invoking no-till, cover crops, regenerative agriculture, precision agriculture, partnerships, cost sharing, conservation tillage, conservation drainage, conservation agronomy, or any other soil health practices. Nor can we simply rely on voluntary adoption of these conservation practices by only some farmers. These are all good practices. However, we need more. What can we do?

Although currently farmers receive funding to install environmentally beneficial practices, there is no coupling of that funding and the practices themselves to a farm's land management. Thus farmers supported by public cost-share funds can, for example, plant beneficial cover crops but pour so much manure on their land that their outflowing waters remain highly polluted. Or they might receive funding to plant diverse buffer strips that absorb flowing water and its pollutants but simultaneously install drainage tiles that increase harmful outflows underneath the buffers. Too often, the negative aspects of industrialized agriculture heavily outweigh the benefits of our state's investment in conservation cost-share programs.

What if the awarding of subsidies for environmental improvements were linked to an environmental performance evaluation or standard for a farm's *entire* environmental performance? Such a link would require farm managers to consider *all* farming practices and their environmental consequences as an integrated whole. The money and effort invested in practices that are known to produce positive outcomes, such as buffer strips, cover crops, or no-till, would then reap demonstrably positive results.

Such standards could be applied on scales both large and small—for example, to individual creeks or to entire watersheds that feed into sensitive streams, rivers, or lakes. Too often the environmental benefits of lake restoration are decoupled from management practices of upland landowners near the lake; this decoupling frequently negates the lake's potential restoration benefits.

Put simply: in most cases, our conservation efforts are not keeping pace with the intensification of agriculture. Each day, we seem to lose a little more ground.

The partners and organizers of the Iowa Watershed Approach had a vision. People got it, and they bought into it. We now need the political will to implement funding of programs that voters have already indicated they support and to adopt environmental standards to fulfill this vision.

BACK TO THE CREEK

Although I'm grown now, the boy who could spend all day playing in the creek still lives within me. I'm older, better educated, and supposedly wiser. But deep down, I am still fascinated by the flow of water through a creek and the ecosystem that grows up around it.

Perhaps that's what inspired me and my wife, Miechelle, to purchase a hundred acres of land along Old Man's Creek near our home in Iowa City. Our efforts here are all focused on improving the water quality of the creek, knowing that as it flows on to the Iowa River and then to the Mississippi, we can have some small positive effect on the larger watershed.

With this in mind, we're in the process of restoring the timber and reconstructing a prairie on the land. Healthy, open, diverse woodlands and deep-rooted prairies have a much greater water-holding capacity than the overgrown woodlands and expansive row crops seen across Iowa.

On this land, we forage for natural foods and tend an orchard, an apiary, and a large garden that produces fresh vegetables for our family. We're working to restore the native upland forests, return early successional woodlands to historic grasslands, manage invasive species, and foster diversity on the floodplains by managing the forests, wetlands, and oxbow remnants along the two creeks on the property.

This work is both my joy and my responsibility. All Iowans enjoy the birthright of our beautiful and productive landscape, but we all also bear the responsibility to care for it and rectify the mistakes of the past. We continue to move forward with hope and determination, knowing that future generations of Iowans are depending on the work we do today.

And every now and then when I'm working on the property, I look up and realize that hours have slipped away as if they were just a moment, while I've been deep in contemplation of the beauty and flow of the creek. My relationship with this place and with its soil, its growing things, and especially its water remains as primal and intimate as it was when I was a boy.

My wish for Iowa is that each of us could reestablish this most important of relationships with the natural world, which has given us so much and asks only to be respected and cared for in return.

NOTES

1. See the "Mississippi River Gulf of Mexico Watershed Nutrient Task Force New Goal Framework," December 3, 2014, https://www.epa.gov/ms-htf/ hypoxia-task-force-new-goal-framework. Iowa and the other states in the Mississippi River watershed were to reduce nutrient loads of nitrogen and phosphorus to the Gulf of Mexico by 45 percent between 2000 and 2015. Because of lack of progress, the goal for reduction was shifted to 2035, with an intermediate reduction goal of 25 percent by 2025. And see C. S. Jones, J. K. Nielsen, K. E. Schilling, et al., "Iowa Stream Nitrate and the Gulf of Mexico," *PloS ONE* 13, no. 4 (2018): e0195930.

2. See Larry J. Weber, Marian Muste, A. Allen Bradley, et al., "The Iowa Watersheds Project: Iowa's Prototype for Engaging Communities and Professionals in Watershed Hazard Mitigation," *International Journal of River Basin Management*, 2017, doi:10.1080/15715124.2017.1387127. And see Genevieve Bennett, Jan Cassin, and Nathaniel Carroll, "Natural Infrastructure Investment and Implications for the Nexus: A Global Overview," *Ecosystem Services*, 2016, doi:10.1016/j.ecoser.2016.05.006.

Section III

• • •

AIR

◆ ◆ ◆

BECAUSE MY PARENTS TAUGHT ME TO OBSERVE SEASONAL changes, Earth's patterns became my way of tracing time and tracking growth. Even as a child, I understood that each month brought its own special gifts: biting snows in January, slow-flowing heat in July, the smell of burning leaves in October as smoke ascended into the skies. March— my birthday month—attuned me to the smells of melting soils, spring's gentle rains, the first tentative calls of chorus frogs.

As I matured, the natural world's cycles shaped my vision of life's progression while nature's symmetries fed my faith in goodness and hope. By middle age, I had no doubt that winter's dimming of light and warmth pulled me into an annual period of rest that prepared me for springtime's energy demands. In troubling times, I listened for Mother Earth's soft yet dependable drumbeat, trusting that nature would sustain me.

I trusted nature's stability and predictability, that is, until they started to fade away. Until December temperatures reached into the seventies and whittled early winter into a thin slice of its former white glory. Until spring's showers became pounding downpours and hurricane-force winds catapulted through our summer woods, breaking massive oaks in half like matchsticks.

This dissolving of climate's time-honored norms has left me with a deep-seated, disquieting anxiety. It's robbed me of the belief that regardless of human blunders, our reliable Earth will roll forward along ancient paths, meeting life's needs as it's always done.

But I think that my malaise must be nothing compared to the uprooting of other species' customary repetitions. In the last few years, I've heard chorus frogs singing out-of-season mating songs in November and found violets bursting springtime's lavender buds in December. I wonder, How will these tiny lives survive as climate change escalates its random provisioning of weather extremes? As it obliterates our native communities' seasonal blueprints and erases Earth's well-honed operating instructions?

Like water, Iowa's air is a receptacle for many unwanted pollutants, such as the disagreeable odors and health-challenging gases and particulates that drift from our state's massive livestock containment facilities. These pollutants are important and concerning, but in this section we focus on the planet's most insidious and disruptive air pollutant: the steadily climbing concentrations of carbon dioxide produced primarily by the burning of fossil fuels. Rising concentrations of this gas hold more and more of the sun's incoming heat within our atmosphere. The result: climate change, also called global warming—the planet's creeping but relentless temperature increase that by 2021 had raised the average global temperature about 2°F above that of 1900. Most of that growth has occurred since 1980.

Iowa's average rise is lower, about 1°F, a seemingly minuscule amount. Yet even that increase has altered Iowa's climate in distinctive ways. It's brought significantly higher winter temperatures and has elevated atmospheric moisture, which in turn has boosted our state's annual precipitation by several inches and produced heavy downpours, especially in spring. The climbing average temperature has pushed weather events including windstorms to their extremes and replaced predictable weather patterns with weather whiplash. These changes magnify the other environmental problems discussed in this book: more soil erosion, water pollution, flooding, soil degradation, and stresses on natural communities.

Around the world, climate change takes challenging problems and makes them worse. Western wildfires become more intense and larger and send more smoke our way. Southern hurricanes grow stronger. The East Coast's rising sea levels surge farther ashore. The costs of climate change are many and large: increased risks to human health, infrastructure failures, military destabilization, disruptions to food systems, and losses from destructive weather events and the expenses of repeated cleanups. Declining quality of life and shrinking ecosystem services. These costs are predicted to increase. What can we do?

First, we must realize that climate change is real and dangerous. Daily, thousands of ever-rising temperature and carbon dioxide measurements, which validate its growing strength, are fed into the research models of scientists around the world who decipher climate change's attributes and destructive potential. These researchers confirm that climate change is now influencing all weather events, that its expressions are accelerating, that some effects are appearing sooner than expected, that it's touching all parts of the world, and that in places it's already redesigning the human experience. For these reasons, many call climate change humanity's largest existential threat.

Second, we must act rapidly to reach net carbon neutrality—that is, by or before 2050 we must produce no net gain in atmospheric carbon—and then we must start to reduce atmospheric carbon levels. We also need to adapt, for example, by strengthening infrastructure to resist damage from intensifying storms. As with Iowa's other environmental problems, we know what to do, but we lack the societal and political will to do it. Reaching carbon neutrality will require action at all levels from international agreements and national policies and programs to each of us doing what we can. Advocacy efforts that put pressure on governments at all levels are imperative. Speed is essential; the faster we act, the more we will decrease climate change's ultimate hold and destruction.

Climate change is a huge and complex subject, replete with new developments. This book barely lays out the basics. I encourage you to keep learning and reading. Avoid fake news by choosing your information sources with care. There are many excellent books, such as Katherine Hayhoe's *Saving Us: A Climate Scientist's Case for Hope and Healing in a Divided World.* Robert Henson has written a string of excellent guides to climate change, the latest being *The Thinking Person's Guide to Climate Change.* As of 2022, the EPA, NASA, and NOAA had excellent websites with trustworthy information presented clearly, often through impressive graphics. The most comprehensive information sources are the websites of the U.S. National Climate Assessment, with major reports published every four to five years, and the U.N.'s Intergovernmental Panel on Climate Change, with massive global reports published every five to seven years—check out their summary reports.

One last thought: facing climate change can be depressing and overwhelming. The internet has suggestions for addressing such emotions. Here's one more: join the millions of people who are decreasing their personal climate impacts—see suggestions on the web, including Project Drawdown's book and website. And take heart from the thousands of passionate professionals around the world who are working to reduce this threat. New technologies appear almost daily. Join the throng. Recognize the excitement and potential of these times. Allow our race to save the world from climate chaos to bring out your creativity and unite us in community.

This section starts with Charles Stanier's focus on climate change as a global phenomenon. We all share the same overheated atmosphere, and its rising warmth affects us all, even though the resulting problems may vary. Stanier realized this when he joined a service project for Guatemalan farmers facing intense climatic warming and drying. Because of their lack of aids to help them adapt to climate change, these rural Guatemalans suffered far more than U.S. farmers would have suffered. Stanier writes that such hydrologic changes as well as the rise in sea level leave large climate change fingerprints. Iowans will increasingly feel the effects of both as climate refugees flee unlivable lands and as the cost of federal aid for seawall construction and flood cleanups increases. Consider the expense, destabilization, and stress of climate-generated political tensions, outbreaks of disease, continuous infrastructure repair, international crises, ecosystem collapse, and the like, and the arguments for aggressive climate change actions are compelling. Stanier adds to that list our moral obligations to others and to the earth, and he also outlines positive climate actions that Iowans can take. We have "the tools and the knowledge," he exhorts. "Let's get to work and use them!"

We then hear how Carole Teator's quiet August day was interrupted by an unexpected derecho. Its hurricane-strength straight-line winds would become the costliest single-day thunderstorm event in U.S. history, screeching across Iowa to topple over 7 million trees, collapse countless buildings and power lines, and level nearly a million acres of crops. Teator's terror during the storm and her later grief are palpable warnings of our own future if we ignore climate change's multiplying strength.

In William Gutowski's chapter on climate change in Iowa, he encourages us to consider our effects on the "web of interacting natural, human, and societal systems" that is critical to our survival. Within that framework, he explains that Iowa's climate is already changing significantly. Winters have warmed on average 2 to 3°F since a century ago. Summer's nighttime temperatures have also risen, although daytime temperatures have been held in check by the cooling forces of increasing humidity and by a tremendous rise in annual precipitation—with gains of 2.5 to 7.5 inches annually, mostly in downpours from April through June. Those rains and the increase in extreme weather including fierce winds have magnified erosion, water runoff and pollution, flooding, and soil degradation and are wreaking havoc on wildlife and native plants. Predictions for future decades depend on how quickly we attain carbon neutrality, but in general they indicate intensification of these challenges plus drought, with increasing dangers and costs for all. These changes will "profoundly disrupt ways of living for people and for the natural world, and they will occur too rapidly for us to comfortably adapt to them," Gutowski warns. He then countermands, "We can choose a better future."

By leading the Winneshiek Energy District and the Clean Energy Districts of Iowa, Andrew Johnson is reaching toward Gutowski's better future in a big way. The Clean Energy District model—active in nine eastern Iowa counties in 2021—is helping residents increase energy efficiency and transition to locally owned clean energy resources. Doing so also generates local jobs and creates communities dedicated to "taking climate stewardship increasingly seriously."

Eugene Takle's chapter asks how Iowa's agriculture has affected climate change and what climate change is doing to our agriculture. The answer to both questions is plenty! Takle writes that agriculture's greenhouse gas emissions soared after World War II due to new fossil fuel–powered machinery, synthetic nitrogen fertilizers, and so on. In turn, crops and livestock in recent decades have been increasingly affected by the changing climate's rising atmospheric humidity and nighttime temperatures as well as extreme rains and flooding, which also boost soil degradation, erosion, and water pollution. Without strong efforts to reduce climate change, in the coming decades extreme heat waves and rainfall will increase some years, flip us into drought in other years, and raise farming costs and difficulties until some producers may abandon corn and soybean farming. But Takle asserts that "agriculture can also be a major part of our climate change solution." He looks toward science-based, visionary information and policies concerning, for example, carbon sequestration in soils and a reduction in methane emissions from livestock operations. These should help protect soil and water while providing a path toward ensuring sustainability for Iowa agriculture and reducing global greenhouse gas emissions.

Francis Thicke is working on this hopeful vision in his farm pastures, where his regenerative grazing system excels in sequestering soil carbon while providing nutritious feed for his dairy cattle. Thicke describes this grazing system as well as his finely tuned regenerative cropping system (which Lisa Schulte Moore also writes about in chapter 4). Add in his renewable energy systems and local marketing of farm products, and he and his wife are truly "making our farm more regenerative, more resilient, and better able to sequester carbon in the soil."

In his closing chapter, Gregory Carmichael first explains why climate change is so important. He points out that without "swift and uncompromising action," we could in this century reach "a temperature that our planet has not experienced in 2 million years." He then traces the changes that Iowans are already experiencing, which if left untended could lead to overwhelming tipping points and compounding catastrophes from which we may not recover. Carmichael's information-rich chapter surveys multiple actions to help us avoid the worst consequences of climate change and create "a soft landing for humanity and for nature." Targeting short-lived pollutants such as the methane produced by Iowa's cattle will produce a relatively rapid drop in emissions. Another powerful climate pollutant, nitrous oxide emissions from synthetic fertilizers, is also an obvious target for action in Iowa. Carmichael then establishes climate literacy education as his vision for the future. He shares how young adults, disturbed by our slowness to act, are pushing for new forms of climate education. He proposes reshaping college- and university-level education across the board to include broad-reaching interdisciplinary climate-related coursework, research, and experiential learning opportunities that prepare students to assume leadership of the changing world they will inhabit.

CHAPTER 9

A Healthier, More Functional Planet

Global Implications of Climate Change

Charles O. Stanier

I AM AN ATMOSPHERIC measurement scientist. For over twenty years, I have been taking measurements to understand air pollution and the atmospheric composition that is tied to climate change. One of my projects as a professor of engineering at the University of Iowa is to assist scientists from the National Oceanic and Atmospheric Administration with greenhouse gas measurements in West Branch, Iowa. Since our start in 2007, we have handled over 2,500 air samples pumped down from an inlet mounted on a tower reaching 1,243 feet above ground level. The goal is extremely high accuracy. High accuracy is necessary so that differences in the gas concentrations measured across the country can be compared meaningfully. For example, if methane readings taken in Colorado and Iowa are slightly different, we need that difference to be due to physics and atmospheric chemistry, not to measurement error.

But high-accuracy measurements and their interpretation are not all that I do. In 2019, I traveled with my family and other midwesterners to Guatemala to do faith-based service and to experience rural Central America. Our destination was the region around Lake Atitlán in the western Sierra Madre highlands—at 1,115 feet the deepest lake in Central America. We were met by welcoming people, a vibrant culture, and stunning natural scenery. We were there to serve families suffering from hunger and illness.

Many of the families we met practiced subsistence agriculture, growing corn, beans, fruit, and vegetables to eat or trade at the market. Plots of coffee bushes were tended for export. Notwithstanding their hard work, many families were very vulnerable. One injury or severe illness, one crop failure, one unexpected shift in commodity prices and their difficult but largely self-reliant existence became even harder and more precarious. While each family's scenario was different, the burdens of poverty, debt, rudimentary farming practices, violence, corruption, lack of job opportunities, and lack of basic infrastructure—for example, medical care, transportation, sanitation, crop insurance, and housing—combined to create and sustain this vulnerability. When we asked how we could help, one response was, "Pray that food is plentiful."

CLIMATE AND HYDROLOGIC CHANGES IN CENTRAL AMERICA

While many factors undermine the ability of Central American farmers and farmworkers to create good lives for themselves and their families, the hydrologic changes initiated by climate change undeniably make it harder to grow a reliable crop and get it to market. Lake Atitlán is on the edge of the Central American Dry Corridor, a region with 2.2 million people in Guatemala, El Salvador, Honduras, and Nicaragua.[1] In the Dry Corridor, both the predicted and already observed impacts of climate change include greater warming and drying on average; more variability in temperature, rainfall, and streamflow; and unpredictability in the timing of the rainy season. These climate changes result in hydrologic changes in the amount and timing of rainfall and snowfall and the fate of precipitation—its evaporation, infiltration into groundwater, and interplay with soils. All these alterations make it harder to know when to plant. They complicate pest and disease management. And they make keeping poultry and livestock healthy and productive more difficult.

Furthermore, the rising frequency of intense rains is increasing mudslides and flash floods. The mudslides are hazards in their own right, but they also disrupt transportation, cutting off remote Guatemalans from markets, supplies, and emergency response crews. On the last day of our visit, we saw the former site of the Mayan village of Panabaj, wiped out in 2004 by a forty-foot-deep mudslide after days of torrential rains.

In circumstances as difficult as those faced by poor farmers and their families in parts of Central America, it is understandable that some choose to leave in search of better lives. While international migration always has multiple causes, one factor in Dry Corridor migration is climate change, which creates climate refugees, also known as victims of environmentally induced displacement.

How do all these threats compare to the effects of climate change in Iowa? The answer lies not only in how big the impacts are but also in each location's social, infrastructural, and ecological vulnerability. Like Iowa, Guatemala has serious negative climate change impacts happening now, and these are anticipated with high scientific confidence to become more severe in the future. But because of the lower overall vulnerability of systems in the United States, Iowa's impacts will manifest themselves in different ways. The U.S. advantages of efficient goods transport, high education levels, agricultural biotechnology, precision agriculture, crop insurance, and the relative ease of implementing irrigation will enable Iowa to absorb and adapt to climate change with less severe disruption than Guatemala. Will the U.S. experience be smooth, with no human suffering and economic losses? Of course not. But it is very unlikely that many Iowans will experience hardship at levels anywhere near those that will be felt in Central America.

CLIMATE CHANGE AND SEA LEVEL RISE

While climate change produces an arm's-length list of serious effects, I believe that two of its most important global consequences, climate processes that everyone should understand, are the hydrologic changes described above and the rise in sea level discussed here. The 10 percent of our population living in low-lying coastal zones, including residents of numerous megacities such as New York City, Tokyo, London, Los Angeles, São Paulo, Buenos Aires, Jakarta, Mumbai, Shanghai, Lagos, and Cairo, are being directly affected by today's global sea level rise. So too are many military installations, especially naval bases. Because of the interconnected nature of global and interstate commerce, our federal system which shares many costs, and the political stresses caused by relocation and competition for resources, we Iowans are by no means immune to the damages anticipated from sea level rise, even though it is happening at a distance.

The reasons for the rise in sea level are simple and straightforward. They are core concepts of middle-school science classes: energy flows, the water cycle, and the effects of energy on matter, specifically on ice and water. At temperatures greater than 39°F, warm water takes up slightly more room than cooler water (and the surface of the ocean averages about 68°F). This thermal expansion is responsible for a bit less than half of the current rise in sea level. The other contribution comes from melting glaciers and ice sheets. While the melting of floating ice such as icebergs does not raise sea level, the melting of ice on land such as Greenland's ice sheets does.

The rate of global sea level rise between 2006 and 2015 was 0.14 inch per year or 1.4 inches per decade.[2] Between 1902 and 2021, the global average sea level rose 7 inches. This does not sound like much, but it is already causing increasingly severe flooding, with the amount of flooding in specific locations dictated by peak water levels during high tides and storm surges. During hurricanes and typhoons, flooding is often compounded by extreme rainfall and swollen coastal rivers and creeks—think Hurricanes Sandy, Katrina, and Harvey. The problem is just emerging and will become more severe as the rate of sea level rise accelerates. We now predict a global average of 11 to 40 inches of *additional* sea level rise between 2020 and 2100.

Why are future predictions so wide-ranging? Part of the uncertainty is due to questions about how the climate system will evolve—how much ice will melt and how quickly, how energy will be redistributed within the climate system, that sort of thing. In addition, we are talking about the future, and we do not know the levels of future greenhouse gas emissions because these depend on our actions now and in the coming years. Finally, the oceans, like a large ship trying to turn, are slow to respond. Even if we eliminate greenhouse gas emissions and stabilize warming of the earth by, say, 2050 or 2100, sea levels will require hundreds of years to stabilize.

Complicating matters further is the potential for an additional 19 to 33 feet of sea level rise should the Greenland or Antarctic ice sheets begin a rapid unstable retreat, a possibility that is not yet well understood. However, even the conservatively anticipated sea level rise and its resultant coastal flooding will be sufficient to cause massive economic and health consequences, which will be coupled with the unprecedented migration of climate refugees away from coastlines.

I want to emphasize that the causes and physics of global sea level rise are extremely well known and noncontroversial among scientists. Greenhouse gases create an energy imbalance because an atmosphere enhanced with greenhouse gases reradiates the heat energy that normally would have escaped into space back to the planet's surface. The oceans absorb that extra energy, causing slow warming and expansion. The energy imbalance at the surface of the planet is known with near-complete certainty to be caused primarily by human-made changes to the atmosphere through the addition of greenhouse gases—principally carbon dioxide—from burning fossil fuels. The associated physics and chemistry date back at least to Svante Arrhenius's 1896 paper on the greenhouse warming properties of carbon dioxide. The energy imbalance is well understood, reproduced in increasingly detailed computer simulations, and measured in at least a dozen independent ways.

What about the detailed effects of sea level rise? How much will it augment coastal flooding, beach erosion, and storm surges? How much property damage and loss of life will these cause? How much will this affect coastal ecosystems and supplies of fresh drinking water? How much will we spend on coastal defenses versus periodic rebuilding? How many people will relocate and who will pay for all this? Although those factors are much more uncertain than the geophysical impacts, economists, social scientists, and military strategists use previous disasters and forecasts of future conditions to try to make useful predictions for planning purposes.

THE CONSEQUENCES OF GLOBAL CLIMATE CHANGE FOR IOWA AND BEYOND

Perhaps more than any other challenge, sea level rise presents us with profound challenges in governance due to the costs, uncertainties, number of stakeholders, and long lifetimes and cascading economic influences of climate change on coastal infrastructure.

Without adaptation and mitigation, coastal flooding could cause damages of over 9 percent of global gross domestic product. The costs of adapting are less than the costs of rebuilding after each flood, but they are still very large. Adaptive efforts can include planned retreating from low-lying areas, hardening of existing infrastructure like transit systems and the electrical grid, and building of coastal defenses such as seawalls. The disasters and costs associated with sea level rise would not be directly incurred in Iowa, but they would ripple through the economy in the form of federal government outlays, supply chain interruptions, stresses on political decision making, business losses, investment losses, and climate refugees. Iowa will share in the price tag through higher prices for goods coming via coastal hubs, higher prices when visiting coastal cities, and higher taxes to pay our part of the government's contributions for remediation and recovery costs. For example, the U.S. Army Corps of Engineers' budget request to Congress for fiscal year 2022 included initial coastal barrier protections for Charleston, Miami, Houston-Galveston, and New York City, totaling over $100 billion.[3]

The climate refugee problem is intimately connected with the rise in sea level. Environmentally induced displacement is happening all over the world and is anticipated to intensify as climate change becomes more severe. In richer countries, climate migration can take the form of in-country migration after disaster evacuations. For example, after Hurricanes Katrina, Irma, Maria, Harvey, and Florence, some evacuees from New Orleans, Puerto Rico, and Houston simply cut their losses and built permanent lives at their evacuation destinations.[4] Other climate refugees follow jobs as businesses relocate. In countries like Guatemala, where farmers are particularly vulnerable, environmentally induced displacement often takes the form of some family members relocating to cities to secure jobs that bring in money to supplement precarious farm income. Or entire families may pick up and move, seeking better opportunities through relocation. Whatever the situation, the relocation may be in-country or it may be international. In the case of Guatemala, many may migrate to the United States.

Environmentally induced displacement does not have an effect on Iowa only when climate refugees move to our state. It also causes financial and political stresses inside of countries and among countries. These stresses can exacerbate existing political tension, feed anti-immigrant violence, and even lead to failed governments, armed conflict, and civil war.

Beyond the specific issue of migration, climate change has a number of implications for U.S. foreign policy that affect Iowans. Military planners and diplomatic experts refer to climate change as a threat multiplier due to the fact that its consequences often exacerbate existing vulnerabilities. Thus, foreign policy must anticipate more complex and frequent international crises connected to climate change. This means being ready with military and humanitarian disaster relief, making investments to secure or relocate low-lying U.S. interests such as naval bases, and adapting to the demands that extreme heat makes on people and equipment. Regional destabilization due to climate change limits the United States' capacity to deal with other important geopolitical and security issues such as disease outbreaks, trade disputes, illegal drugs, human trafficking, and terrorism.

In this chapter, I have focused on arguably the two most important effects of climate change—changes to rainfall patterns and global sea level rise—because they create so many expensive, destabilizing, and cascading problems. But climate change is transforming life across the country and around the world in many other significant ways. While I was writing this, in summer 2021, extreme heat (with a heat index of 105 on day 4 of RAGBRAI) and air-quality problems from western wildfire smoke were capturing Iowa headlines.[5] Other serious effects include ocean acidification, mountain and arctic ecosystem collapse, and fisheries and coastal ecosystem degradation. Some of these will be felt directly in Iowa, others we will witness at a distance, but all will affect us in some way.

WHAT OF OUR RESPONSE?

I believe it is important that we keep these many global consequences in mind as we consider how we, as Iowans, choose to respond to the challenges and opportunities of climate change. The question of whether we strive to reduce emissions now to prevent these significant effects or whether we put them aside for possible future action is partly a utilitarian one. The research shows that with aggressive action, I can pass a healthier, more functional planet on to my children. Furthermore, by investing in mitigation and early adaptation, I can lessen the financial burden of disaster response that I pass on to my kids.

But for me these are also moral decisions. I believe that natural places and the plants and animals in them have inherent value and that it is spiritually impoverishing to degrade them through unnecessarily severe climate change. Whether you believe that the earth was a gift from a benign creator or a beautiful cosmic accident, isn't the conclusion the same?

The potential solutions to these problems, the sorts of investments in demonstration projects, and the additional research and development needed to build them at scale are well understood. Some of the most relevant solutions in Iowa are more energy-efficient buildings, wind energy, solar energy, bioenergy, soil carbon sequestration, and the reduction of methane and nitrous oxide emissions from livestock and crop production. Iowans can also help address Guatemala's problems by mitigating climate change here in the Midwest and by helping Central Americans increase their resilience through improved agronomic practices, conservation agriculture, crop diversification, water management, and crop insurance.[6]

In my Green Chemical and Energy Technologies class at the University of Iowa, I engage students by using a list of twenty-two ways to stabilize the climate system.[7] I teach them how to evaluate potential greenhouse gas–reduction projects and recommend the best ones for a given scenario. I share tests that solutions must meet for long-term success as well as research showing that authentic partnerships with stakeholders are necessary for effectiveness and equity. Solutions must also demonstrate truly effective and equitable partnerships among all stakeholders, including business owners, faith communities, workers, agricultural producers, local governments, and nonprofits. The most effective partnerships are long-standing ones that take on increasingly ambitious challenges while trust and mutual respect develop.

As a scientist and an engineer carefully monitoring the atmosphere and climate system, I have come to terms with the fact that serious climate change can no longer be avoided. But we still have the tools and the knowledge to avoid its most severe consequences going forward. Let's get to work and use them!

NOTES

1. UN World Food Program USA, "The Dry Corridor," https://www.wfpusa.org/emergencies/dry-corridor.

2. H.-O. Pörtner, D. C. Roberts, V. Masson-Delmotte, et al., eds., *IPCC Special Report on the Ocean and Cryosphere in a Changing Climate* (Cambridge: Cambridge University Press, 2019). This report contains historical sea level rise data through 2015. The historical record was extrapolated out to 2021 using an annual rate of 0.14 inch per year to create past and future sea level rise values with a transition year of 2021. Information on sea level rise in this chapter is based on this report.

3. See J. Hinkel, D. Lincke, A. T. Vafeidis, et al., "Coastal Flood Damage and Adaptation Costs under 21st Century Sea-Level Rise," *Proceedings of the National Academy of Sciences* 111, no. 9 (2014): 3292–3297, doi:10.1073/pnas.1222469111. And see Gary Griggs, "For Flood-Prone Cities, Seawalls Raise as Many Questions as They Answer," *Conversation*, June 23, 2021, https://theconversation.com/for-flood-prone-cities-seawalls-raise-as-many-questions-as-they-answer-162587. The largest of these is the New York–New Jersey seawall; its cost estimate can be seen at the U.S. Army Corps of Engineers website: https://www.nan.usace.army

.mil/Missions/Civil-Works/Projects-in-New-York/New-York-New-Jersey
-Harbor-Tributaries-Focus-Area-Feasibility-Study.

4. Oliver Milman, "'We're Moving to Higher Ground': America's Era of Climate Mass Migration Is Here," *Guardian*, September 24, 2018, https://www.theguardian.com/environment/2018/sep/24/americas-era-of
-climate-mass-migration-is-here.

5. Philip Joens and Sarah Kay LeBlanc, "A Day That Came with Warnings of Extreme Heat Turns into What Nobody Expected: A Great RAGBRAI Ride," *Des Moines Register*, July 28, 2021.

6. J. Hansen, J. Hellin, T. Rosenstock, et al., "Climate Risk Management and Rural Poverty Reduction," *Agricultural Systems* 172 (2019): 28–46, doi:org/10.1016/j.agsy.2018.01.019.

7. My solutions, developed and taught over the years, started with the stabilization wedges of Stephen Pacala and Robert Socolow; see https://cmi.princeton
.edu/resources/stabilization-wedges. To these I added control of short-lived climate forcers such as methane and airborne soot; see Steven J. Smith and Andrew Mizrahi, "Near-Term Climate Mitigation by Short-Lived Forcers," *Proceedings of the National Academy of Sciences* 110, no. 35 (2013): 14202–14206. These were further updated using the comprehensive assessments in chapter 4 of V. Masson-Delmotte, P. Zhai, H.-O. Pörtner, et al., eds., *Global Warming of 1.5°C: An IPCC Special Report on the Impacts of Global Warming of 1.5°C above Pre-industrial Levels and Related Global Greenhouse Gas Emission Pathways, in the Context of Strengthening the Global Response to the Threat of Climate Change, Sustainable Development, and Efforts to Eradicate Poverty*, 2018, https://www.ipcc.ch/sr15. A more approachable coverage of solutions can be found in Paul Hawken, ed., *Drawdown: The Most Comprehensive Plan Ever Proposed to Reverse Global Warming* (New York: Penguin, 2017).

Forty-Five Minutes of Sheer Terror

Carole Teator

ON AUGUST 10, 2020, I was working from home, as were most of my colleagues, due to the COVID-19 pandemic. My employer at the time, the Iowa Natural Heritage Foundation, is a statewide conservation land trust with staff in several locations across Iowa. The majority live and work in the Des Moines area, 130 miles west of where I live in Cedar Rapids.

We had an online staff meeting that morning and as the meeting ended, several of my central Iowa coworkers mentioned that the sky had gotten very dark. As they spoke, notifications on their phones alerted them to severe weather in their area. Over the next hour, many of them texted that the storm had left them without electricity and had caused a great deal of damage to trees.

None of us realized at the time that a violent band of thunderstorms 50 to 100 miles wide was carving a path across the Midwest. This line of storms would travel more than 700 miles from Nebraska to Ohio and was detectable on radar for fourteen hours, about the time it takes to drive an automobile the same distance.

This weather system was not a tornado or even a cluster of tornadoes, which midwesterners might expect on a hot and humid day in August. Instead it was a derecho, a long-lived and fast-moving band of thunderstorms with sustained and intense straight-line winds. Derechos are not rare in this part of the Midwest, but without question no one alive today had ever experienced one of this magnitude and duration.

The storm careened across the state, flattening nearly a million acres of crops, collapsing buildings, tearing off roofs, shredding utility lines and communication towers, and killing at least three people. As it reached Cedar Rapids, wind gusts topped 140 miles per hour, the equivalent of a Category 4 hurricane. Unlike a hurricane, however, people in the derecho's path had minutes, not days, to prepare.

Knowing what my coworkers in central Iowa had experienced, I texted friends and neighbors to alert them to the storm heading our way. As soon as the clouds darkened and the wind picked up, I retreated to the basement with my dog to wait out the storm in relative safety.

What happened next was forty-five minutes of sheer terror. As my dog and I huddled in the basement, the wind pummeled the house with such force and unrelenting fury that I expected the walls to collapse. I feared that all the towering trees surrounding my house would fall and crush my home. I heard the house groan and something—I assumed a window—making a ratcheting sound as the wind torqued it in its opening in the wall. I later realized that large tree limbs and whole trees were snapping and falling all around the house, but all I heard or felt during the storm were the howling wind and the vibrating house.

After the storm subsided, I left my house through the only door not blocked by storm debris and crawled under and over broken trees to assess the damage to my home and neighborhood. Trees were strewn everywhere, on top of houses and vehicles and blocking the street. I learned later that hundreds of homes and businesses throughout the city had been partially or completely destroyed. Hundreds more sustained extensive damage that would take a year or more to repair due to supply shortages caused by the pandemic and weather disasters in other parts of the country.

My neighborhood was without power for nearly two weeks. The electricity in nearby neighborhoods wasn't restored for three weeks or more. Without electricity, gas stations were inoperable those first days after the storm, forcing people to drive several miles to buy gasoline for their vehicles, chain saws, and generators.

Incredibly and thankfully, my house sustained only minor damage. But the trees that surrounded it—the best part of my home and my companions during the preceding months of pandemic-caused isolation—were devastated. The majestic white pines and stately oaks and maples that had been growing in this spot for eighty years or more were destroyed, their trunks snapped or twisted, with the bark on some slit open like a zipper. I counted twenty-five trees on my one-acre property lost to the storm before I forced myself to stop counting. The loss was just too much to quantify.

Because I have worked for more than two decades in the conservation field, I know that the loss of trees is more than just a loss of beauty. Trees cool our homes, reduce soil erosion, clean our air and water, and provide wildlife habitat. In addition, numerous studies have shown that neighborhoods with trees experience less crime, better public health, and increased home values. Now, because of the destructive power of the derecho, my generous tree neighbors and an estimated 65 percent of the large trees in Cedar Rapids are no longer with us, and over 7 million trees across the state were either destroyed or damaged, bringing the estimated cost of lost services such as removal of air pollutants and carbon sequestration by these trees to over $20 million a year in urban areas alone.[1]

Even more troubling, as Cedar Rapids and other communities step up to address the climate crisis, local efforts to mitigate the carbon we contribute to the atmosphere have suffered a tremendous setback. The U.S. Forest Service estimates that one large tree growing in a park or other public space for twenty years can sequester 109 pounds of carbon dioxide in one year.[2] But such an amount of sequestration is achieved only once the tree has gained its mature mass and height. This means that it will take at least two decades for the trees planted today to grow large enough to match the carbon storage capacity of the trees lost to the derecho.

The good news is that the Cedar Rapids community is moving quickly to replace its lost trees. City leaders have committed $1 million a year for ten years to replant trees along streets and in parks. Conservation organizations are sourcing good-quality affordable saplings for owners of homes and small businesses. A youth employment program was launched to deploy young people to plant and care for the young trees in public spaces. Tree equity is being prioritized, ensuring that trees are planted in all neighborhoods so that all residents will enjoy the benefits they provide. And diverse native tree species are being promoted because of the food and shelter they supply to beneficial insects, birds, and other native wildlife.

The National Oceanic and Atmospheric Administration determined that the August 2020 derecho was the costliest single-day thunderstorm event to hit the United States in recorded history, causing $11 billion in damage, mostly in Iowa.[3] But that record will likely be broken. Climate scientist Eugene Takle tells me that as Earth's temperature continues to rise, the amount of heat energy in the lower atmosphere is building up, just as it does in a pressure cooker. That excess energy is known to make normal weather events such as hurricanes more extreme. So it seems inevitable that tornadoes and derechos will become more powerful under climate change. It is therefore critical that we strengthen both rural and urban landscapes to increase their resilience if we are to prevent worsening repercussions of these and other extreme weather events as the climate crisis intensifies.

For me, cleanup of tree debris continues even a year after the storm. But like so many others in my community, I am committed to replanting trees around my house. I'm determined to do what I can to make sure that anyone living in my home eighty years from now will know the joy that I have known living among big trees.

NOTES

1. See *Our CR: Weathering the Storm*, page 4, https://issuu.com/cityofcedarrapids/docs/our_cr_nov_2020_web. And see Thomas C. Goff, Mark D. Nelson, Greg C. Liknes, et al., "Rapid Assessment of Tree Damage Resulting from a 2020 Windstorm in Iowa, USA," *Forests* 12, no. 5 (2021): 555, https://doi.org/10.3390/f12050555, and Nick McGrath, "Assessment of Urban Tree Canopy Damage in Incorporated Communities Resulting from the August 2020 Midwest Derecho" (Des Moines: Iowa Department of Natural Resources, 2021), https://www.iowadnr.gov/Portals/idnr/uploads/forestry/DerechoReport.pdf?utm_medium=email&utm_source=govdelivery.

2. See page 28 in E. Gregory McPherson, James R. Simpson, Paula J. Peper, et al., *Midwest Community Tree Guide: Benefits, Costs, and Strategic Planting*, https://www.fs.fed.us/psw/publications/documents/psw_gtr199/psw_gtr199guide.pdf.

3. See NOAA National Centers for Environmental Information, *Billion-Dollar Weather and Climate Disasters: Events*, https://www.ncdc.noaa.gov/billions/events.

CHAPTER 10

Choosing a Better Future
Climate Change in Iowa

William J. Gutowski, Jr.

WHEN I ARRIVED IN Iowa in 1991 to begin teaching at Iowa State University, human-caused climate change was considered plausible but still somewhat uncertain: were there unknown factors we had not yet considered? As I explored Iowa in those early years, often on my bicycle, I came to appreciate again the beauty of a landscape I had first admired when passing through many years earlier, a landscape that had a sense of quiet, ordered permanence to it. Of course, the climate of the place we call Iowa has changed slowly but substantially in the past, as I will describe below. And we now know with great certainty that Iowa's climate will be changing in the future, much more rapidly than in past centuries, because humans are causing climate change worldwide. That landscape I've admired is changing significantly as the weather that gives us our climate alters the land and how we live on it.

These changes will pose challenges to our agriculture and soils, water resources, natural systems, and health as our climate transitions from the familiar to a potentially very different future. How different will that future be? That will depend on the choices we make. The choice before us now is how much and how fast we are willing to prevent further increases in the greenhouse gases we are emitting and even to remove some of them by carbon sequestration. Lack of action to curtail the growth of greenhouse gases will have dangerous impacts on our lives and even more so on the lives of our descendants. These impacts should be viewed not individually, piecemeal, but collectively, as forces that are reshaping and ultimately endangering Iowa's web of interacting natural, human, and societal systems. That web must be considered and sustained as a whole; otherwise our Iowa community will fall apart. But we can produce a better future.

Climate and weather are key intertwined elements of that endangered web that surrounds and supports us. Weather, such as warm sunny days, thunderstorms, or cold blustery days, is what we experience day to day. Climate is the collective behavior of all those weather events. Climate creates expectations of what range of weather to expect at any time of the year or, as is often said, "Climate is what you expect, weather is what you get."

Historically, Iowa's weather patterns and thus climate were shaped by our location in the middle of North America. We've tended to have large temperature changes—as much as 50 to 60°F—between typical summer and winter temperatures.[1] These seasonal changes were much greater than those in places close to a temperature-moderating ocean. Typical Iowa summer days were in the seventies and eighties, and typical winter temperatures were in the teens and twenties, with extremes occasionally taking temperatures beyond these limits. Because warmer summer air can contain much more moisture than cold winter air, precipitation has usually been greatest during the warmest half of the year.

But today, because our climate is changing, we do not always get what we expect. It's changing because we are burning fossil fuels and increasing the concentration of the highly potent greenhouse gas carbon dioxide in the atmosphere. Additional human activities are increasing other greenhouse gases such as methane and nitrous oxide. And atmospheric carbon dioxide is also emitted when forests are cut and land is tilled. But burning fossil fuels is clearly the predominant cause of this increase. Greenhouse gases trap heat in Earth's atmosphere and warm our climate. Increasing greenhouse gases are creating the phenomenon we call climate change.

HASN'T IOWA'S CLIMATE ALWAYS BEEN CHANGING?

The climate of today's Iowa has always been in flux.[2] Geologists point to far-distant times when Iowa's climate was tropical and warm pulsing seas bathed our land. At different times, dinosaurs, camels, and mastodons all roamed here. Then starting about 2.6 million years ago, the climate became cooler, and massive glaciers periodically advanced and retreated across portions of Iowa's landscape. Major climate transitions occurred relatively slowly, giving organisms and ecosystems time to respond to changing conditions. But the climate and the natural systems that are part of our supporting web did not exist here in their present forms.

As time moved on, data extracted from mineral deposits in caves and buried pollen indicate that the climate gradually warmed, and by 10,000 years ago modern prairies, which over time produced Iowa's deep rich agricultural soils, started moving into the region: the natural world's part of our sustaining web was starting to take shape. The prairies gradually migrated eastward, shifting the boundary between prairie and forest. The climate was roughly similar to today's, with a wide range of temperatures between summer and winter, yet with sufficient rainfall to support our region's ecosystems.

Humans producing agriculture appeared about 3,000 years ago, suggesting that the climate was providing a stable base for raising crops. We know that even over the past 2,000 years the climate has changed somewhat, but the changes have been relatively small. Thus the climate was relatively stable and dependable, allowing prairie plants and animals to thrive and human settlement to flourish. Our supporting web of interacting natural, human, and societal systems was in place. I've seen signs of this myself when visiting Native American mounds at scattered places in Iowa. This same stable, predictable climate made the land attractive to Euro-American settlers when they started arriving in the 1830s and established farms.

IOWA'S NEW CLIMATE

Our climatic stability, however, has started to change. Iowa winters in the first two decades of this century have been warmer on average than the first two decades of the previous century, as much as 2 to 3°F warmer depending on your exact location. These changes are consistent with winter changes around the world, showing that what we are experiencing is part of a global change, not a local anomaly. That warming may not seem like much, but shifts in average temperature are often accompanied by much larger changes in the frequency of extreme temperatures. Thus, persistent cold snaps have decreased. Severe cold snaps with temperatures of minus 15°F or colder occurred with far greater frequency a hundred years ago than they have in the current century. The bitter winter weather that I've experienced occasionally occurred much more regularly a century ago.

In contrast to winter, something different has happened with summer. Summer average temperatures in the first two decades of this century have changed little compared to those of a hundred years ago, perhaps even decreasing a little. The summer behavior illustrates the complexity of climate change and its effect on people and their lives. In recent summers, the average humidity of the air has increased, very likely because more atmospheric moisture is coming into Iowa after evaporating from the warming waters of the Gulf of Mexico. This moisture is increasing precipitation, which has two important effects on temperature. Rainy weather means cloudy weather, so sunlight that might normally warm the ground and air gets blocked. In addition, if there is more rain, the ground is wetter, and water evaporating from its surface has a cooling effect. (Think about the chill you experience when stepping out of a pool in the summertime.)

The increase in annual precipitation has been substantial: over most of Iowa, the first two decades of this century have had 2.5 to 7.5 inches more precipitation than the first two decades of the previous century. Annual precipitation now ranges from 30 to 40 inches across the state, so these increases are significant. Most of that increase has occurred over the past forty years. There has been little time to adapt to this new reality. Moreover, for most of the state, the increase has been greater in April through June than in other months, leading to more spring downpours. This change is especially important for Iowa's farmers. In spring, crops are just starting to grow. They aren't tall enough nor do they have deep enough root systems to prevent substantial soil erosion. Furthermore, because of this erosion, Iowa's waterways now carry more sediment as well as the fertilizers applied to the soil to help the young crops grow. The increases in humidity and rainfall promote increased flooding.

Increased flooding and other changes stress and even break some of the strands of our supporting web of interacting natural, human, and societal systems, so these changes in themselves are important even without looking toward the future. For example, higher summer humidity, even without rising summer temperatures, causes problems. It increases heat stress when temperatures are high. I can't enjoy bike rides on those days. Higher humidity also promotes mold growth, which can be bad for human health, agriculture, and natural ecosystems. In particular, higher humidity promotes higher summer nighttime temperatures, which harm agriculture (see the next chapter). In these ways and others, our warming climate imposes substantial costs that will increase in the future as climate change intensifies.

WHAT IS IOWA'S CLIMATE FUTURE?

Some of the changes occurring around the world, like rising sea levels or glacial lake outburst floods and landslides, will not directly affect us here.[3] But other high-impact events now seen elsewhere, like extreme heat and extreme downpours, are signs of our own future. Many of the trends we're experiencing already will continue to intensify but more rapidly, unless we start dramatically decreasing greenhouse gas emissions.

Overall, Iowa winters will get warmer. By midcentury, there may be 30 fewer days per year with temperatures dropping below freezing, lowering the annual average number to 120 such days compared to the current number of 150. Cold snaps could still happen but much less often, as recent decades have already shown. The portion of the year with no frost, the frost-free season, could increase by two to three weeks. While a longer frost-free season may reduce risks such as frostbite or hypothermia, it will produce a yet longer period for harmful invasive plants and disease-transmitting vectors like ticks and mosquitoes to thrive. (The longer frost-free season has already allowed ticks to spread Lyme disease to Iowa.) Human health will be hurt. Other changes, though not as dire, will affect recreation. For example, winter activities favored by many in Iowa, such as ice fishing and outdoor ice skating, will become much more limited. Days when I can engage in one of my favorite activities, cross-country skiing, will occur less and less often.

Summer climate shifts will amplify the high-impact changes Iowans are already experiencing. And they will pose new and more extreme risks. Heat waves are expected to be more frequent—and hotter. The cooling effect of increased precipitation, which limited daily maximum temperatures over most of the twentieth century, will be overridden by a general warming. By midcentury, the number of days above 90°F could nearly triple from twenty-three per year in recent decades to sixty-five or more. Still-warmer days, above 95°F, will also increase significantly. Currently, these very hot days are relatively infrequent, but there could be ten to fifteen more per year by midcentury, with some years having a good deal more. High heat creates dangerous conditions for human health, crops, livestock, and natural ecosystems. Heat stress that threatens crop viability, livestock health, and outdoor working conditions will have significant negative economic impacts.

Effects of increasing high heat on people will be uneven. Those with sufficient incomes and indoor jobs will be able to cope in air-conditioned environments. Those with lower incomes may not have air-conditioning and, moreover, may live in areas where they are reluctant to leave windows open for safety reasons. Inequities in responses to heat waves have already played out in major cities, often with significant negative public health consequences, including death from heat stress. Future challenges will be yet more dire.

Hot summer temperatures by themselves create problems for agriculture. But their impact is amplified by the changes they impose on the crops' water use. The maximum amount of moisture that can be in the atmosphere (the saturation vapor level) increases markedly with temperature—by about 4 percent per °F. Higher temperatures mean that the atmosphere can contain more moisture. Hotter air can pull more water than cooler air out of plants and the ground, drying them. Indeed, projections of Iowa's future climate show a significant decrease in soil moisture by midcentury. Not only will plants tend to lose water more rapidly, but there will be less water in the soil to be drawn into the plant to replace this loss.

We might think that with summertime's greater atmospheric moisture, there would also be more rainfall that would balance heat-induced drying. But computer simulations of future climate show summer rainfall tending instead to decrease, not increase, through the twenty-first century. Moreover, the warmer air appears to need a longer time for moisture to build up to saturation, condense, and yield rainfall. Thus, on average, the periods between rainfalls are expected to become longer, leading to more droughts, which will further amplify the moisture-deficit stresses on plants.

Once water vapor does accumulate to saturation levels, there is much more moisture in the atmosphere than there would be if the climate were cooler. Thus the heavy downpours that can occur occasionally in our current climate will occur much more frequently in a warmer climate: when it finally rains, it will more often pour, soaking the land. The net effect of this drying and the buildup of atmospheric moisture will create a seemingly contradictory situation: more drought and yet more flooding. Understanding the above-explained processes that lead to more drying and to heavier rainfall and their timing differences provides a key to resolving this apparent contradiction.

The crucial lesson to be learned from all these projected changes is that they will profoundly disrupt ways of living for people and for the natural world, and they will occur too rapidly for us to comfortably adapt to them. The changes will upset our normal patterns of living and working; they will fray and tear apart our supporting web of natural, human, and societal interactions. We must work to reduce these negative impacts and the inequities they entail by approaching our world as that web of truly intertwined parts. Just as the problems are integrated with one another, so too must be our ways of taking action.

WHAT CAN WE DO ABOUT CLIMATE CHANGE?

We have an opportunity to counteract the effects of increasing atmospheric greenhouse gases, especially carbon dioxide. Some have also proposed ways of blocking sunlight from reaching Earth, thus causing a cooling effect to counteract the warming from increased greenhouse gases. A problem with this approach is that about half of the carbon dioxide we put into the atmosphere goes fairly quickly into the oceans. This dissolved carbon dioxide has gradually made the oceans slightly more acidic, especially in the polar regions. (Think about how your can of pop retains its fizziness, its dissolved carbon dioxide, much longer when it's cold.) Making the oceans more acidic is hurting marine organisms, a key element of our global food network.

We need other means of reducing greenhouse gases. There are global efforts that are attempting to stop the growth of atmospheric greenhouse gases to achieve carbon neutrality by midcentury. How can Iowans contribute? We can reduce the emissions of greenhouse gases into the atmosphere by adopting more and more renewable sources of energy such as wind and solar power. Iowa is already a national leader in this movement with our growth of wind and solar farms.

We can also reduce atmospheric carbon dioxide by drawing it out of the atmosphere. One means of doing this, under active research in Iowa, is to use our land to store carbon. Tilling our former tallgrass prairies has caused our soils to lose about half of the carbon that had been in the ground, suggesting that there is an unfilled reservoir under our feet within which we can store carbon. One way of recarbonizing our soils, now under exploration, is to add biochar (akin to charcoal) to agricultural land.

An even better solution might be to expand farming methods that promote carbon storage in the ground. See the chapters by Kathleen Woida and Lisa Schulte Moore and the farming essays in the soil section as well as the other chapters and Francis Thicke's essay in this section for more information on returning carbon to the soil and other climate-healing agricultural methods. However it is accomplished, increasing soil carbon is beneficial for crop production because the recarbonized soil better resists compaction and thus better holds water and nutrients while maintaining a rich and diverse population of organisms that support plant life. The soil is healthier and more resilient in the face of increasing extreme weather events. As a further benefit, recarbonized soil, especially when combined with the greater use of prairie strips, can reduce agricultural soil erosion and water pollution.

THE FUTURE IS UP TO US

How large will the changes be as we move through this century? That depends strongly on our choices, on what we as humans do to reduce greenhouse gas emissions and, further, to pull carbon dioxide out of the atmosphere. The more we act to limit greenhouse gas emissions and draw carbon dioxide out of the atmosphere, the less harmful these changes will be. The more we recognize that we are embedded in a web of interacting natural, human, and societal systems, the better our chances of success.

I think about this as I ride my bike through Iowa's landscape and consider all the ways that we are connected with each other and with nature. And I think about my daughter going about her daily life in the future, hoping that the supportive web that has sustained me will still be there to sustain her. She will experience climate changes far more than I will, and they will extend farther into her future. Will she be able to ride through a landscape of quiet, ordered permanence like that which I admired when I first viewed Iowa? Or will it be too hot and muggy to be outside on a summer day? And if she ventures out on her bike, will she see a landscape scoured by floods in some years and desiccated by droughts in others?

Answers to these questions come down to how we and our fellow humans decide to respond to the growing threat of climate change and how seriously we consider the legacy we want to leave to our children and our children's children. We can choose a better future.

NOTES

1. Statistics on Iowa's climate over the past hundred years are from the Iowa Environmental Mesonet at https://mesonet.agron.iastate.edu.

2. Information in this section comes from several sources. See R. Baker, E. A. Bettis III, R. Denniston, et al., "Holocene Paleoenvironments in Southeastern Minnesota: Chasing the Prairie-Forest Ecotone," *Palaeogeography, Palaeoclimatology, Palaeoecology* 177 (2002): 103–122, doi:10.1016/S0031-0182(01)00354-6; E. A. Bettis III, Stephanie Tassier-Surine, and Deborah J. Quade, "Quaternary Geology of the Iowa City Area," in Thomas Marshall and Chad L. Fields, eds., *The Geology of Klein and Conklin Quarries, Johnson County, Iowa*, 135–151 (Iowa City: Iowa Geological Society, 2010); and Shirley J. Schermer, William Green, and James M. Collins, "A Brief Cultural History of Iowa," 1995, https://archaeology.uiowa.edu/brief-cultural-history-iowa-0.

3. Information on future climate projections comes from several sources. See J. M. Melillo, Terese Richmond, and G. W. Yohe, eds., *Climate Change Impacts in the United States: The Third National Climate Assessment* (Washington, D.C.: U.S. Global Change Research Program, 2014), doi:10.7930/J0Z31WJ2; D. J. Wuebbles, D. W. Fahey, K. A. Hibbard, et al., eds., *Fourth National Climate Assessment*, vol. 1: *Climate Science Special Report* (Washington, D.C.: U.S. Global Change Research Program, 2017), doi:10.7930/J0J964J6; and D. R. Reidmiller, C. W. Avery, D. R. Easterling, et al., eds., *Fourth National Climate Assessment*, vol. 2: *Impacts, Risks, and Adaptation in the United States* (Washington, D.C.: U.S. Global Change Research Program, 2018), doi:10.7930/NCA4.2018.

Clean Energy at the Universal-Local Level

Andrew Johnson

I HAVE LONG BEEN fascinated by how change happens: as a parent watching my kids grow, as a conservationist and farmer partnering with the land community, as a citizen believing in both liberty and the common good, and now as executive director of the Winneshiek Energy District and the Clean Energy Districts of Iowa.

I grew up milking cows and shearing Christmas trees on our family farm in northeast Iowa. Then, like so many, I left—to attend college in Indiana and graduate school in Michigan, to enter the Peace Corps in Guatemala, and to work in natural resources conservation with the U.S. Department of Agriculture in Georgia.

Twenty years later, it was time to come home. Upon returning to the family farm with my wife and daughters, I was fortunate to join conversations already happening in our rural community about the major challenges of energy economics and a changing climate. It was the summer of 2008, and Middle America was deep into the Great Recession. Unemployment was rising, gasoline was nearly $4 a gallon, households were struggling to pay electric and gas bills, and the cost of energy was increasingly understood to be a perpetual drain on local economies.

That same summer, much of Iowa was hit with sustained torrential rains. The state was experiencing its own form of sea level rise, and heat waves were growing. Was hell or high water coming to the heartland?

While most people in the change-making business turned toward state and federal policy solutions, our local conversations were asking more can-do questions. How can we move our entire community and region toward clean energy benefiting all? Can we create a successful and truly replicable model and then scale it up?

We were struggling to find ways not only to mitigate climate change but also to invest in the health, wealth, and resilience of our communities. We barely had the language back then, but today these ideas have become part of a national conversation around a clean energy transition that is more just, inclusive, and democratic than today's energy systems.

You see, energy has always been an extractive industry. Where fossil fuels are produced, jobs are certainly created but natural systems are destroyed. In much of Iowa and the Midwest, the vast majority of every dollar spent on energy leaves our communities. This extraction of wealth is significant and nearly universal, but what if it could be reversed?

We decided to build an organization that focused not only on accelerating the transition to clean energy but also on making that transition an opportunity for local investment, job creation, and community self-reliance. Because we believed that every community and county should own part of its clean energy future, we created a county-level nonprofit organization dedicated to implementing the transition toward this future. We wrote grants, raised money, and rolled up our sleeves, and the Winneshiek Energy District went to work.

The Winneshiek Energy District and subsequent Clean Energy Districts in eastern Iowa are not utility companies. We sometimes partner with them, but mostly we work directly with consumers to save energy through efficient practices and to invest in consumer-owned energy resources such as rooftop solar panels. We also work at the community level on projects and initiatives such as public ownership of solar panels and the electrification of transportation.

A core strategy is energy planning, also known as energy auditing. Every energy user—farms, homes, businesses, institutions—has an opportunity to invest and save through energy efficiency and solar, yet few even know where to start. With sound technical assistance, we can help energy users understand and prioritize investments in, for example, heating and cooling, insulation, solar, and electric vehicles. We have served hundreds of farms, businesses, and households with this comprehensive energy planning with tremendous results.

Since our inaugural year in 2010, we have hosted an annual team of Green Iowa AmeriCorps members. We train, equip, and empower them to conduct a first-step home efficiency assessment and to install energy-saving light and water fixtures throughout a household. Our inspiring young teams have now served well over a thousand households whose owners qualify for free service due to their elderly, disabled, veteran, or low-income status.

We've all heard it from our grandparents: a penny saved is a penny earned. Widespread adoption of energy efficiency in our buildings could prevent millions of energy dollars from leaving our communities every year. That's money that would then strengthen our households, farms, and businesses as it recycles through the local economy. Efficiency isn't easy, and it generally isn't a high priority for utilities—whose business model is, after all, built on growing sales—but we make it work.

In addition to saving energy, every Iowa energy consumer and community can also be an energy producer. Rooftop and on-site solar is financially viable and good for the grid, but markets need cultivation, and consumers need trusted advice. We have worked with our local community college to train contractors, with banks on solar loans, and with the public on education, and we have provided solar site assessments for homes, farms, and businesses. We now have over 400 customer-owned solar systems in Winneshiek County, which is roughly ten times the per capita average in Iowa and the Midwest.

Advocacy was not initially in our strategy tool kit, but we quickly realized the necessity of engaging in the policy arena. From partnering with local officials on ordinances related to energy efficiency and renewable energy and collaborating with other organizations on state policies such as net metering (which gives fair credit to rooftop solar owners) to submitting hundreds of pages of testimony in Iowa Utilities Board dockets, the growing energy district network has been an important voice for local ownership and leadership of the clean energy future.

While celebrating the ten-year anniversary of the Winneshiek Energy District in 2020, we took stock of some high-level outcomes. We documented over $20 million invested in energy efficiency and solar power in our county, resulting in a reduction of over $35 million in utility bills and the creation of dozens of good jobs. Simultaneously, we have lowered greenhouse gas emissions by over 120,000 metric tons, and our community is taking climate stewardship increasingly seriously.

This combination of local clean energy prosperity (one green benefit) and climate stewardship (another green benefit) is a key principle behind the Clean Energy District movement: when green meets green, communities unite and thrive. Another key principle is that local leadership exists everywhere. Energy districts create independent nonprofit county organizations that empower those who are passionate about clean energy and dedicated to driving change. With appropriate state and federal support, they can become local institutions in every county in the state and beyond. Finally, energy districts are geographically and socioeconomically inclusive. They work hard to find resources that serve *all* energy consumers of a given county—urban and rural, in all social groups, at all economic levels.

Our vision of 100 percent local, renewable, and efficient energy for Iowa by midcentury is big and bold, and it requires local ownership of both processes and outcomes. Energy efficiency and solar power that are locally implemented and owned create local jobs and keep energy dollars in the community. They replace the historically extractive model of the energy industry, in which resources and wealth leave communities and accumulate in large corporations, with a model that helps our communities transition to a healthier climate and a more livable home place for our children and all the other forms of life we depend upon. Our vision unites people. It's the right thing to do.

We invite you to join the movement. Consider organizing a county-level energy district in your neck of the woods, or get involved if one already exists near you. Look up the Clean Energy Districts of Iowa online to learn more.

CHAPTER 11

Ongoing Transformation
Climate Change and Agriculture

Eugene S. Takle

MY FAMILY'S INTERACTION with climate change goes back to 1892, when my great-grandfather moved his family from an island in the fjords of southeast Norway to the marshy landscape of Linn Grove in northwest Iowa. While searching for affordable land, he and his family stayed with his brother, and my great-grandfather helped him transform the prairie to agriculture. In spring 1893, his brother hired a contractor with an excavating machine pulled by twenty oxen that cut a drainage ditch from a prairie pothole to a nearby stream, an action being duplicated by many others. These drainage efforts transformed ponds and marshes into fertile carbon-rich agricultural land.

Draining the prairies was part of the massive transformation of Iowa's deep-rooted grasslands to cultivated croplands, a transformation that has culminated in today's intensive and pervasive agricultural system. Cultivating the prairies released nearly half of its soils' organic carbon into the atmosphere as carbon dioxide, which has since fed climate change.

Before my family's arrival, the region's human population had a long but minimal history of interplay with climate through its soils, water bodies, landforms, plants, and animals. Indigenous cultures, which relied on only local plants and animals for food, clothing, and shelter, were founded on respect for the land and a synergistic relationship with Mother Earth. However, an enduring climate legacy of Native Americans was their use of prairie fires to suppress woody vegetation and improve prairie quality for the grazing mammals that supplied them with meat. These intentional fires created a form of carbon called biochar with a lifetime of thousands of years in the soil. Although the activity's impact on global atmospheric carbon was likely small, it is an example of early human-caused carbon sequestration.

Euro-American settlement of the region in the nineteenth century, with its harnessing of animal power for agricultural purposes, created a new chapter in landscape manipulation on a scale that could influence climate. Oxen, horses, mules, and cows delivered power to break prairie sod, grind grain, and provide transportation while producing meat and milk. The expansion of animal agriculture added a need for feed grain and specialized forage crops that fueled the prairie's transformation and thus multiplied the release of carbon dioxide from its soils.

The introduction of steam engines replaced animal power with stationary mechanical power for threshing grain and grinding it into flour. And steam locomotives and ships expanded markets for agricultural products well beyond Iowa. Thus began the modern era, where populous regions of the world flourished because of large-scale transportation systems. The invention of the internal combustion engine expanded the use of liquid fossil fuels, and by 1950 the network of roads, rails, and waterways allowed even larger separations between producers and consumers of agricultural products.

Although such uncompensated costs of transforming the prairie as soil erosion, loss of soil carbon, and water pollution were high, their contributions to climate change were at first modest. It's safe to say that other than the release of carbon dioxide from cultivation, Iowa's climate was not much affected by agricultural practices before 1950.

The post–World War II economic recovery initiated many of the transformations that made agriculture a significant contributor to global climate change. These transformations included electrification of rural Iowa, the expanded use of nitrogen fertilizers and chemical weed control, increasingly larger and heavier equipment, and the consolidation, specialization, and expansion of row crop agriculture and confined feeding operations for cattle, hogs, and poultry. Collectively these changes increased agriculture's carbon dioxide emissions from fossil fuels. Other highly potent greenhouse gas emissions—methane from animal production facilities and nitrous oxide from tillage and the expanded use of synthetic fertilizers—also increased tremendously.

Iowa's favorable climate and deep fertile soils with their high water-holding capacity permit crops to be grown successfully without irrigation. Furthermore, much of its landscape is flat or gently rolling, which allows agriculture to be practiced with large and efficient machinery. A wide range of crops flourish and can potentially be grown profitably under these conditions, but both the choice of crops and the changing climate are increasing the costs of production.

Having spent my entire career in Iowa, I have seen the ways that changing climate trends and extremes have made our state's agriculture increasingly vulnerable. The changes that have affected agriculture between 1980 and 2020 include increased humidity (especially during the growing season), increased nighttime temperatures in summer, more intense and more frequent storms in the early part of the growing season, and increased frequency of extreme rains as well as floods.[1]

In the 1950s, my family's diversified farm raised wheat, oats, rye, barley, alfalfa, clover, and flax in addition to corn and soybeans. All these except corn and soybeans are usually planted in March, when soils are still cold, and complete their forage biomass and grain production by mid-July for harvest in early August.

In contrast, corn and soybeans are planted during rain-free periods after early April, when soil temperatures exceed 50°F. These crops reach their full height by late July, after which time photosynthesis primarily creates seed biomass instead of vegetative growth, and they are harvested between late September and early November. During July and August, these crops require about an inch of rain weekly or moisture from deep soil to reach today's average production levels.

The diverse crops of the 1950s, except for corn and soybeans, were planted before the spring rains and harvested before the thunderstorms, heavy rains, or droughts of late summer. But the vast expanses of corn and beans that now dominate our croplands are more vulnerable to heavy rains and water-logged soils during their planting season and to droughts and high winds, hail, and the heavy rains of thunderstorms in mid- to late summer. These vulnerabilities, all of which are increasing with climate change, were not so pronounced in the past. Corn planted on diversified farms before 1950 could be fed as silage to cattle even if, due to late planting delayed by spring rains, it did not fully mature into feed grain. And soybeans, having more tolerance to heat and high winds, are not as vulnerable as corn to these climate extremes.

Another problem is atmospheric moisture, which like carbon dioxide prevents near-surface heat from dissipating into the outer atmosphere. Thus Iowa's increasingly humid summers tend to produce increasingly warmer nighttime temperatures, which bring discomfort to both livestock and farmworkers. I have witnessed the effects of Iowa's increasing weather extremes, especially high nighttime heat, humidity, and rainfall, on farm animals. Milk cows, for instance, eat substantially less feed and thus give less milk during heat waves, particularly when these are accompanied by high humidity.[2]

Cattle and hogs raised for meat production can tolerate moderately high daytime temperatures if nighttime temperatures and humidity are low enough to provide a reprieve from daytime stress. However, rising nighttime temperatures and humidity have put more stress on these animals, and the higher feed inputs needed to provide weight gains increase metabolic heat, which is harder to dissipate given higher temperatures and humidity.[3] In response, meat animals drink more water, eat less feed, and gain less weight. Laying hens produce eggs with thinner shells that are more vulnerable to breakage. The panting behavior I have observed in beef cattle, hogs, and even chickens on extremely hot days signaled that their normal body-cooling functions were inadequate.

The rise in summer nighttime temperatures has not been widely recognized as a yield-impairing factor, even though they are known to regulate both plant respiration (which releases carbon dioxide into the atmosphere) and the length of time a plant devotes to producing seed. The observed rise in Iowa's nighttime temperatures during July and August shortens this grain-filling period and increases respiration for corn, thereby suppressing the amount of carbon transferred into each seed. The net result is that a bushel of corn that normally weighs fifty-six pounds might weigh fifty-one pounds or less and has less market value, since grain is marketed by weight, not by volume. The actual amount of these reductions has not been measured, but the plant respiration process is well understood, and the rise in nighttime temperatures is clearly related to global climate change, so the impact will continue to increase.

Precipitation patterns such as seasonal total, timing, and intensity significantly affect both crop growth and the critical management activities of planting, managing pests, and harvesting. Favorable corn yields require eighteen to twenty inches of rain from April through August. Timeliness and intensity of rainfall during the growing season are optimal if water infiltrates to depths where crop roots are abundant and able to use the moisture for growth. Intense rains—daily totals of more than two inches—lead to increased soil erosion, ponding, and waterlogged soils. Additionally, intense rain events may be accompanied by strong winds and hail that damage crops and can lead to infections caused by, for example, the fungus that produces aflatoxin.

The climate change of highest impact to Iowa agriculture in the last thirty years has been the rise in rainfall from April through June. A stronger flow of moisture from the warming Gulf of Mexico during this critical planting season has led to humidity increases in Iowa that are four times the global average.[4] This has enhanced both the frequency and the intensity of rain events, resulting in a 19 percent increase in the three-month total rainfall. In Iowa, every extra inch of rain in April and May reduces the time suitable for fieldwork by 2.6 days, which means that the number of fieldwork days per planting season has decreased by 5.5 days over the last thirty years.

Although over the last thirty years Iowa's growing season precipitation, *on average*, has become more favorable to agricultural production, our year-to-year variability—both higher *and* lower annual statewide averages—has become increasingly unfavorable, both economically and environmentally. Increased humidity and changing storm characteristics have led to more years with heavy rain events but also more years and more parts of the state with insufficient rain for good crops. So despite the increase in annual average total precipitation, we are experiencing more floods *and* more droughts.

Today Iowa's soils can absorb up to about 1.25 inches of rain over twenty-four hours if they are not already saturated.[5] More daily rainfall totals exceeding this threshold are being reported, many being 3 to 6 inches or more, leading to runoff and the loss of water for crops. The increase in the number of rain events with more than 1.25 inches per day causes more erosion, waterlogging of soils, and flooding, and it lowers the number of harvested acres. Drought years, in contrast, produce lower average yields and leave unused nitrogen fertilizer in the soil that may leach into groundwater or be washed into rivers and lakes.

Some recent climate changes, however, have benefited agricultural production. The frost-free season has increased by ten to fourteen days since the 1950s, allowing farmers to plant longer-season hybrid corn for increased yields. Increased spring and early summer rains in the last thirty years have filled deep soil reservoirs that corn can draw upon during dry conditions in July and August. More cloudiness and precipitation in summer have lowered daily high temperatures, with fewer corn pollination failures. An estimated 28 percent of annual corn yield increases since 1981 has resulted from more favorable weather, with the balance being attributable to better plant genetics and better management.[6]

Since 1960, Iowa's corn yields have risen about two bushels per acre per year. This long-term increase has been punctuated by isolated years with substantial reductions in yields—for example, severe and widespread droughts in 1983, 1988, and 2012, excess rainfall in July and August of 1993, and the derecho in August of 2020. Only a few years have had yield reductions from other factors. And since higher winter temperatures reduce cold-weather stress for milk cows, Iowa's recent warmer winters likely have contributed to higher milk production.

THE FUTURE: MORE EXTREME HEAT AND MORE EXTREME PRECIPITATION

Archaeological studies have documented numerous flourishing civilizations that died out when protracted climate changes or associated abrupt landscape changes disrupted food production on a large scale.[7] Could this happen to us? Today's climate trends are likely to intensify and bring new challenges on multiple fronts. What will be our fate? Let's consider how future climate change may affect Iowa by looking specifically at our major crop, corn.

According to the *Fourth National Climate Assessment*, temperatures during five-day summer heat waves are projected to increase more in the Midwest than in any other region of the country.[8] Higher July temperatures interfere with corn pollination, and extreme heat in August reduces the length of the grain-filling period for corn. Increases in midwestern growing season temperatures are projected to be the largest factor contributing to declines in the productivity of U.S. agriculture.[9]

Beyond 2050, Iowa is likely to experience more years with extremely high precipitation interspersed with years of less than twenty inches per year. During wet years, waterlogged soils will interfere with tillage, planting, pest and pathogen control, and harvesting of both corn and soybeans. During dry years, yields will suffer significant declines unless sparse rain events are well timed with periods of critical needs of plant growth and reproduction.

Changes in climate by midcentury will inevitably lead to higher costs to prevent declines in yields. Installing irrigation systems, updating field drainage systems, increasing chemical control of pests and pathogens, and devoting more acreage to controlling overland water flow are examples of costly changes that may become necessary to prop up yields. At some future point, parts of the state may see producers abandon corn and soybean farming because of these costs.

WHAT CAN AGRICULTURE DO TO ADDRESS THE PROBLEM?

Since around 1950, agriculture has increasingly been part of our climate change problem. About 29 percent of Iowa greenhouse gas emissions are caused by agriculture, either directly by burning fossil fuels or as nitrous oxide emissions from soils, fertilizers, manure, and urine from grazing animals and methane production by ruminant animals or indirectly from changes in land use.[10]

But today agriculture can also be a major part of our climate change solution. For example, carbon can be sequestered in soils by soil amendments such as biochar, alternative tillage practices that retain more crop residues, and an increase in deep-rooted native perennials by planting prairie strips in row crop fields. As a bonus, these healthier soils will help buffer agricultural lands from the effects of climate change such as heavier rains. And changes in animal agriculture can reduce greenhouse gas emissions through the use of manure digesters that capture methane from dairy farms and concentrated animal feeding operations.

Farms are becoming common sites for solar panels that power on-farm needs and often generate extra power that's returned to the grid. In addition, Iowa's farmland is used for utility-scale wind turbines, which require a remarkably small site and are likely to benefit crop growth and grain weight by increasing the plants' carbon uptake from the atmosphere.[11] In the coming years, electric tractors and trucks could tremendously reduce the production of greenhouse gases by agricultural equipment. Other innovative practices and future opportunities to address climate change through agriculture are discussed in the other chapters and Francis Thicke's essay in this section and in the chapters by Kathleen Woida and Lisa Schulte Moore and the farming essays in the soil section.

Finally, I should note that growing up on a farm as I did ingrains in a young child a sense of optimism and a can-do spirit coupled with a recognition of and respect for the rhythms of nature. Both curiosity and necessity have led farmers to look for and adopt transformative practices. Climate change presents some daunting challenges for Iowa agriculture. It becomes increasingly urgent that our farmers and agribusiness leaders have access to the latest science-based information on the plants, soils, and animals that underpin Iowa agriculture and that they are willing, perhaps with science-based incentives, to make transformative changes. Visionary policies based on projections of future climate trends will promote wholesome food production and sustainability for Iowa agriculture, even as such policies lower global greenhouse gas emissions.

NOTES

1. Personal analysis of data from Iowa Environmental Mesonet, "Climodat Reports," 2021, https://mesonet.agron.iastate.edu/climodat. And see Eugene S. Takle, "Climate Changes in Iowa," in *Climate Change Impacts on Iowa 2010: Report to the Governor and the General Assembly*, 2011, https://www.iowadnr.gov/conservation/climate-change.

2. Current research shows that as the temperature-humidity heat index rises above 72°F, milk cows experience increasing discomfort and lowered milk production. If the average daily temperature rises above 78°F, stress on cows can become severe. Over recent decades, the summer daily average temperature in Iowa has gone up and the humidity has gone up, so a higher temperature-humidity heat index increases stress on cows and lowers their milk production. (Temperature and humidity information from personal analysis of data from the Iowa Environmental Mesonet.) See also M. K. Walsh, P. Backlund, L. Buja, et al., "Climate Indicators for Agriculture" (Washington, D.C.: USDA–Climate Change

Program Office, 2020), https://www.usda.gov/sites/default/files/documents/climate_indicators_for_agriculture.pdf.

3. T. L. Mader, L. J. Johnson, and J. B. Gaughan, "A Comprehensive Index for Assessing Environmental Stress in Animals," *Journal of Animal Science* 88, no. 6 (2010): 2153–2165, doi:10.2527/jas.2009-2586.

4. Eugene S. Takle and William J. Gutowski, Jr., "Iowa's Agriculture Is Losing Its Goldilocks Climate," *Physics Today* 73, no. 2 (2020): 26–33, https://doi.org/10.1063/PT.3.44.

5. J. Hatfield, E. S. Takle, R. Grotjahn, et al., "Agriculture," in J. M. Melillo, Terese Richmond, and G. W. Yohe, eds., *Climate Change Impacts in the United States: The Third National Climate Assessment* (Washington, D.C.: U.S. Global Change Research Program, 2014), 150–174, doi:10.7930/J02Z13FR.

6. E. Butler, N. D. Mueller, and P. Huybers, "Peculiarly Pleasant Weather for US Maize," *Proceedings of the National Academy of Sciences* 115, no. 47 (2018): 11935–11940, www.pnas.org/cgi/doi/10.1073/pnas.1808035115.

7. Examples include the Akkadian Empire in Mesopotamia (collapsed after a 300-year-long drought beginning about 2200 BC), the Mayan civilization of Mesoamerica (lasted about 3,000 years until AD 1000), the 600-year Khmer Empire of southeast Asia (ended in 1431 due to drought alternating with extreme monsoon rains), and the 500-year Viking settlement of Greenland (abandoned due to harsh climate of the Little Ice Age in the 1400s). These demises included both long-term climate trends and changes in climate extremes. See World Economic Forum, "Climate Change Helped Destroy These Four Ancient Civilizations," 2019, https://www.weforum.org/agenda/2019/03/our-turn-next-a-brief-history-of-civilizations-that-fell-because-of-climate-change.

8. The average temperature for a five-day heat wave in Iowa in the late twentieth century was about 92°F; by the mid-twenty-first century, this is projected to rise to 103°F if greenhouse gas emissions continue at rates of the early twenty-first century. Even under a scenario with modestly reduced carbon dioxide emissions, projections indicate that, on average, by the mid-twenty-first century one year out of two in Iowa will have at least one summer five-day period when pollination of corn and soybeans will fail. See J. Angel, C. Swanston, B. M. Boustead, et al., "2018: Midwest," in D. R. Reidmiller, C. W. Avery, D. R. Easterling, et al., eds., *Fourth National Climate Assessment*, vol. 2: *Impacts, Risks, and Adaptation in the United States* (Washington, D.C.: U.S. Global Change Research Program, 2018), 872–940, doi:10.7930/NCA4.2018.CH21.

9. See Butler, Mueller, and Huybers, "Peculiarly Pleasant Weather." And see Xin-Zhong Liang, You Wu, Robert G. Chambers, et al., "Determining Climate Effects on US Total Agricultural Productivity," *Proceedings of the National Academy of Sciences* 114, no. 12 (2017): E2285–E2292.

10. Iowa Department of Natural Resources, "Greenhouse Gas Emissions," 2020, https://www.iowadnr.gov/environmental-protection/air-quality/greenhouse-gas-emissions.

11. D. A. Rajewski, E. S. Takle, J. K. Lundquist, et al., "CWEX: Crop/Wind-Energy Experiment: Observations of Surface-Layer, Boundary-Layer and Meso-scale Interactions with a Wind Farm," *Bulletin of the American Meteorological Society* 94, no. 5 (2013): 655–672, doi:10.1175/BAMS-D-11-00240.

Curtailing Climate Change on the Farm

Francis Thicke

MY WIFE, SUSAN, and I are owners and operators of an organic dairy and crop farm near Fairfield in southeast Iowa. We process our milk on the farm and market our dairy products in our local community through grocery stores and restaurants.

We are taking three kinds of action on our farm to help mitigate climate change: we reduce fossil fuel use wherever possible, we are installing renewable energy systems, and we are adopting regenerative pasture and cropping practices that sequester carbon in the soil and make our farm more resilient to the effects of climate change. I will write mostly about this last point. Key elements of regenerative farming systems are having living plants covering the soil at all times, reducing or eliminating tillage and chemical applications, increasing plant diversity, and integrating crop and animal production systems.

Our cows get most of their feed by grazing pastures from spring until winter. The design and management of our regenerative grazing system are key to its success. We have divided about 200 acres of our farm into many small pastures—paddocks—that provide grazing for our 160 dairy animals. Additionally, we have the flexibility to graze adjoining hayfields in case of drought and to lengthen the grazing season in the fall. Twice a day the milking cows are turned into a fresh paddock of lush pasture. The cows rotate through the paddocks, allowing the diversity of grasses, legumes, and forbs in each paddock ample time to rest and regrow before the next time it is grazed. We have a portable shade for the cows that we move daily to wherever they are grazing.

This grazing system provides our cows with nutritious feed and helps sequester carbon in the soil. When pasture plants have time to regrow before being regrazed, they put down deeper roots and sequester more carbon as organic matter. This happens in two ways. First, when plants take carbon dioxide out of the atmosphere through photosynthesis, they transfer a large amount of that carbon down through their roots and exude it into the soil as a liquid that feeds the underground bacteria that are cycling soil nutrients, making them more available for plant uptake. Second, each time the pasture plants are grazed off, they slough some of their root mass into the soil, which becomes food for the soil food web. Then, as the plants regrow, they also grow new roots. Thus, each grazing episode contributes more carbon to the soil's organic matter.

This kind of grazing management contrasts with the more common practice of keeping cows in the same large pasture all summer. In that system, by midsummer the grass has been grazed very short, which means that its roots are shallow, making that system more prone to drought, less productive, and inefficient at sequestering carbon.

Most dairy cows today are kept in confinement by the milking facility. All the feed they eat must be harvested in distant fields and hauled to the cows, and their manure must be collected and hauled back to distant fields. Each of these steps requires fossil fuels for powering machinery and for manufacturing the fertilizers and pesticides used to grow the feed.

A friend once observed, "It is the nature of cows to move about and graze, and it is the nature of grass to stand in one place. But with today's industrial agriculture, we have made the cows stand in one place and made the grass move to the cows." By taking animals off the landscape, we have amplified the pollution problems inherent in both industrialized crop production and industrialized livestock production. Regenerative agriculture, instead, is based on the principles of mimicking nature and harnessing the energy and the organizing power of nature's ecology, rather than trying to overpower nature with fossil fuels.

A regenerative grazing system not only sequesters carbon in the soil and reduces fossil fuel use, but we have also found that our cows are healthier because they are in their natural environment, eating their natural diet. We have not needed a veterinarian on our farm in several years. Also, cows on pasture naturally deposit their manure on the same land where they graze, thus directly cycling nutrients back to feed soil bacteria and to regrow plants.

When cows are on well-managed pastures with a diversity of forages, the health of the whole system is optimized: soil health is improved; landscape biodiversity increases, contributing to improved wildlife habitat; grazing animals are healthier; and the milk and meat from cows on pasture are higher in omega-3 fatty acids, conjugated linoleic acids, and other beneficial nutrients, making them more healthful for the people consuming them.

Our farm is about 800 acres. In addition to our regenerative pasture system, we raise a diversity of crops and are striving to integrate regenerative practices into our cropping system. Some of these crops are grown for winter feed for our livestock, and some are sold to commercial markets. Because our farm is certified organic, we do not use chemical fertilizers, herbicides, or pesticides.

A number of practices on organic farms sequester carbon in the soil, including the use of cover crops and diverse crop rotations and the addition of animal manure and compost back into the soil. These practices also help improve soil health, maintain soil fertility, and prevent pest problems. However, one major challenge for organic crop farmers—a challenge that works against sequestering carbon—is the fact that organic crop farming often uses tillage to control weeds. Conventional farmers control weeds with chemical herbicides and therefore generally use less tillage than organic farmers. Tillage disrupts soil microbiological communities and breaks up soil aggregates, thus degrading soil organic matter and causing a loss of soil carbon.

We are excited about adopting some new technologies to reduce and perhaps even eliminate tillage on our organic farm. One such technology is a roller crimper. For example, cereal rye can be planted as a cover crop in the fall, allowed to overwinter, and in spring allowed to continue growing toward maturity. Just before the rye begins to make a seed head (at anthesis), it is rolled down and killed with a roller crimper, and a cash crop like soybeans is planted into the rolled-down rye without our having to till the field. The flattened rye serves as a mulch that conserves soil moisture and controls weeds. This system eliminates the need to make multiple tillage passes to prepare a seedbed and control weeds in organic soybean production.

Another new technology that we are investing in is a weed zapper, which consists of an electric generator mounted on the back of a tractor and connected to a wide wand on the front of the tractor. The wand is positioned to run just above the canopy of the cash crop, so any weed that is taller than the crop is killed with electricity.

We have some renewable energy systems on our farm and plan to install more over time. Because our on-farm dairy-processing plant requires a lot of hot water, we have installed solar hot-water panels to preheat water for our water heater, thus saving on propane fuel.

We also have a solar-powered water-pumping system in the middle of our farm. Solar panels near a pond power a pump that feeds pond water to a 6,500-gallon tank on top of a nearby hill. That water then runs through pipes by gravity to water cows in all the paddocks scattered around the farm.

And we have a 40-kilowatt wind turbine, which is able to provide about half of our electricity needs. Our renewable energy goal is to install enough solar panels—and battery storage when it becomes less expensive—to meet all our needs. These energy systems, our regenerative farming practices, and the fact that we sell our dairy products locally all help us reduce fossil fuel use.

We are excited about our progress toward making our farm more regenerative, more resilient, and better able to sequester carbon in the soil. However, we recognize that climate change will likely bring even more extreme weather events in the future. If temperatures rise as much as predicted, our whole system will have to become even more resilient, including selecting cows with genetic traits that can handle hotter temperatures.

CHAPTER 12

A Soft Landing for Climate Change
A Vision for the Future

Gregory R. Carmichael

MY INVOLVEMENT IN climate change work came about indirectly. I grew up in a small town in northern Illinois where my father owned a farm implement dealership. The first Earth Day and the passage of major amendments to the Clean Air Act coincided with my senior year in high school in 1969–70. I was very interested in environmental issues and was coming to understand that many environmental problems were related to the production, use, and disposal of human-made chemicals. So I chose to enroll at Iowa State University to study chemical engineering with the goal of finding ways to reduce the environmental impact of chemicals and to design better chemicals and better manufacturing processes.

This was several decades before green engineering became mainstream in education and practice. In fact, when I was learning engineering at ISU, carbon dioxide was still thought of in a good light. The accepted goal when burning fossil fuels to provide steam and electricity was to maximize the conversion to carbon dioxide to reduce the pollutants emitted through incomplete combustion, such as black soot and carbon monoxide. No one was thinking or teaching about the negative effects of the buildup of carbon dioxide in the atmosphere.

After graduating from ISU in 1974, I went on to graduate school, also in chemical engineering, at the University of Kentucky. At this moment the world was presented with the undeniable fact that air pollution had global consequences; the emerging problems with acid rain and stratospheric ozone depletion taught us this in no uncertain terms. Immediately, I became focused on these issues and their impact on human health and ecosystems.

Four years later, I accepted a teaching position at the University of Iowa. Within a few years, by the mid-1980s, the threat of climate change became clear. Again I adjusted my views, this time to include carbon dioxide, yet another key air pollutant harmful to both human health and the health of our planet. Understanding the long reach of air pollution became the focus of my career, expressed both through my international research and leadership and more locally through my position as a professor and administrator at the university. As such, my remarks come from dual—some might say dueling—local and international concerns.

WHERE IS OUR SENSE OF URGENCY?

We need to address climate change now. But why aren't we? Why are countries and too many adults not seeing this? The looming threats of climate change were already known in the 1980s. Since 1994, the United Nations Framework Convention on Climate Change has been bringing the world's countries to the discussion table to assess and implement greenhouse gas reduction policies and negotiate country-specific commitments. Yet greenhouse gas emissions have *increased* by 70 percent since that time, and our planet's temperature has continued to rise.[1] How could this have happened? Was it because we thought that the consequences of climate change wouldn't be felt until many decades later? Or because no single nation wanted to be first to make changes for fear of economic harm? Or because governments lacked the support of their citizens? Or because powerful fossil fuel lobbies were allowed to take precedence over the common good?

Whatever the reasons, without a sense of urgency we lost decades in terms of reducing greenhouse gas emissions. Instead we proceeded in the wrong direction: as of 2021, we have experienced 2.2°F of warming since 1750. Our global average temperature rise has been speeding up since 1970, and it is now increasing faster each year than at any time in the past fifty years. As things stand, without dramatic cuts in carbon dioxide emissions, Earth's average temperature will undoubtedly rise another 0.5°F in a few decades, and in this century the total temperature rise since 1750 may exceed 5.4°F—3°C—greatly surpassing climate change mitigation goals and producing a temperature that our planet has not experienced in 2 million years.

Why must we care about such small and seemingly insignificant changes in global average temperatures? The reasons are many. Even these small temperature rises are sufficient to increase the difficulty of life for humans and animals and increase climate extremes. They cause more droughts, heat waves, wildfires, and severe windstorms. As temperatures rise, the atmosphere holds more water vapor, leading to heavier rainfall events, more flooding, and more severe storms. High humidity has its own consequences for human and animal health, as those of us who live in Iowa know too well because of the increasing danger of heat exhaustion and heatstroke and worsening allergies and asthma.[2] In fact, climate change is now recognized as the biggest threat to human health globally, and it is linked to a diverse set of problems such as heat-related mortality, infectious diseases, and adverse mental health outcomes.[3] Climate change also exacerbates the health impacts of air pollution from, for example, increases in wildfires and exposure to smoke with warming temperatures. These are disproportionately felt by the most vulnerable, including children, older populations, the poor, and those with underlying health conditions. We are clearly already experiencing the effects of rising temperatures in Iowa, with noticeable increases in heavy precipitation, strong winds, and flooding.

We also need to worry about the existential threats of rising temperatures: threats to the continued survival of human civilization. As the globe gets hotter, sea levels rise and glaciers melt, and regional climate extremes become more serious. Without swift and uncompromising action, we may reach a tipping point where glaciers collapse and sea levels rise several meters, making coastal cities dysfunctional—half of the largest cities worldwide are coastal—and tropical areas too hot for outdoor work and recreation. These combinations will lead to increased immigration, exacerbation of geopolitical conflicts, and cataclysmic losses in biodiversity. Ultimately, these crises could proliferate into a compounded catastrophe from which we might not be able to recover. This could all happen in this century if we stay on the path that we are on.

The younger generations see the urgency and recognize climate change as a crisis multiplier, and they are calling for action now. "The time for small steps in the right direction is long gone," climate activist Greta Thunberg said at the 2021 World Economic Forum. I agree with her. Yet while many have heard her message and those of other young activists, we are still not moving toward solutions quickly enough.

The solution is hard but simple: we need to reduce carbon dioxide emissions dramatically, dropping them to near net zero by 2050. Focusing on carbon dioxide is crucial because it represents 76 percent of global greenhouse gas emissions and 63 percent of Iowa's.[4] But how can we accomplish this as worldwide energy consumption continues to rise? It has doubled during these past few decades even though we have become more aware of climate change![5] Fossil fuels have lifted the standard of living for half of the world and now the other half has similar desires and plans. As a result, energy consumption will undoubtedly continue to grow. Our "Mission: Impossible" is to reduce carbon dioxide emissions in the face of growing energy consumption.

A soft landing for humanity and for nature, one where we avoid the worst consequences of climate change, is still possible because the oceans, ice sheets, and other parts of the climate system change slowly: with so much mass, they have what climate scientists call large inertia. But once they hit their tipping point, everything will speed up. We can't let this inertia mislead us into thinking we have more time than we actually have. We need to proceed as if we were at the precipice of the tipping point. Still, this means there is time for hope if we have the will to act on a global scale.

We know what we need to do. We need to reduce our use of fossil fuels by electrifying everything we can as quickly as we can and then getting that electricity from renewable energy sources that do not release carbon dioxide. And we need to increase energy efficiencies and expand nature-based removal of carbon dioxide from the atmosphere. But to move forward with the urgency needed, we must also reshape our politics and policies by, for example, putting a fee on taking fossil fuel carbon out of the ground and paying to put organic carbon back into the soils, turning movements into actions through our votes, demanding transparency in business and government reporting of emissions, and increasing the scope and number of government and private programs that invest in clean energy and carbon removal technology. These actions will enhance our resiliency to climate change and simultaneously reduce health and economic inequities.

Iowa has a few special roles to play in this effort. Our state has become a national leader in the adoption of renewable energy. Iowa is the nation's leader in renewable fuels production. Iowa also ranks number one in the percentage of electrical energy produced from renewables, exceeding 60 percent in 2020.[6] Investments in wind and solar energy have helped diversify the state's energy portfolio, stabilize costs, create jobs, and stimulate economic growth.

Wind generation accounts for the vast majority of Iowa's renewable energy production, with solar currently being a small contribution. However, the solar potential in Iowa is large and exceeds that for wind by a factor of 7. Achieving this potential requires advances in technology and ways to address siting challenges. It takes eight acres of land to generate 1.5 megawatts of solar energy while wind generation requires less than an acre to generate twice that amount of power. Large-scale solar installations require significant land, and in Iowa land is a political and cultural as well as an economic issue. Perhaps the way to change the energy landscape is to appeal to Iowa's owners of rural land and make them partners in energy production so that their land will remain viable for their family's future generations. Advances in energy storage technology, such as batteries and further investments aimed at strengthening Iowa's electrical grid, are also pivotal in making a 100 percent wind and solar portfolio for Iowa a reality.

Iowa can also make significant contributions to addressing climate change by reducing emissions from agriculture, our state's largest source of greenhouse gases. Climate change is caused by multiple climate pollutants, with carbon dioxide, methane, and nitrous oxide being the three largest individual contributors to global warming. Food production is associated with all three of these gases, but direct agricultural emissions are dominated by methane and nitrous oxide. In 2020 these two gases together accounted for more than 30 percent of Iowa's total greenhouse gas emissions.[7]

Fortunately, we can also use agriculture to solve climate change problems. Cutting the overuse of nitrogen-based fertilizers would reduce our greenhouse gas emissions dramatically. The manufacture of these fertilizers has a very large carbon footprint. In addition, Iowa's rampant overfertilization in the last thirty years has resulted in large nitrous oxide emissions from the soil. To decrease nitrous oxide, we must develop green alternatives to industrialized corn and soybean production. Regenerative cattle grazing, reductions in the use of chemical fertilizers and pesticides, and the other strategies presented in the other chapters and farming-related essays in this book are also imperative.

Targeting the short-lived pollutants that increase greenhouse gas emissions is another critical goal that Iowans can work toward. In my career, I have consistently identified climate change solutions by looking at air pollutants in a novel way, and I have examined the interaction between climate and pollution. It is hard to believe this now, but at the start of my career, just as carbon dioxide wasn't thought of as a pollutant, air pollutants in general were not part of climate discussions. Unfortunately, many of today's government climate policies are still oriented this way, although this is changing.

My research has helped establish that air pollutants such as black carbon or soot, ozone, and methane collectively contribute as much warming to the atmosphere as does carbon dioxide. Black carbon, ozone, and methane stay in the air for only a few days, a few weeks, and about a decade, respectively, so their warming impact is short-lived. Reducing the emissions of these short-lived climate pollutants must be a priority for our near-term efforts because these pollutants can be removed relatively quickly from the atmosphere, and doing so will give us a head start toward averting climate disaster. This may help us create my aforementioned soft landing. In other words, removing short-lived atmospheric pollutants can buy us time to work through the logistically complex problem of eliminating our dependence on fossil fuels, whose carbon dioxide emissions will inevitably continue to warm Earth for a century or more.

I am happy to say that many actions are being taken nationally and internationally to reduce these three climate pollutants. These include reducing black carbon emissions from trucks and cookstoves, the flaring of natural gas associated with oil extraction, decreasing ozone through decreasing the emissions of primary air pollutants—nitrogen oxides and hydrocarbons, including methane—that produce it, and reducing methane leaks from natural gas pipelines and capturing methane from landfills.

More ambitious actions to reduce methane emissions are needed since such actions could avoid an additional 0.5°F of warming by 2050.[8] Agricultural livestock are the main source of methane emissions globally, accounting for about 40 percent of the total. Here in Iowa livestock account for 83 percent of methane emissions, created mainly by ruminating cattle and manure.[9] How could we significantly reduce the methane emissions of Iowa's millions of cattle? Better diets, supplements to slow down methane production, breeding (not all cattle breeds emit the same amounts—cows in India emit just a fraction of those in Iowa), capturing methane from the air in confinement buildings, better manure management including manure stockpile aeration, and on-farm biogas capture and use could all play a role.

To stretch our consideration still further, our food delivery system needs to be fixed. Currently, about a third of the food we produce is wasted. All the food thrown out by grocery stores, restaurants, homes, and so on worldwide represents 8 percent of the total global greenhouse gas emissions. This amount of wasted food is sufficient to feed 2 billion impoverished children every year![10] This statistic exemplifies our moral obligation to address climate change now. Better labeling—including associated greenhouse gas emissions—better inventory systems, and better-organized donations to food banks are necessary fixes for our food delivery system.

Given the path we are on, addressing climate change is going to require more than reducing emissions of carbon dioxide, nitrous oxide, and methane. We also need to actively remove carbon dioxide in the atmosphere that originated from human activities. Here, too, Iowa has an important role to play by, for example, adding biochar to the soil to enrich organic matter and drawing down atmospheric carbon dioxide into the soil through prairie plantings that enhance biodiversity, enrich the soil, and contribute to climate healing.

To sufficiently control atmospheric carbon dioxide, we will also need to develop new technologies and approaches to use as bridges to carbon-free energy supplies. Some of these might employ carbon capture and storage methods that pull carbon dioxide directly from the atmosphere, from the oceans, or from production streams, such as the stacks of fossil fuel–fired power plants, and then store the captured gas in geological, terrestrial, or ocean reservoirs or use it in products like cement.

Finally, a soft landing for climate change requires that electricity be truly carbon-free by 2050. Society's perception of nuclear power will play a key role in the transition to a clean energy future. Of all major sources of energy, modern nuclear reactors have been shown to be the safest on a death-per-kilowatt-hour basis and to have the smallest environmental footprint.[11] Advanced small nuclear reactors may be a game changer.[12]

These modular reactors, with their innovative engineered features, are designed to be built in factories and shipped to utility companies for installation as demand arises, making them affordable. They are also easier to site and can be integrated with solar and wind power.

MY VISION FOR THE FUTURE: EDUCATION FOR CLIMATE LITERACY AND SOLUTIONS

In combating climate change, I've learned that every world citizen has a role to play and that every action, no matter its size, makes a difference. However, more of us need to exercise our passionate environmental beliefs through advocacy that moves beyond words. Fortunately, today's youth are pushing us to change our teaching and learning models; they want to know more so that they can become more responsible leaders soon. I think it is the responsibility of higher education, worldwide, to educate students into climate literacy.

Iowa's universities and colleges have important roles to play in addressing climate change. In 1990, fellow professor Jerry Schnoor and I founded a resource organization, the Center for Global and Regional Environmental Research, based at the University of Iowa. Promoting interdisciplinary efforts that focused on global environmental change, the center gathered a membership of a hundred-plus scientists from colleges and universities across the state. Those scientists' educational and research efforts have increased our understanding of climate change and decreased their institutions' carbon footprints. For example, the center aided the transition to renewable fuels at the university's power plant.

These efforts have been a good start. It is beyond doubt that today's young people will have to live with and adapt to the effects of climate change, and they will have to take up the mantle of leadership toward combating it. They will have to push forward the actions that we must take to create a soft landing. Younger generations are already unsettled by government and corporate leaders' slowness to adapt, as documented in a recent United Nations poll of 21,000 youth from around the world, which showed that 75 percent believe governments should work together across borders and take immediate actions to address global warming.[13] Here in Iowa, the students and young professionals whom I know are deeply concerned about the politics, aesthetics, and technological practices of adaptation. And they feel that their needs, experiences, and knowledge are too frequently ignored or passed over by their elders in climate change deliberations.

I believe that universities and colleges have a moral mandate to listen to their students and to prepare their minds and bodies to meet future challenges. At present this means seizing the opportunity to meet student demands that we recognize pressing climate change challenges. Shouldn't we be doing all we can to ensure their future safety and their sense of hope for their future? Perhaps this is a new role for higher education, but perhaps it is also time to revamp educational policy, just as it was after the tumultuous years of the Vietnam War, when students internationally called for a more relevant education that placed their future realities at the center of their educational activities.

I feel passionately that our educational institutions should become hubs for research and policy development and undertake initiatives that will spur the innovations in technologies, policies, and governance we need to meet the challenges of climate change. Because climate change affects all human experience and all academic disciplines, including artistic fields, it is essential that universities and colleges do not relegate it to isolated scientific centers or a few courses. While climate science is clear and it doesn't lie, sustainable solutions require greater understanding of the social dimensions of mitigation and adaptation. We need holistic, campus-wide approaches to meet the demands of today's students and secure their future well-being.

Specifically, I envision Iowa's colleges and universities becoming destinations for all-campus initiatives, such as the following, which could be developed and targeted at climate solutions. First, we need cohesive portfolios of climate-related courses from across campus that involve engineering, natural sciences, social sciences, health sciences, arts, and humanities, as well as interdisciplinary seminars that bring climate-focused students and faculty together. Next, a Climate Corps of undergraduates could engage in research and experiential learning around climate solutions and community involvement. New interdisciplinary degree and certificate programs could expose students to the breadth of climate issues, connect them with community members, and promote climate-related solutions across campus. Climate solutions institutes could be designed to expand competitive research in climate-related areas and coordinate climate-focused activities across campus. Targeted areas of research could include climate change and human health, resiliency studies (applied, for example, to transportation systems, extreme weather events, and land-use changes), societal impacts such as equity and migration, ways to monitor climate change, and carbon removal and storage. Experiential learning opportunities and community-based activities should be stressed whenever possible.

IT'S TIME TO PULL TOGETHER

When I came to Iowa for the first time in 1970, I had no clue that I would still be here more than fifty years later. I also could not have imagined that half a century later we wouldn't have solved more environmental problems related to the use and manufacture of chemicals. But here we are, now facing the grand challenges of climate change.

We cannot be daunted by these challenges. Rather, we need to seize the opportunities available to us to achieve a soft landing for humanity and for nature. Iowa can play a big role in piloting us toward this soft landing. Iowans need to urgently address climate change by working together and making strategic investments that continue to champion our leadership in renewable energy; reduce carbon dioxide, methane, and other greenhouse gas emissions; and establish higher education hubs for climate solutions that empower our youth and their actions. These opportunities offer the prospect of a bright future for Iowa.

NOTES

1. IPCC, 2021: *Climate Change 2021: The Physical Science Basis, the Working Group I Contribution to the Sixth Assessment Report of the Intergovernmental Panel on Climate Change*, ed. V. Masson-Delmotte, P. Zhai, A. Pirani, et al. (Cambridge: Cambridge University Press, in press).

2. D. Peden and C. E. Reed, "Environmental and Occupational Allergies," *Journal of Allergy and Clinical Immunology* 125, no. 2 (2010): S150–S160.

3. *BMJ*, "Call for Emergency Action to Limit Global Temperature Increases, Restore Biodiversity, and Protect Health," September 6, 2021, *BMJ* 2021;374:n1734.

4. Iowa Department of Natural Resources, "2020 Iowa Statewide Greenhouse Gas Emissions Inventory Report," 2021, https://www.iowadnr.gov/Portals/idnr/uploads/air/ghgemissions/Final%202020%20GHG%20REPORT.pdf.

5. U.S. Energy Information Administration, "Iowa: State Profile and Energy Analysis," 2021, https://www.eia.gov/state/analysis.php?sid=IA.

6. Ibid.

7. J. Lynch, M. Cain, D. Frame, et al., "Agriculture's Contribution to Climate Change and Role in Mitigation Is Distinct from Predominantly Fossil CO_2-Emitting Sectors," *Frontiers in Sustainable Food Systems* 4 (2021): 518039, doi:10.3389/fsufs.2020.518039.

8. IPCC, 2021: *Climate Change 2021.*

9. Iowa Department of Natural Resources, "2020 Iowa Statewide Greenhouse Gas Emissions Inventory Report."

10. Food and Agriculture Association of the United Nations, *The State of Food and Agriculture 2020: Overcoming Water Challenges in Agriculture,* 2020, https://doi.org/10.4060/cb1447en.

11. A. Markandya and P. Wilkinson, "Electricity Generation and Health," *Lancet* 370 (2007): 979–990.

12. See U.S. Department of Energy, "Advanced Small Modular Reactors (SMRs)," https://www.energy.gov/ne/advanced-small-modular-reactors-smrs.

13. UNICEF, "The Changing Childhood Project," 2021, https://changing childhood.unicef.org.

Section IV

◆ ◆ ◆

LIFE

◆ ◆ ◆

CENTURIES AGO, MIDCONTINENTAL NATIVE AMERICANS relied on nothing beyond natural ecosystems for food, clothing, shelter, medicines, everything they needed for life. They surely knew well the diversity, distribution, and abundance of prairie and woodland plants and animals, as must have some settlers arriving in the 1800s. But today we rarely think about biodiversity, even though it's omnipresent. Our very bodies, composed of trillions of cells, are colonized by a similar number of microorganisms. I've read that micro-animals inhabit my eyelashes and eyebrows, my face and body skin. Whether I like it or not, I am never alone.

Many of these tiny organisms are vital to our health and survival. Just like the microbes that populate soils, our body's microbes carry out vital functions without our knowledge. Kill them off and things fall apart. The same thing happens when native biologically diverse communities are badly degraded or disappear.

Consider Iowa's preeminent native ecosystem, the tallgrass prairie. For thousands of years before Euro-American settlement, diverse prairie plants and animals and their soil-based representatives purred through time like a massive fine-tuned engine, providing near-miraculous eco-system services. I like to think that Iowa's earliest human residents knew the land they roamed as sacred ground, astonishing in its ability to create and sustain life, wondrously complex and beautiful.

Today we are so inured to the idea of human importance that it can be difficult for us to conceive of any system surviving without our tinkering and additives. Yet that's exactly what healthy diverse natural systems do and what the prairies did in spades. Using only sunlight, water, air, and minerals in the soil, the prairies generated thick rich topsoils, cleansed water and governed its flow, moderated flooding, generated oxygen, captured and stored carbon underground, cycled nutrients, decomposed wastes, enhanced landscape productivity, and did so much more. Each community spilled these benefits out to surrounding areas. And each spring, birds, bats, butterflies, and other animals returned to seek healthy

193

habitats for reproduction. Our tallgrass prairies exemplified the ultimate in long-term sustainability. They ensured life's continuation just as healthy natural systems still do wherever they have survived.

The tallgrass prairie's innate functionality relied on its multiplicity of organisms, each one playing its own role. In doing so, each species contributed to the survival of other prairie organisms and the community's self-perpetuation. When biodiversity was reduced and the community was pushed toward simplification, its functionality decreased. Eliminating too many species could cause ecosystem collapse. This is the concern that scientists voice about today's quiet but unyielding loss of species and shrinking natural communities: a collapse of our world's functionality and the loss of the many ecosystem services that safeguard and tend all lives, including our own. For this reason, some scientists consider biodiversity loss equal to, if not more important than, climate change in its destructive potential.

I summarized the history of Iowa's rapid loss of native biodiversity at the beginning of this book. That discussion is expanded in this section. Plowing, logging, grazing, draining wetlands, and removing natural regulators such as fire enabled a rapid and thorough conversion of prairies, wetlands, and open woodlands to farmlands, which was the intended consequence. What wasn't expected were the reduction of numerous ecosystem services and the environmental problems that followed—increased runoff, erosion, flash floods, declining soil health and porosity—all problems that today plague the agriculture that instigated them. The loss of aboveground biodiversity was mirrored by a loss of underground biodiversity as soils were plowed, organic material declined, and soil organisms disappeared. Climate change likewise is driven by the loss of carbon storage in diverse natural ecosystems. Thus the problems initiated by Iowa's lost biodiversity run deep and spread far.

Section I focused on the loss of diverse life from Iowa's soils. Here we consider Iowa's aboveground loss of diverse communities and the tremendous decline of many native species. Much of this section looks at ways to rebuild our landscape's native communities. Thus a note on terminology. *Remnant* preservation and management remain our gold standard. These refer to holding on to and restoring today's irreplaceable intact native snippets that provide models and seed sources for future restorations. *Restoration* and management, which refer to bringing health back to sites with vestiges of native elements, are also crucially important. Restoration plus *reconstruction* of native ecosystems—reestablishing them from scratch—are critical for expanding nature's diversity in Iowa's transformed landscape. All these actions envision sites, small to large, with identifiable native communities.

A growing number of books share practical information on prairie restoration. See, for example, *A Practical Guide to Prairie Reconstruction* by Carl Kurtz and *The Tallgrass Prairie Center Guide to Prairie Restoration in the Upper Midwest* by Daryl Smith and his colleagues. In *Timberhill: Chronicle of a Restoration*, Sibylla Brown tells of her adventures restoring a rich oak savanna in south-central Iowa. The Iowa Natural Heritage Foundation provides information on the preservation of natural lands.

Where re-creation of entire native communities is not possible, we can work toward functional restoration of the landscape by introducing elements of original biodiversity to achieve a reduced subset of results— for example, planting a limited number of prairie species to hold the soil and protect fragile agricultural lands, to feed the soil and sequester carbon, or to support pollinators. Even nonnative cover crops or perennial plantings can, to a degree, be used to this end. And we should not forget regenerative agriculture's efforts, which Lisa Schulte Moore describes in chapter 4, to rebuild underground biodiversity and thus restore soil function and health.

Wherever any of these efforts are undertaken, they are good. And whenever they are done in an agricultural setting, they help modern farming turn a corner ever so slightly back toward a healthy and self-sustaining landscape. This then should be our ultimate goal: to use agriculture, which caused much of the loss of one of this continent's most sustainable ecosystems, to return resilience and health to the land by reincorporating biodiversity in the many ways suggested in this book—for the benefit of both nature and agriculture, for the sake of our descendants, for the health of our planet.

Elizabeth Lynch begins the section by introducing us to the multiple aspects of biodiversity. We learn that this term encompasses genetic, species, and community diversity and that all these have declined dramatically in Iowa—from the ecosystems that "form the backdrop to our lives" to the genetic variety of wildflowers that delight us in spring. Lynch describes Iowa's major biological communities and then explains how, to our detriment, they have been degraded and lost. Extinction is the extreme form of this loss—the disappearance forever of a given species' millions of years of adaptation to place. She states that we are now in Earth's sixth mass extinction—the only one caused by human activities rather than natural disasters. After presenting an Iowa-centric explanation of what these many losses mean to us—the irreplaceable losses of future possibilities, resilience, beauty and wonder, educational and recreational resources, economic and resource benefits, and life-sustaining services—she concludes, "It is urgent that we commit resources to properly assess what remains of our native biodiversity and then find the will to identify and control the factors that threaten it. Much could easily be done if we decide to do it. . . . Our lives depend on doing so."

Rebecca Kauten's essay tells us how her family's farming and economic challenges were compounded by a purchase in the 1980s of land that would not succumb to tillage. In the end, this led to the preservation of one of Iowa's highest-quality fens, a rare wetland that today boasts over 200 native species. Her story reflects the tenuous existence of native communities in Iowa, the significance of personal action, and nature's resilience when given the opportunity to survive if not thrive.

Pauline Drobney's tallgrass prairie chapter introduces us to Iowa's preeminent native ecosystem by inviting us to the 160-acre Kalsow Prairie State Preserve and traveling back to a time when similar wildlands stretched to the horizon. She stands with us as we imagine underground lives, watch the seasons change, and hear the crackling of prairie fires. She then returns us to the present, all the while describing the prairie's demise and its consequences. Given her evocative tour, we are ready to consider "the roles we must play to restore balance to our troubled natural and cultural landscapes. These remnants teach us to see." But equally important, she describes how we might re-create extensive prairies from scratch, on cropland, which she helped accomplish as the first refuge biologist at Neal Smith National Wildlife Refuge near Des Moines. Although this restoration is "still in its infancy," such larger plantings may be "our best chance of preserving a vestige of Iowa's natural heritage in perpetuity" and thus creating hope for Iowa's future.

Ronald Eckoff follows with an essay describing his retirement project: staying physically and mentally active by restoring native prairie and savanna remnants on his 75 acres (later 116 acres) of hilly pasture near

Des Moines. The enthusiasm and pleasure he expresses about identifying new native plants, sharing the land with others, "making a difference," and even tackling invasives are both contagious and inspiring.

James Pease, who from his youth has shared adventures with wild animals, has seen numerous changes in wildlife in his lifetime. Thanks to conservation efforts, animals such as wild turkeys and beavers that once were rare are now common. But birds and insects, among others, have suffered major collapses: North American birds dropped 29 percent in abundance between 1970 and 2018, and grassland birds—former prairie nesters—have declined the most. Pease discusses such key causes as pesticides and habitat degradation. To counter ongoing wildlife losses and potential extinctions, he looks to strengthening prairie, wetland, and woodland complexes as well as our riverside lands, which he asserts comprise "the only reasonably continuous wider ribbons of wildlife habitat remaining in Iowa." His emphasis on riverside restorations blends nicely with suggestions made in Larry Weber's chapter 8 and Mary Skopec's chapter 5. Expressing his concerns for wildlife's future in our much-transformed state, Pease challenges us: "Are we up to the task...? Will we continue to make room for the wild species with whom we share this state?"

Marlene Ehresman's lifelong passion for wild animals serves her well as cofounder and director of the Iowa Wildlife Center, a wildlife rehabilitation and education organization. The center strives to deepen people's connections to nature and the land as well as aid injured animals. Her essay shares what it means to take care of needy wild animals even as she privileges us with her wisdom about what we can learn from wildness and the lives that can often seem alien to us.

Thomas Rosburg concludes this section—and our explorations of Iowa's environmental problems—with a bold vision for the future focused on dedicating 30 percent of Iowa's land to biodiversity. He stresses that he is not suggesting the removal of productive land from agriculture. Rather, he adopts the Working Landscape model that balances agriculture with nature's needs and livelihoods. Building on earlier chapters, he promotes compliance with Lisa Schulte Moore's regenerative agriculture practices on row-cropped lands. And he furthers Larry Weber's suggestion of taking marginal and frequently flooded farmlands out of intensive row crop farming.

These marginal agricultural lands could be restored to native or other perennial cover that could, for example, pasture livestock as well as sequester carbon. Rosburg concedes that this plan depends on government incentives and programs and thus on political support. But it's totally feasible: he calculates that restored marginal farmlands, when added to existing conservation lands, would create the 30 percent of nature that is crucial for making both agriculture and Iowa's landscape economically viable and ecologically resilient, thereby ensuring agriculture's long-term survival. With each such fusing of nature and the human landscape, Iowa moves a bit closer toward the healthy balance that will be needed by our children and grandchildren and by the world.

CHAPTER 13

The Ties That Bind

Biodiversity's Critical Importance

Elizabeth A. Lynch

I SPENT MOST OF MY formative years seeking ways to explore the wildest places I could find. Somewhat improbably, I ended up settling down in northeast Iowa, where I now live on a run-down old farm and teach ecology at the local college. At first, all that I could see here was the absence of the wildness that I craved, but over time my perspective has changed.

Behind my house is a degraded oak woodland. In front is an old field where row crops grew until so much topsoil was lost that farming was no longer possible. Despite the grim condition of the land immediately surrounding my house, it is possible to find treasures within a short walk from home. In May, showy male bobolinks hurl skyward from perches in the pasture; last April, I found a badger dozing in the sun at the entrance to her sett while her two cubs roughhoused nearby; last week, I watched brook trout stealthily cruising the cold dark pool of a spring-fed stream. In the woods and wetlands of neighboring farms, I have found at least a dozen plant species that are very rare in Iowa. These sightings thrill me and keep me going back for more, often with a neighbor or two in tow.

The fact that once-common badgers and bobolinks excite me so deeply is an indication of an unfortunate reality: Iowa has suffered enormous biodiversity losses over the past two centuries, and by all signs this trend will continue as populations of native species continue to decrease. In this chapter, we'll look closely at biodiversity in Iowa—what it is, why it is important, and why it is being lost. I will focus on the loss of our original native communities and the character of the remnants that survive in nooks and crannies of our agriculture-dominated state. Later chapters in this section examine in more detail trends in wildlife as well as efforts to counteract the losses of the native remnants and species that I discuss here. Iowa's efforts to restore and reconstruct native plant assemblages, which in turn can provide habitat for native animals, are crucial to returning environmental health and wholeness to our state.

The term "biodiversity" was coined to describe the variety and diversity of life in all its forms and levels from genes to ecosystems. The term is neither precise nor easy to define, but it is useful shorthand for all the living biological stuff of nature. Most often, biologists use the term to refer to the number and relative abundance of species in an area, though the genetic diversity within species and the diversity of ecological communities across the landscape are also important considerations. All three forms of biodiversity have experienced dramatic losses in Iowa since 1830.

COMMUNITY DIVERSITY AND HABITAT LOSS

Biological communities are composed of the species that live in a given place. They are defined by their species and the interactions among them. Some species are eaten by others—mayflies are food for brook trout. Other species have mutualistic relationships—soil fungi partner with oak trees to exchange mineral nutrients scavenged by the fungi for the energy-rich sugars produced by photosynthesis in a tree's leaves. I participate in this network of interactions, too. Native bees and wasps pollinate my fruit trees. Later in the summer, I forage under the oaks for chanterelles, the mushrooms produced by the mycorrhizal fungi that are nourished by the oaks.

Ecosystems are biological communities plus the nonliving parts of the environment, including water, nutrients, and energy. Around my house are a diversity of ecosystems, including the degraded oak woodland, grassy pastures, and small spring-fed wetlands and streams. These ecosystems provide habitat for a wide variety of wild species: pileated woodpeckers and wood ducks in the oak woodland, bobolinks and dickcissels in the pastures, skunk cabbages and marsh marigolds in the seepage wetlands, mayflies and brook trout in the streams.

Diverse ecosystems form the backdrop to our lives, something that we take for granted. They are the neighborhood parks where, after a busy week at work, we refresh mind and body; they are the woodlots where we take our kids hunting and the patches of tall grasses where we watch fireflies on a summer evening. In addition to providing opportunities for recreation, learning, and relaxation, ecosystems perform many other essential services: controlling pests, pollinating plants, generating soil, decomposing waste, turning solar energy into food and timber, and cleaning the air and water.

Consider, for example, the tiny wetland across the road from my house that is fed by clear water that seeps out from under the ground, creating moist conditions favored by marsh marigolds, skunk cabbages, and black ash trees. The constant trickle of water emerging from the hillside keeps the soil here constantly wet and cold. As a result, decomposition is extremely slow, and a thick layer of spongy organic peat has accumulated, locking up carbon and keeping it out of the atmosphere. Bacteria in these soggy soils remove nutrient pollution from the water, cleaning it before it flows into the Upper Iowa River. Wetlands across Iowa similarly store carbon and regulate the flow of water. These ecosystem services reduce the effects of extreme rainfall events and droughts, both of which have become more frequent and more severe as a result of human-caused climate change.

Iowa owes much of its pre-nineteenth-century biodiversity to its position at the border between the eastern deciduous forests and the grasslands of the central plains. The broad transition zone between these two major biomes was a crazy quilt of diverse ecosystems shaped by the interactions among climate, topography, fires, and floods. Indigenous peoples probably also influenced the patchwork of ecological communities through the use of fire and by planting and tending useful species. In hillier portions of Iowa, the landscape supported an extraordinarily rich mosaic of ecosystems, including oak woodlands and savannas, maple-basswood forests, and an assortment of prairies and wetlands. In flatter areas, shrub thickets, swales, sloughs, and strips of forests and woodlands along major rivers created diversity within the tallgrass prairie.

At the time of Euro-American settlement, grassland ecosystems composed about 80 percent of Iowa's patchwork quilt. More than 99 percent of the prairies have since been destroyed. Wetland ecosystems—prairie potholes, marshes, fens, and oxbows—composed a much smaller percentage of the landscape, although they played a large ecological role by providing habitat and regulating the flows of nutrients and water. Most of these were also eliminated as the land was drained for agriculture and urban development. In 2020, remaining fragments of once-extensive prairies and wetlands were ghosts of their former manifestations. At 240 acres Hayden Prairie State Preserve, Iowa's largest tallgrass prairie remnant outside the Loess Hills, lacks essential prairie ecosystem functions; it is too small to support migrating herds of bison or natural wildfires. The many native species missing from the habitat fragments that remain have been replaced with other species that can withstand the conditions of our human-dominated landscape: red-winged blackbirds, killdeer, gray dogwood, and reed canary grass. The trend has been toward simplification and homogenization. This is true of forests and woodlands, too.

At the time of Euro-American settlement, about 18 percent of the landscape of Iowa had some amount of tree cover. Exposed uplands with regular fires had thickets and oak barrens, oak savannas, and oak openings. Better-protected sites supported open oak woodlands and mixed hardwood forests. Hardwood forests dominated by sugar maple and basswood occurred on cool north-facing slopes, and broad floodplains along major rivers supported a variety of tree species that could withstand brief periods of flooding during the spring and early summer.

The forests and woodlands in Iowa have undergone substantial changes over the past century. Some oak woodlands and savannas are now being managed to restore their native biodiversity and character, but the species composition and structure of most Iowa forests and woodlands bear little resemblance to those of the past. Fire suppression in upland oak-dominated woodlands and savannas favors species better adapted to shady conditions and high deer browsing—primarily elm, hackberry, bitternut hickory, sugar maple, and basswood. Gnarly grandmother oaks are succumbing to old age, disease, and severe storms while young oaks, struggling to grow in the shade, fail to replace them.

Carpets of invasive garlic mustard create additional problems for many tree species by releasing toxins that kill the fungi that help trees take up essential nutrients from the soil.[1] And extraordinarily large populations of white-tailed deer are browsing many plant species out of existence, including many native shrubs and wildflowers. Like the remnant prairies and wetlands, the degraded forest and woodland remnants are vestiges of their former selves. Some species persist; others are already missing or will be lost soon. Despite these problems, it is still possible to find surprisingly high levels of native species diversity in Iowa: oak woodlands and savannas treated with prescribed fire host a spectacular diversity of plant, insect, and fungal species, and sugar maple–basswood forest remnants on steep, inaccessible slopes have lush understory plant communities thanks to their relative protection from deer and invasive plants.

The loss and degradation of prairies, wetlands, woodlands, and forests have compromised essential ecosystem services, making cities, towns, and rural valleys more vulnerable to flooding, reducing carbon storage, and harming native pollinators and natural enemies of crop pests such as wasps, beetles, and birds. While restoration and conservation create hope on some sites, the loss of ecosystem services comes with significant monetary cost, and the decline of beauty, inspiration, and educational and recreational opportunities is impossible to account for. All these losses will be felt only more profoundly as we continue to grapple with the challenges of climate change and increasing human demands for food, fuel, water, timber, and other natural resources.

SPECIES DIVERSITY, GENETIC DIVERSITY, AND EXTINCTION

When ecosystems become increasingly compromised, this diminishes both species diversity within remaining communities and genetic diversity within species, making them more fragile. Communities and species that appear healthy may be in more trouble than we realize. As high-quality habitat remnants become increasingly small and isolated from one another, they function more and more like tiny islands surrounded by a sea of uninhabitable terrain. Each tiny island can support only a small population of any particular species, making each isolated population even more vulnerable to extinction. Extinction can happen suddenly in the event of disaster—a windstorm, chemical spill, or outbreak of disease. A manure spill into the spring-fed stream near my place would eliminate one of four native brook trout populations remaining in the state.

When populations get very small, their genetic diversity can be lost. Genetic diversity refers to differences in the genetic makeup of individuals within a population. Some genetic diversity is visible, such as variation in the color, size, or behavior of individuals. Much of it is hidden in biochemical pathways that affect the physiology of organisms; for example, individuals within a species vary in the ways they can tolerate extreme temperatures, pollution, or diseases. Genetic diversity increases the chance that a species can evolve in response to environmental changes. Populations of most species have a good deal of genetic variation, allowing them to adapt to some changes in environmental conditions like climate change and new diseases. In very small populations, however, isolation and inbreeding can cause the elimination of genetic variation, making these populations particularly vulnerable to extinction.

Scientists say that we are currently witnessing the sixth mass extinction event in Earth's geological history. During most former periods, the rate of new species formation roughly equaled the rate of extinction. Five times in the past, dramatic disruptions of natural systems caused mass extinctions. The current mass extinction is human-caused. We have logged, grazed, mined, and paved more than 50 percent of Earth's land surface, and commercial fishing, drilling, and pollution have devastated ocean habitats and marine fish stocks.[2] Globally, two in five noncrop plants are threatened with extinction, and hundreds of species of vertebrates are currently on the brink of extinction.[3] In a geological blink of an eye, Earth has lost an extraordinary number of species and varieties of organisms, each the product of millions of years of evolutionary history. Once gone, these species are lost forever. Technological wizardry may someday allow us to clone extinct individuals, but it cannot resurrect the genetic diversity and cultural memory of populations pushed to extinction. Even if it could, the root causes of their extinction would still not have been addressed.

At first glance, the sixth extinction doesn't appear particularly devastating in Iowa. Only a handful of known species have gone extinct since 1800, including the passenger pigeon and the Carolina parakeet. The list gets longer if we consider species that have been extirpated from Iowa but still survive elsewhere: wolves, elk, Say's phoebes, the lichen *Lobaria pulmonaria*, and several types of mussel are a few of the more than one hundred species known to have been lost from Iowa since the arrival of Euro-Americans.

The situation is more troubling, however, when we consider population trends caused by habitat loss and degradation. The populations of many species in Iowa have declined to very low numbers. Vascular plants illustrate the scope of the problem: of the 1,508 vascular plant species native to Iowa, 26 percent—386 species—are rare enough to be labeled endangered, threatened, or of special concern.[4] Many of the species that we see around us today are unlikely to persist for much longer if we do not address the factors causing population declines. Ecologists refer to these impending extinctions as extinction debt. It is safe to say that we are not aware of the true size of the extinction debt we have accumulated since the 1830s.

Each June, I hear a wood thrush in the woods by my house. Its beautiful song is mournful to my ear. Research conducted on small woodlots like mine shows that wood thrushes often don't reproduce successfully because their nests are parasitized by brown-headed cowbirds or their eggs and young fall prey to raccoons, crows, and blue jays, all of which are more abundant in small woodlots than in large forest tracts.[5] Even though I still hear the wood thrush each spring, the long-term survival of this species in most of Iowa is not secure.

Ecologists have learned important lessons about the loss of species diversity. One lesson is that some species are absolutely dependent on the presence of another species. For example, leatherwood, a somewhat rare shrub in Iowa, is the only host for the larval stage of the tiny moth *Leucanthiza dircella*. Clearly, if very hungry deer drive the leatherwood to extinction, this moth will also become extinct. Another lesson is that certain foundation species are extremely influential and their elimination ripples through a community. Oaks are foundation species in Iowa; acorns are an important food source for a wide variety of birds and mammals, and the canopies of oak trees host a high diversity of insects that, in turn, attract a variety of bird species. Keystone predators can keep prey populations in check: wolves and other predators once regulated populations of deer and other prey in Iowa. Without this regulation, deer and raccoon populations have soared, affecting other species in Iowa ecosystems. Ecosystem engineers create habitat for other species: bison wallows in prairies, for example, become important habitat for certain prairie plants and invertebrates.

Yet another lesson is that communities with more species are often more resilient than communities with fewer species. For example, severe drought affects diverse grasslands less than species-poor grasslands. On a recent visit to a remnant sugar maple–basswood forest brimming with spring ephemerals such as squirrel corn, Dutchman's breeches, toothwort, spring beauty, and Virginia bluebells, I spotted a bumblebee queen searching for an abandoned chipmunk burrow where she could establish a nest. I wondered if it would matter to the bumblebee if one or two of these wildflower species were to disappear. I think that it could. Perhaps in a year when an ill-timed frost decimated the bluebells, other plant species would be available to provide pollen and nectar. If the number of flowering species were reduced, then bee populations could become more vulnerable to year-to-year fluctuations in the abundance of remaining food sources.

Even if impressive displays of spring ephemerals were not essential to bumblebees, I would be inconsolable without such diversity close at hand. Rambling through the woods and fields, looking for spring wildflowers, foraging for mushrooms, and searching for unusual birds and unfamiliar insects are essential to my well-being. Study after study has demonstrated that contact with biodiversity makes people happier and healthier, reduces stress, alleviates anxiety and depression, and improves cognitive function. Biodiversity offers spiritual connection and inspiration for artistic expression. When the COVID-19 pandemic abruptly upended our lives in 2020, we flocked to parks and nature preserves seeking solace, relief, inspiration, and recreational opportunities. The disruption of a pandemic provided a timely reminder of the importance of biodiversity to our bodies, minds, and souls.

WHAT SHOULD WE DO NOW?

Human actions have resulted in the dramatic loss of high-quality habitats and severe reductions in the extent and size of populations of many species in Iowa. Not only are populations of many native species still responding to past losses of high-quality habitats, but climate change, invasive species, continued habitat losses, and increasing pollution pose serious threats. Despite this bleak state of affairs, it is still possible to find remnants of remarkably diverse ecological communities and populations of rare species persisting on the landscape. We depend on the ecosystem services provided by these remaining fragments of original biodiversity.

It is urgent that we commit resources to properly assess what remains of our native biodiversity and then find the will to identify and control the factors that threaten it. Much could easily be done if we decide to do it. We are smart enough to manage deer populations and invasive species; we have the technology and the techniques to reduce pollution from agricultural chemicals; it is possible to restore prescribed fire to the small fragments of natural communities that remain. We even have the ability to limit the amount of future climate change, perhaps the ultimate threat to Iowa's biodiversity. Our lives depend on doing so.

NOTES

1. V. L. Rodgers, K. A. Stinson, and A. C. Finzi, "Ready or Not, Garlic Mustard Is Moving In: *Alliaria petiolata* as a Member of Eastern North American Forests," *BioScience* 58, no. 5 (2008): 426–436.

2. R. Hooke, J. Martin Duque, and J. de Pedraza, "Land Transformation by Humans: A Review," *GSA Today* 22 (2012): 4–10.

3. See A. Antonelli, C. Fry, R. J. Smith, et al., *State of the World's Plants and Fungi 2020* (Kew: Royal Botanic Gardens, 2020), doi: https://doi.org/10.34885/172, and G. Ceballos, P. R. Ehrlich, and P. H. Raven, "Vertebrates on the Brink as Indicators of Biological Annihilation and the Sixth Mass Extinction," *Proceedings of the National Academy of Sciences* 117, no. 24 (2020): 13596–13602.

4. Data are from a manuscript in progress by T. Rosburg, P. Drobney, D. Lewis, et al., "Floristic Quality Assessment for the State of Iowa," and Iowa Administrative Code, "Endangered and Threatened Plant and Animal Species," Natural Resource Commission 571, chapter 77, 1994.

5. S. K. Robinson, F. R. Thompson III, T. M. Donovan, et al., "Regional Forest Fragmentation and the Nesting Success of Migratory Birds," *Science* 267 (1995): 1987–1990.

Preserving the Fen

Rebecca L. Kauten

MY NAME IS REBECCA, but many people call me Becky due to a sign that bears my name on a wet prairie hilltop, a fen in northeast Iowa. These rare and distinctive prairie wetlands exist due to a seldom-found combination of groundwater, bedrock, and plant material. My story describes how one of Iowa's highest-quality remnant fens survives today in spite of alternative plans.

In 1981, my family purchased eighty acres of land for $190,000 or $2,375 per acre. This was when interest rates on property loans had skyrocketed to nearly 20 percent. Heavy debt put many farmers at risk, and we felt the economic crisis firsthand. On rural roads, you know the people who drive past your farm. During this time, it was not unusual for tractors and other equipment to go by on semitrailers to a bank foreclosure auction. Times were tough. We were struggling but getting by. As fate would have it, the new land purchase yielded thirteen acres essentially incapable of producing a crop. Little did my family know that this cursed yet resilient landscape was actually a small but mighty remnant of Iowa's ancient natural history.

A bit of time travel helps explain what makes this land both so unfarmable and so special. During the last glacial period, a spring likely formed there. As millennia passed, plants lived, died, and decayed on saturated substrate, creating a hill of soil that holds water like a wet sponge. Minerals from the sand, gravel, and decaying plant matter kept conditions just calcareous (chalky) and anaerobic enough for rare plant species to thrive, undisturbed, for ages.

Today more than 200 vascular plants grow here, including more than two dozen species classified as threatened or endangered. The sage willow, far shorter than any willow you might see near water, was thought to have disappeared from Iowa. Other rare plants include grass of Parnassus and four species of gentian. If you find a sage willow along with Riddell's goldenrod on a hilltop awash with cattails, odds are good that you are in a fen. And if you're at our place, you're visiting one of the highest-quality fens remaining in Iowa.

Let's now return to my parents and their new farmland in the 1980s. Economics drove management decisions and money was tight. No farmer stuck with a nearly $200,000 debt wants unproductive land. With sod busting as his goal, my father installed drainage tiles every thirty feet throughout the fen, trying to wring water out of the saturated soil as efficiently as possible. Under normal conditions, this would have rendered almost any hilltop wetland in Iowa exceedingly dry. He also sprayed herbicides to kill off the vegetation. To my father's chagrin, both attempts failed to produce a viable site for growing corn and beans. Instead, many of the native plants that should have been eradicated remained relatively intact. Following a single spraying, the hilltop would go from green to black and then back to green again in a matter of weeks, seemingly fighting back against any attempted transformation.

In many ways, serendipity led to the next chapter of the story. Coincidentally, a multiyear study to locate remaining fens in Iowa was underway. Two botanists from the Iowa Department of Natural Resources, John Pearson and Mark Leoschke, were scanning hard-copy soil maps for all ninety-nine counties with a hand lens and much patience. Without the aid of computers, they searched for soil type 221, a code identifying what was known as Palms muck, on every paper soil map of Iowa. Where this soil occurred, fens historically existed. The question was, How many remained? The two identified approximately 200 appropriate locations and embarked on a statewide tour of possible remnant fen sites. Ours made the list. One day the phone rang, and a few days later a car drove up and everything changed.

Both botanists would visit our fen many times over the coming years. Local conservation groups also got involved, especially when conversations about protecting the site began. As word got out that this special place had survived the test of time, people came from throughout the Midwest to see it in person. Tour buses filled with people excited to learn about prairie also joined the mix. Eventually, my parents agreed to a conservation easement to protect the fen in perpetuity. Today my family owns the fen, but management is shared with the Fayette County

Conservation Board and the Iowa Department of Natural Resources. The fen exists as it does today because of the timing of a scientific study, regular communications among local partners, and the trust that came with years of shared conversations and shared experiences.

Jump now to 2020. The fen is alive and well. In fact, it's also experiencing a bit of regeneration thanks to experimentation and another key local partner. In the early 2000s, the initial conservation easement with my family expanded to include an additional seven acres as a protective buffer for the fen. This took seven more acres out of agricultural production but created an opportunity to restore native plants on the added land. A total of twenty acres remain privately owned yet perpetually protected from future disturbance.

I was in my thirties when this happened, with a stronger voice in decision making than I'd had in my childhood years. Standard procedures for such upland conservation efforts typically include a native plant seeding using a standard mix of twenty-five species to encourage habitat for ground-nesting birds. I requested that there be no seeding at all. "Let the land do its own thing and let's see what happens," I suggested. We were able to skip the seeding and instead relied upon prescribed burning of the buffer zone every few years to encourage natural reestablishment. The experiment generated amazing results. The buffer zone had been covered with corn and soybeans for decades. Not one speck of seed was planted on the site when farming stopped. Yet today a walk through the buffer zone includes sightings of Riddell's goldenrod, gentians, and even nodding lady's tresses orchids, which commonly reside in the wettest spots of the fen. In this case, the best treatment for the land was no treatment at all.

What began with a poorly timed land purchase ended with an unintended expansion of one of Iowa's highest-quality fens. Compared to the 5,000 years it took for the fen to establish itself, decades flew by. Patience, tenacity, and a little creativity applied to both management and planning were what it took to get to where we are today.

Just as the fen grew and transformed, I found myself in a series of educational and career transformations that took me out of Iowa and back again. Throughout those times, I drew on my enthusiasm for the outdoors and my curiosity about the natural world, which had been fostered by the people who visited over the years. It led me to graduate school and a number of professional experiences exploring and teaching about the natural world. I remain curious about the world around me and appreciate nature's capacity to endure if not outlast our human efforts to change it.

Becky's Fen remains private property. However, if you wish to visit, contact either the Fayette County Conservation Board or one of my family members. And every September, rain or shine, we host a fen field day to give people the opportunity to see a sample of Iowa's historic landscape. It starts at the farm, moves to the fen, and ends with a walk through the reestablished buffer zone. Lucky visitors also get to feel the ground shake when someone hops up and down on the quaky hilltop. It's a chance for all of us to be a kid again, if only for a brief moment, on a patch of Iowa that, miraculously, hasn't changed too much since the last ice age.

CHAPTER 14

Knitting It Back Together

Iowa's Tallgrass Prairie

Pauline Drobney

I GREW UP AROUND some of the richest soil on the planet. Farmers on the flat plains of Pocahontas County, Iowa, love this black soil because it grows crops so well and, as a consequence, what I saw around my little farm town was farmed land. I barely noticed the deep straight ditches carrying water away from those fields except when I played in them. I thought that they were streams. That they were normal. But this was the prairie-pothole region of north-central Iowa and these ditches were part of the bargain made to exchange prairie, shallow lakes, and wetlands for dry fertile farmland.

One of my earliest jobs was walking beans to hoe cockleburs, thistles, and other weeds out of soybean rows. It was hot, hard work, but I loved feeling strong and alive and part of something bigger than myself. Clearly, I was a member of a farm community. What I didn't know was this: the black soil that squeezed between my toes was the legacy of the tallgrass prairie and its deep, dense roots. And how could I know? Prairie was nearly absent from the landscape, though traces of former prairie were in plain view all around me, had I but known how to see them.

At sixteen, I jumped at the chance to use my newly minted driver's license to transport my aging grandpa to the nearby town of Manson to get coveralls to fit his ample build. On the way back, he asked if I'd ever been to "that piece of ground they never plowed." It was Kalsow Prairie, a now-rare deep blacksoil type of prairie that had somehow escaped the plow and was preserved for posterity. And so we went there. Standing together on the gravel road that separated this ancient prairie on one side from a modern cornfield on the other, my grandfather in old age and wisdom and I in youth and naivete, I recognized that he wanted me to understand something. But what did he want me to see? What was this place? From my vantage point on the prairie's edge, it just looked like a bunch of weeds. Grandpa had come from another time when prairie-chickens and more prairie were still around. In the span of two generations, however, much had been lost, including the prairie-chickens and nearly all the prairie that supported them. But Grandpa had planted a seed in me. He had shown me the essence of prairie in Pocahontas County. I just needed to learn to see it.

WHAT WAS IOWA LIKE BEFORE CORN AND BEANS?

Kalsow Prairie is a remnant, a fragment of something formerly complete. If we imagine following this remnant back in time, as if we were tracing a colored thread leading to an intricate tapestry, we would discover a very different Iowa.

As we travel back a couple of centuries, farms, cities, and roads melt away. The mantle of soil grows thicker, rivers become shallower and clearer, and channelized and eroded waterways disappear. Between natural rivers and streams, native grasslands with unfathomably complex plant and animal diversity seem to stretch endlessly in all directions, and it becomes easy to lose your bearings.

Standing amid the raucous prairie in spring, you might be overwhelmed by the immensity of the natural world. But you are clearly not alone. Flocks of migrating passenger pigeons are so dense, they blot out sunlight as they pass overhead. When the pigeons roost, oak limbs sometimes break under their weight. Meadowlarks, dickcissels, bobolinks, and other prairie birds sing enthusiastically, vying for mates and nesting sites. Prairie-chickens whirl wildly in misty morning courtship rituals on traditional dancing grounds, booming eerily. Herds of bison thunder across the prairie and majestic elk browse beneath branches in ancient oak savanna.

Underground, microorganisms and small animals productively hum away, feeding plants and manufacturing deep rich soils. Aboveground, butterflies, bees, and all manner of insects fly, buzz, or crawl about in great abundance, each species with its own particular roles and interactions with other species and with the land itself. Everything seems busy. All life-forms in the natural landscape ultimately depend on one another and on a functioning natural system. And ecological function, health, and resiliency largely depend on natural processes like pollination, hydrology, and fire.

In the cool moist springtime, big bluestem, Indian grass, and switch-grass wait for more heat to begin a growth spurt. But species like needle grass, with its sharp needle-and-thread-like seeds, and grass-like sedges with their telltale triangular stems already thrive. The vernal prairie is spangled with a dizzying array of colorful wildflowers blooming at full tilt. Every two weeks, more species bloom, overtopping the previous suite in the race for sunlight until finally in late summer species like big bluestem twelve feet high are in their full glory. Their objective is to perpetuate the species and survive for another season by making seeds and sending energy to roots. In the process, new roots grow and bits of old roots die, banking carbon in the soil in this interconnected and self-replicating system. Finally frost comes, plants grow dormant, and crisp brown leaves and stems rattle in the wind.

This is when native people ignite the landscape. Burning is a sensible action for them. They burn to provide good forage for their wild herds of bison and elk and to clear away dead grass, shrubs, and trees. In exchange for invigorating the native grasslands, they gain meat, berries, roots, and all the provisions they need to live. Native grasslands are sustained by bright sunlight, an essential condition assured by frequent fire. And humans, a key species of the prairie, provide fire.

Across nearly all of Iowa is tallgrass prairie so high you might tie a knot in big bluestem over a horse's back. Willa Cather in *My Ántonia* aptly described it as the running country, for prairie vegetation undulating in the wild wind looks for all the world like waves chasing waves, running to the horizon.

But this similarity does not mean that all prairie is the same. Where soils are so soggy that water pools, the land gives way to wet prairie, sedge meadow, and wetland. More rarely, deposits of sand and gravel provide haven for species adapted to dry environments. Here where vegetation is shorter with more space between plants, little bluestem often dominates. Dry prairie on towering limestone bluffs in eastern Iowa suggests a native rock garden, while tall dry bluffs of fine loess soil in western Iowa sport a blend of tallgrass prairie species mixed with species more typical of the Great Plains over a hundred miles west of Iowa. From the tops of these rugged bluffs, you look down past circling hawks to the broad Missouri River in the valley.

Where fire is less intense, park-like oak savanna thrives with light-seeking tree limbs reaching like open arms in all directions. Some oaks grow alone or sparsely, but others grow close together with intermingling limbs. Light filters easily through the airy branches to the understory below, allowing wildflowers to bloom throughout the growing season. Savanna is more diverse in plant and animal species than any other natural community in Iowa because differences in light levels provide a wide variety of habitats.

WHAT HAPPENED TO WILD IOWA?

As we follow our thread back to current times, we watch as prairie is divided, plowed, or heavily grazed by livestock. Oak trees are cut for firewood and building materials or are grubbed out to make farm fields. The natural landscape becomes fragmented into smaller and smaller parcels as more land is plowed. Towns and cities are constructed, and streams and rivers are straightened and deepened to serve agriculture, transportation, and other purposes. Water, the lifeblood of the system, becomes brown and laden with soil sediment, and it is quickly shunted off the land like refuse. Soils grow thinner and lose their health. The increased water volume and velocity scour the earth, cutting deeper and deeper waterways. Native people, bison, and elk are expelled, and passenger pigeons are hunted to extinction. Fire is suppressed and can no longer keep trees and shrubs at bay or renew the remaining bits of the natural systems. Prairie remnants become overgrown with trees and wither. Oak savanna and woodland remnants are now considered to be forests and fire is excluded, allowing fire-intolerant trees to proliferate between the oaks, causing dense shade. This seals the demise of savanna communities, for without bright light oaks cannot regenerate, and the sun-loving mid- and late-season wildflowers languish.[1] Only spring flowers can bloom in these dark and dying savanna remnants during the seasonal pulse of light before tree leaves are fully formed.

European settlers of the mid-1800s and their descendants had no context for and perhaps limited interest in the dwindling natural landscape. We have come to believe the myth that this altered condition is normal. By the time we reach the present, only *one-tenth of a percent* of the original prairie remains to represent Iowa's formerly vast and incredibly intricate native grassland ecosystems. Remaining plants and animals survive where they can, many species have been extirpated, and some have become extinct. Some native ecosystems have become imperiled.

This is extreme simplification of the landscape. For every species removed, each natural process interrupted, each prairie parcel erased, the ecosystem that supports us and all other species becomes simpler and less functional. Its ability to cleanse water and hold soil declines with the loss of the huge network of roots from more than a thousand native plant species. Water runs off exposed topsoil instead of being directed down prairie leaves and carried into the soil to replenish a supply of clean groundwater. With exposure to air, carbon formerly stored in the soil is oxidized and released into the atmosphere or eroded and carried downstream, recklessly spending our banked savings of carbon. Native pollinators, once so diverse and abundant, are reduced to a relative few, and many are in a struggle for survival. The services formerly provided by the prairie now become our responsibility to maintain, a nearly impossible task without the support and ecological wisdom of native ecosystems.

The consequences of this simplification can be imagined if we think of an elaborate and beautiful piece of music. Remove one note throughout the song, and perhaps the effect is not strongly noticed. Remove another, and it sounds a bit off. Continued removal of notes eventually renders the music unrecognizable and perhaps even disturbing. The simplified song no longer works as the musical composition it was designed to be. Our landscape has likewise been simplified. We will never truly understand the degree of diversity, structure, or function that we have lost. We can, however, reverse the trend of degradation if we learn to read the land and establish ourselves as thoughtful, healing, and sustaining members of a recovering natural community.

WHY SHOULD WE PRESERVE REMNANTS?

Remnant prairies, savannas, and wetland meadows are our Rosetta stones. Remnants are mostly small, degraded, and isolated like islands in a sea of agriculture, much different from the vast continuous grassland of the past. Their edges are raw and ecologically frayed from a constant onslaught of invasive species, erosion, and pesticide damage from adjacent farmland. Most remnants are too small to persist in the long run. And yet these remnants are our teachers because they contain the essence of the ancient native landscape. As ecologist Frank Egler wrote in *The Nature of Vegetation: Its Management and Mismanagement*, "Ecosystems are not more complicated than you think, they are more complicated than you CAN think." How true! These remnants are precious because here we can learn about ecological functions, species interactions, and the roles we must play to restore balance to our troubled natural and cultural landscapes. These remnants teach us to see.

But what do these remnants look like and where are they? To answer this question, we must learn the language of prairie. Learning to know a few prairie plants is like learning a few words of prairie. Lead plant, rough blazing star, big bluestem, compass plant. Recognizing a few helps us see remnant prairie, and as we learn the names of their companions our understanding grows.

Sometimes we see a few plants of just a single species, like pale purple coneflower whose deep roots can help it survive adversity. These are important, but a true remnant includes many species even if its roster is incomplete. Hayfields, pioneer cemeteries, inaccessible corners between crop fields, pastures, railroad rights-of-way, roadsides, and places too rocky, wet, or steep to plow might harbor prairie plants or even a prairie remnant. The tenure of these remnants is fragile. I have repeatedly celebrated the discovery of a diverse remnant only to later mourn its loss to the plow. I imagine that it must have been wonderful for early botanists to experience large expanses of prairie, and I hope that remnants will remain for my grandchildren to nurture and enjoy. These remnants must be actively preserved if we are to have enough prairie material to help regenerate viable examples for posterity.

But it is not enough to simply cherish and preserve native prairie remnants. Invasive trees must be removed, invasive species controlled, and fire reinstated. In this process of actively restoring remnants, we also restore our place as a species of native prairie.

But if remnants are already too small to persist, aren't these efforts futile?

CAN WE KNIT IT BACK TOGETHER?

In the 1980s, several efforts to rebuild prairie from scratch were attempted via a planting process called prairie reconstruction. Early reconstructions were mostly small and limited to a few species. But in 1991, a bold new approach was embraced with the establishment of Walnut Creek National Wildlife Refuge, later renamed Neal Smith National Wildlife Refuge.[2]

The goal was to emulate natural conditions on the entire 8,654-acre refuge. That was a tall order and had not yet been attempted at this scale and scope. Small degraded remnants on the refuge had to be restored, and large tracts of formerly farmed land had to be planted with seeds from nearby remnants that matched refuge conditions. The effort would require ecological restoration, a process that uses both remnant restoration and ecosystem reconstruction to knit the pieces back together to recover the land's natural qualities.

As the refuge's first biologist, I was charged with guiding the initial ecological restoration efforts. Many people were skeptical because conservation efforts had previously focused on preserving remnants. Plantings were considered second-rate. A project like this was simply and utterly untried, daunting, and frankly more than just a little weird. But in a state formerly dominated by prairie where 99.9 percent of it was gone, no large examples of typical tallgrass prairie remained. Because Iowa is arguably the most ecologically devastated state in the union, doesn't it make sense to figure out how to reconstruct prairie here? Ecological restoration done well could enlarge our prairie remnants, making them viable in the long term. It could also be our best chance of preserving a vestige of Iowa's natural heritage in perpetuity.

This refuge became a proving ground, an experiment to understand the degree to which ecological restoration could be successful on former farmland. Professionals, seed producers, and just plain folks were invited to lend perspective and help solve problems because this project was bigger than us. It needed a community. We learned to find local remnants and harvest seeds, thus assuring that we used the right species and had sufficient genetic variation to sustain plantings in the long run. We planted seeds, cut trees, and removed invasive species. And we celebrated together, dancing seeds into the ground. Volunteers, staff, students, teachers, researchers, seed producers, artists, and practitioners became a new people of the land, learning, working, and rejoicing together. The refuge became a touchstone, inspiring others to find and restore remnants or reconstruct prairie themselves.

Today windblown prairie again runs wild in endless waves to the horizon, and in savanna light filters through oak branches to the ground. Coyotes, badgers, beavers, bobcats, herds of bison and elk, over 200 species of birds, and hundreds of native plant species are at home on thousands of refuge acres. Early efforts to reintroduce regal fritillary butterflies worked, and now this rare butterfly floats above flowers in August cruising for mates. Monarch butterflies abound, and rare pollinators like the rusty patch bumblebee have been spotted.

As we expected, controlling invasive species has been our biggest challenge, and we need to introduce and nurture more native species, but already some interesting things are happening. Research has demonstrated that soil health and water quality are improving incrementally, and some plantings are beginning to look and function almost like prairie remnants.[3] This ecological restoration is still in its infancy because restoring resilience and function requires ongoing learning, persistence, and time. After all, this refuge is only a few decades into a thousand-year project!

BRINGING IT HOME

People become passionate about the natural world when they become part of it. I think we have an innate need for this elemental connection, but exposure is often difficult. My friend and volunteer seed collector Rayford Ratcliff wisely summed it up by saying, "In order to understand prairie, you have to get your back up agin it." And he was right. You don't fall in love with prairie by standing on the edge looking in. You have to get into it and let it get into you.

It is easy to feel helpless when confronted with the staggering loss of Iowa's native landscape, but we have tremendous power to help reverse that loss. On the thirty acres of land where I live, I have chosen to ecologically restore prairie and savanna despite the land's initial state of profound degradation. I have found deep peace seeing wildflowers and pollinators return and knowing that, at least here, rain falling on the land enters the soil and roots are slowly banking soil carbon. The fires I've lit, the seeds I've sown, and the invasives I've removed help fulfill my part of the sacred bond I feel with the land. In return, I claim it as home.

And if my neighbor would install prairie strips on his cropland in order to hold the soil and farm chemicals on his fields and provide habitat for pollinators and wildlife, then the water draining onto my land and traveling downstream would be cleaner. Our combined efforts would be amplified. I imagine an Iowa with prairie plantings in farmlands, gardens, roadsides, and schoolyards. Iowans without their own land might volunteer to work on conservation lands, or perhaps they would celebrate their natural heritage by singing, dancing, creating art, advocating, or just quietly walking through prairies and learning to see them. And so my advice to you, dear reader? Go out and get your back up agin some prairie!

NOTES

1. J. Nowaki and D. Abrams, "The Demise of Fire and 'Mesophication' of Forests in the Eastern United States," *BioScience* 58, no. 2 (2008): 123–138.

2. See P. Drobney, "Iowa Prairie Rebirth: Rediscovering Natural Heritage and Walnut Creek National Wildlife Refuge," *Restoration and Management Notes* 12, no. 1 (1994): 16–22.

3. K. E. Schilling and P. Drobney, "Hydrologic Recovery with Prairie Reconstruction at Neal Smith National Wildlife Refuge, Jasper County, Iowa" (Washington, D.C.: U.S. Fish and Wildlife Service, 2014), https://www.iihr.uiowa.edu/igs/publications/uploads/2015-04-30_13-04-00_hydro%20synthesis%20report%20-%20final%20(print%20ver)%20-%2004-23-2014%20(2).pdf.

Making a Difference

Ronald Eckoff

I CAME TO IOWA IN 1965 on a two-year assignment with the U.S. Public Health Service. In 1967, I began a thirty-five-year career with the Iowa Department of Public Health. My wife and I built a house on a small acreage southwest of Des Moines and happily raised our two daughters.

When I began to think about retirement, we started to look for a larger acreage where I could putter around after I retired. I grew up on a fruit farm in Michigan and have always enjoyed working out of doors. I knew I wanted to stay physically and mentally active—my father was very active through age ninety-six. In January 2000, after looking at several properties, we purchased seventy-five acres of hilly pasture in western Warren County about twenty minutes down I-35 from our home. The previous owner was an area farmer who had had the property for twenty-five years and had used it only for grazing cattle and making hay. We named it Twin Oaks for a pair of old bur oak trees near the center of the property.

The first spring we discovered numerous ephemerals in one of the wooded gullies. The second year we found what we called an unusual grass growing between the cedar trees on one hillside. It was big bluestem, and we began to find other native prairie plants. We were soon hooked on prairie, joined the Iowa Prairie Network, bought books about prairie, started attending prairie meetings, and took a restoration ecology independent study class at our local community college.

Conferences, field trips, and books are useful teachers, but I needed something more personal. In 2004, I made a donation at an Iowa Prairie Network auction in exchange for having prairie expert Tom Rosburg, a biology professor at Drake University, spend a day on our land. In July, Tom walked the property with me and talked about management. He prepared a species list (which more than doubled what I had developed) and provided a written report. He also told me that he and his students, the Drake Prairie Rescue and Restoration Interns, could help do a pre-scribed burn of my prairie the following spring. Soon I started to acquire the equipment necessary to do prescribed burns myself and recruited grandsons and friends to help. We have burned portions of our prairie all but two years since then.

Our original seventy-five acres probably had fifteen acres of prairie remnants. While working on these, we noted more and better prairie on land adjacent to ours, where I saw white wild indigo, pale purple cone-flower, and compass plant growing. In 2006, we purchased that forty-one acres just south of our land, about half of which was significant prairie. In July 2007, after another Iowa Prairie Network auction, Tom surveyed the new purchase and added quite a few native prairie plants to our list.

In addition to prairie and wooded gullies, our original purchase had a bur oak savanna along its north border. Much of my early effort went into clearing cedar trees, multiflora rose, honeysuckle, box elder, and other invasive vegetation from this savanna. The new purchase included three areas Tom labeled as early successional forest. Each had large bur oak trees along with lots of understory. Tom also provided a 1930 aerial photo from which we identified many of those same oaks in 2007, over seventy years later. We could see that in 1930 the area had been open and was probably heavily grazed.

I have now cleared all the invasive understory from these three areas, leaving only the original large oaks. I am anxious to see how many native species recover in these areas. I have also been clearing understory from under three other scattered bur oaks. These trees once grew in fairly open areas and developed a massive horizontal spread—one reaches out almost a hundred feet. Freeing these wolf oaks is exciting, and I am looking forward to showing them off to visitors.

My plant list now includes over 200 native species. That's not terribly impressive to a prairie enthusiast, but for me starting at zero it is mean-ingful. It is fascinating how once you identify a certain species for the first time, you begin to see it repeatedly. I attended a prairie conference in northwest Iowa and saw nodding lady's tresses on a field trip. Back on our own land, I suddenly discovered several of these orchids in one area. I have now seen them in at least seven spots, sometimes finding just one or two and sometimes many. But they may not be there every year.

I have also watched our prairie plants multiply. Our original land had just one butterfly milkweed. That one plant has now increased to about fifteen scattered plants. The new land has many on one hillside. Many years ago, I saw false foxglove on a Sierra Club service trip in the Loess Hills. I then discovered eared false foxglove and slender false foxglove on our land. We now have lots of eared false foxglove in at least three areas. Unfortunately, I have not found slender false foxglove in recent years.

It is easy to get excited about showy plants like butterfly milkweed, compass plant, white wild indigo, and New England aster or impressive grasses like big bluestem and Indian grass. But I also get excited about many others that may not be as spectacular. I just think plants like palespike lobelia, biennial gaura, flowering spurge, dwarf larkspur, prairie sage, prairie ragwort, late horse gentian, bottlebrush grass, and many others are neat. There are probably five plants on my species list that I have not seen in recent years. I mourn each apparent loss and hope they still might be there somewhere.

Early on, I decided that I would not plant additional prairie species but would see what I could accomplish with remnant management. It has been exciting to see the prairie forbs and grasses spread on their own and even more exciting to identify new native species. Even with all my past efforts, I continue to have plenty to do cutting cedar trees, multiflora rose, and brambles and trying to reduce bird's-foot trefoil and cool-season grasses. Other than burning, I do the great majority of the work by myself at my own pace. Some days I may do little but walk around and enjoy nature.

I continue to identify new native species on our land and enjoy sharing these with others. I try to have two to three informal prairie walks for friends and my burn helpers each year. Tom has also led a public field trip at Twin Oaks, and the Madison County group For Land's Sake has toured twice. Any time you want to visit Twin Oaks, I will be happy to show it to you.

I have always believed in trying to leave the world a little better than I found it. I think the restoration work I am doing at Twin Oaks is bringing native prairie and savanna communities back to health. At age eighty-four, I hope to spend another ten years working on that before passing the land on. When I consider the results we have had on our land as well as the native plant restoration efforts of many other individuals in south-central Iowa and throughout our state, I know that we are making a difference.

CHAPTER 15

Survival Struggles, Survival Hopes
Wildlife in Iowa

James L. Pease

I GREW UP IN southeast Iowa in Burlington bordering the Mississippi River. Southeast Iowa is home to the mouths of many of Iowa's interior rivers that drain the eastern two-thirds of the state: the Cedar, Iowa, Skunk, and Des Moines Rivers all end within thirty miles of my birthplace. My brothers and I explored those rivers by wood-and-canvas canoe as young teens. Our parents trusted us to paddle the lowlands and camp on the sandbars of these rivers since no formal campsites were then available. We hiked when we weren't canoeing, noting where red-tailed hawks had their nests, where pileated woodpeckers had excavated their rectangular feeding holes in trees, and where great blue herons had established a nesting colony. In winter we ice-skated the backwater sloughs, noting where muskrat lodges poked through the ice or where a rare mink track crossed our path. We sometimes crawled into a makeshift log blind in the cold of early morning to watch bald eagles grab fish from openings in the river ice.

We had the freedom and carefreeness of youth to explore, and we knew the wildlife that shared those adventures. But in retrospect, growing up in the Iowa of the 1950s and 1960s was more notable for what we didn't see than for what we did. Beavers were beginning to return, but we never saw them along the rivers or in the sloughs. No river otters ever slid along the shorelines. No wild turkeys gobbled in the woodlands. No trumpeter swans were ever seen or heard. White-tailed deer were a rarity; spotting one might land you in a local newspaper column, and harvesting one during the hunting season would assure you a photo in the newspaper. The honks of Canada geese were heard only in the early spring or late fall, as their V-shaped skeins headed north or south along the river flyway. Wood ducks were seen only by those fortunate enough to know where Fred Leopold had erected a nest box in town. And the bald eagles we watched along the river in the winter were nearly all white-headed adults that were never present in other months. They nested only in states and provinces to the north. Bobcats and mountain lions were animals you saw in the movies, not in the woodlands of Iowa.

It is hard to believe today that white-tailed deer were essentially absent from Iowa at the dawn of the twentieth century. Equally difficult is realizing that the geese now considered nuisances on golf courses and ponds were not nesting in Iowa just fifty years ago. In his book *A Country So Full of Game: The Story of Wildlife in Iowa*, James Dinsmore details what happened to Iowa's once-abundant wild species. For most, it boils down to this: Iowa's great diversity and abundance of wildlife were rapidly depleted by Euro-Americans settling in Iowa from 1830 onward. A combination of commercial market hunting, few or no regulations, and lax enforcement of the few game laws led to dramatic declines or disappearances of wildlife species over about fifty years.

By 1900, the herds of bison, elk, and white-tailed deer that were so common in 1830 were gone. The vast flocks of ducks and geese were greatly diminished. The amazingly abundant greater prairie-chickens were in steep decline, despite initially having increased in numbers with Euro-American settlers' planting of small grains. Wolves, bears, and mountain lions, seen as competitors for other wildlife resources, had been eliminated. The flocks of passenger pigeons that once darkened the skies were gone forever. Wild turkeys were once found statewide but, being delicious, they were gone from most of Iowa by the 1880s. The cranes, herons, and egrets that once waded the shallow waters had their numbers greatly reduced by demand for meat and for feathers for the haberdashers of the world.

Human need and human greed, however, were not the only reasons for the decline of wildlife in Iowa. Three additional reasons account for Iowa's loss of species: habitat loss and degradation, habitat fragmentation, and pesticides.

WHAT HAPPENED TO IOWA'S WILDLIFE?

Prior to Euro-American settlement, Iowa was largely tallgrass prairie dotted with millions of acres of wetlands, woodland savannas, and forests along streams and rivers. Today less than 0.1 percent of those original prairies still exist. Wetlands have declined about 92 percent through drainage, straightening, and other landscape modifications. Woodlands have declined about 75 percent.[1] These kinds of absolute loss of habitat as well as the degradation of remaining habitat dictated that the wildlife populations that were once so common would suffer dramatic decreases, even without the unfettered killing of wildlife of the period. While restorations and reconstructions of some habitats have occurred in the last forty to fifty years, the decline and alteration of natural habitats continued throughout most of the twentieth century.

The conversion to a human-dominated landscape of row crops, towns, and cities represents an absolute loss of habitat. But the fragmentation of remaining habitats further stressed wildlife. Fragmentation is the breakup of large natural landscapes into increasingly smaller and more isolated patches. Today's largest prairie remnants are small—from 100 to 200 acres—and the few natural wetlands are small and degraded. These remnants are far from other prairie or wetland patches, isolated geographically and genetically, unable to mix and renew their genetic makeup, and thus less able to adjust to environmental changes. The landscape has been further subdivided by public roads, nearly 115,000 miles of them by 2014, challenging the remaining wildlife species and guaranteeing that some may never return.[2] While birds and some mammals and insects can travel long distances, many smaller and less mobile animals cannot, and ensuring their genetic diversity is problematic. For some, even finding mates may be difficult.

World War II caused a leap in research in chemistry. This led to a new group of synthetic chemicals that proved to be very useful for controlling agricultural and urban pests. These pesticides include insecticides, herbicides, larvicides, avicides, and nematicides, which target (respectively) insects, plants, larvae, birds, and nematodes. Many pesticides increase the ease of growing large acreages of a single crop. Some help make humans safer from biting insects and disease.

Tragically, many pesticides also affect nontarget insects, birds, mammals, reptiles, and amphibians. Among the most famous unintentional effects were those caused by the synthetic organochlorine insecticide DDT. This insecticide was thought to be ideal in some ways: one application killed a lot of pests, and a single application lasted a long time. It was also inexpensive.

But DDT's consequences reached well beyond the species it was intended to control. These unplanned consequences were documented by scientist Rachel Carson in her 1962 book, *Silent Spring*, which helped spark the modern environmental movement. DDT and other organochlorine pesticides and their breakdown products persist in nature and thus travel through food chains to wildlife several steps removed from the original target. In particular, animals at the top of aquatic and other food webs are both directly and indirectly affected. A significant indirect effect was the thinning of eggshells of many avian species, because birds with DDT in their systems could not properly metabolize calcium. Thus eggs might be laid but they cracked when they were incubated. As a result, few young birds hatched, and populations of bald eagles, brown pelicans, ospreys, and many other birds began steep declines. That's why, as a boy, I had seen only adult eagles from our log blind on the Mississippi. Few young eagles were entering populations across North America. America's national symbol was in real trouble.

There are many other unintended consequences of widespread pesticide use. Organophosphates and carbamates replaced most organochlorines in the 1970s after DDT was banned, and pyrethroids became popular later. All have unintended side effects. Some are absorbed through the shells of bird eggs, causing malformations or death of the embryos. Others affect the adults' ability to parent, causing eventual starvation of the young. And while some pesticides have little effect on birds, they may harm mammals or be deadly to fish.

More recently, a new set of pesticides, the neonicotinoids (meaning "new nicotine-like"), has been widely adopted. Neonics are now the most widely applied insecticides in the world, used in agriculture, on lawns, and in some pet collars. In Iowa, they are commonly used as seed coatings on corn and soybeans for protection from soil insects and nematodes, and they may be sprayed on crop leaves to kill sucking insects like aphids. Like DDT, neonics have broad unintentional effects on a broad range of species, including pollinators like bees, wasps, beetles, and butterflies. As neurotoxins that persist in nature for weeks to months, they damage insect nervous systems. In bees and other pollinators, they seem to impair navigational ability, thus preventing insects from returning to their home colonies.[3]

While many species have disappeared from our state, others are still here but in far reduced numbers. Consider the U.S. Fish and Wildlife

Service's lists of endangered and threatened species, which include species in trouble across their entire U.S. range. In 2021, those that are (or were) found in Iowa included two mammals (both bats), a bird, a reptile, a snail, three mussels, two fish, and two insects (a butterfly and a bee). The Iowa Department of Natural Resources' list of endangered and threatened species adds many other animals and plants that may be found elsewhere but have severely declined in Iowa. Included in 2021 were five mammals, three birds, fourteen reptiles, four amphibians, eight snails, thirteen mussels, fifteen fish, and six butterflies. The DNR also lists species of special concern that, without proper management, could become endangered or threatened or could disappear from the state in the future. Included were one additional mammal, four birds, two reptiles, two fish, and twenty-five more butterflies.

This part of the story is not static, however. Many argue that we are in the sixth major extinction event in Earth's history, this one caused by human activities. A 2019 review of insect population research documented huge losses in insect biodiversity across the planet, with more than 40 percent of insects in decline. Such precipitous losses in our most abundant phylum portend similar losses for many other species in both plant and animal kingdoms. Birds, too, have experienced recent massive losses in abundance and in species. Studies show a North American net loss of 2.9 billion birds—a 29 percent decline in abundance—between 1970 and 2018. Declines are the worst in grassland species: more than 50 percent.[4]

RESTORATIONS AND RECONSTRUCTIONS

Since my childhood, local and state conservation efforts have restored many species to the state: white-tailed deer, river otters, wild turkeys, trumpeter swans, Canada geese, peregrine falcons, and ospreys now grace our lands and waters. Others have come back due to regional and national efforts: bald eagles, bobcats, wood ducks, sandhill and whooping cranes, beavers, and others. These species have thrived due to a combination of public and private efforts such as increasing habitat and funding sources, employing scientifically sound management practices, and passing and enforcing hunting laws and regulations.

In addition, a large number of reconstructed prairie and wetland acres now approximate habitats that once dominated Iowa's landscape. From

1990 to 2021, the Iowa Department of Transportation, county conservation agencies, and the Integrated Roadside Vegetation Management program planted over 50,000 acres of roadsides with native grasses and prairie wildflowers.[5] County conservation agencies, local organizations, and private individuals have reconstructed thousands of acres of prairies on other lands. Private landowners in 2020 enrolled about 1.68 million acres of reconstructed grasslands in the federal Conservation Reserve Program.[6] Thousands of acres of wetlands and adjacent uplands have been restored in Iowa under this program, the Wetlands Reserve Program, and other programs. Some have been assembled into complexes of wetlands and prairies, a result of cooperation between public and private landowners. Habitat complexes have been important in recovering many wildlife species, especially those that need larger spaces for roaming and protection from predators that linear habitats like roadsides do not provide.

All these laudable efforts can help restore Iowa's wildlife diversity. They do so by providing habitat for pollinators and other insects, mammals, birds, reptiles, amphibians, mussels, and other creatures. However, no human reconstruction, whether prairie, wetland, savanna, or woodland, can ever match the species or habitat diversity of 1830s Iowa. The vast majority of Iowa is now a landscape dominated by row crop agriculture, towns and cities, roads, businesses, and other human-centric purposes. Existing habitat patches are often interrupted by croplands and roads. Wildlife is largely an afterthought.

In fact, the only reasonably continuous wider ribbons of wildlife habitat remaining in Iowa border our rivers. I believe that, without the habitat along our river corridors, many of the wildlife species we have today would not have recovered and even expanded their ranges. Instead, they would have remained restricted to the areas where they were released.

THE FUTURE

The future of wildlife in Iowa is closely linked to the future of our rivers and streams. Iowa will remain a predominantly agricultural state, subdivided by thousands of miles of roads and other trappings of human civilization. If we fail to protect, improve, and widen our riverine ribbons of habitat—in addition to other complexes of prairies, wetlands, and woodlands—wildlife unable to adapt to a human-dominated landscape will continue to decline both in abundance and in numbers of species. Species with specialized nesting, feeding, or space needs will suffer the most and may disappear from Iowa. In contrast, species that can adapt to our highly altered landscape will remain and perhaps even thrive. These are the generalists, the animals that are most flexible in fulfilling their food, water, shelter, and space needs. They can coexist with humans and may even become pests in some situations.

Fortunately, I am not the only one to have thought about this. The Iowa Wildlife Action Plan was approved in 2006 after several years of work by a cross section of wildlife professionals and organizations. The plan sets goals for species recovery and for human education about and interaction with wildlife. By 2015, only about 2.7 percent of Iowa's natural lands had been permanently protected—895,000 acres by public ownership and 107,000 acres on private land in permanent easements.[7] If we are to double that, as the action plan envisions, we must convince a large cadre of private landowners to enroll their land in permanent easements.

Perhaps the bald eagle's story in Iowa informs us about what we must do. The eagles that, as a youngster, I watched fish in the Mississippi River were all adults—the bald eagle doesn't get its distinctive white head and tail until its fifth year. By the 1960s, DDT had decimated eagle populations across the lower forty-eight states. In 1972, the newly established Environmental Protection Agency banned the use of DDT in the country. Politically, socially, and economically, this was one of the most difficult decisions made by the EPA at the time. Up until that point, DDT had been widely used for over thirty years. Banning it meant, among other things, rapid research and development of replacements.

Bald eagles had not nested in Iowa since the early 1900s. But in 1978, just six years after DDT was banned, a pair nested along the Mississippi River in eastern Iowa. As a young wildlife biologist, I thought that was wonderful, and I hoped that someday Iowa might welcome a handful of nests along its biggest rivers, the Mississippi and the Missouri. Eagles were too wild, I thought, and Iowa too tamed to ever support more eagles than that.

I couldn't have been more wrong. By 2020, we had over 400 bald eagle nests in Iowa, one or more along nearly every interior river in the state. Every year, more than 200 of the nests are active and successfully fledge one or two eaglets. The bald eagle population is steadily increasing, and the bird has been removed from both federal and state endangered species lists.

Why this success? Because of one very difficult but right decision: banning DDT.

Many more difficult decisions lie in our future. Climate change will modify wildlife habitats dramatically. Invasive species of plants and animals will further challenge the livelihoods of native species. Continuing human population growth and its resulting needs emphasize the importance of protecting wild places now to support wildlife species in coming years. Will we make the right decisions even when they are difficult politically, socially, and economically? Are we up to the task as a state? Will we continue to make room for the wild species with whom we share this state?

Another Iowa native, noted conservationist Aldo Leopold, in his 1949 book *A Sand County Almanac*, expressed my own sentiments: "I'm glad I shall never be young, without wild places to be young in. Of what avail are forty freedoms, without a blank spot on the map?" May we continue to have lots of blank spots and wild places for a wild future in Iowa.

NOTES

1. See F. Samson and F. Knopf, "Prairie Conservation in North America," *BioScience* 44, no. 6 (1994): 418–421; D. Smith, "Iowa Prairie: Original Extent and Loss, Preservation and Recovery Attempts," *Journal of the Iowa Academy of Science* 105, no. 34 (1998): 94–108; V. Evelsizer and J. L. Johnson, "Wetland Action Plan for Iowa," Iowa Geological and Water Survey, Special Report No. 4, 2010, Iowa Department of Natural Resources; Earl C. Leatherberry, W. Keith Moser, Charles Perry, et al., "Iowa's Forests 1999–2003" (Washington, D.C.: USDA–Forest Service, 2006); G. Hightshoe, "Iowa Woodlands," *Ames Forester* 66 (1980): 7.

2. Iowa Department of Transportation, "Miles of Public Roads in Iowa by Surface Type as of December 31, 2014," https://iowadot.gov.

3. N. Tsvetkov, O. Samson-Robert, K. Sood, et al., "Chronic Exposure to Neonicotinoids Reduces Honey Bee Health near Corn Crops," *Science* 356, no. 6345 (2017): 1395–1397.

4. See G. Ceballos, P. R. Ehrlich, and P. H. Raven, "Vertebrates on the Brink as Indicators of Biological Annihilation and the Sixth Mass Extinction," *Proceedings of the National Academy of Sciences* 117, no. 24 (2020): 13596–13602; F. Sánchez-Bayoa and K. A. G. Wyckhuys, "Worldwide Decline of the Entomofauna: A Review of Its Drivers," *Biological Conservation* 232 (2019): 8–27; and K. V. Rosenberg,

A. M. Dokter, P. J. Blancher, et al., "Decline of the North American Avifauna," *Science* 366, no. 6461 (2019): 120–124.

5. See https://iowadot.gov/lrtf/integrated-roadside-vegetation-management/irvm.

6. USDA–Farm Service Agency, "Conservation Reserve Program Monthly Summary December 2020," https://www.fsa.usda.gov/programs-and-services/conservation-programs/reports-and-statistics/conservation-reserve-program-statistics/index.

7. The 2006 Iowa Wildlife Action Plan and the 2015 version that looks back on what was accomplished in the first ten years are available on the Iowa Department of Natural Resources website at http://www.iowadnr.gov/Conservation/Iowas-Wildlife/Iowa-Wildlife-Action-Plan.

Wild Calls for Help

Marlene Warren Ehresman

I'VE ALWAYS BEEN interested in wild lives and wild land. My parents had a hand in seeing to that, although from much different perspectives. Mom was my emotional response guide. When I presented her with a listless robin, I vividly remember her fear (I might catch its sickness) and sadness (she felt powerless to help). She had me put it back outside to "let nature take its course." Dad was my outdoor experience guide. When I was wandering through our local woodland one warm day, my sneakers were suddenly covered by a writhing ball of garter snakes. Panicked, I looked up and saw Dad's expression of calm delight as he told me to just stand still for a very long minute. That would not have been my mother's reaction.

I am a wildlife biologist and rehabilitator. I started as the latter in the early 1980s and went back to college in the 1990s to become the former. I eventually combined the two in my work as the cofounder and director of the Iowa Wildlife Center, a wildlife rehabilitation and education organization. In 1991, I envisioned a wildlife center that would not only help the wild lives that had no owners, no veterinary care, and no shelters devoted to them but would also give people opportunities to deepen their connections to and understanding of wildness.

Our motto—Healing Wild Lives, Wild Land, and the Human Spirit— carries the essence of the Iowa Wildlife Center. With guidance from a dedicated steering committee and a working board of directors, we have created a path toward this vision, including purchasing land on which to give it life. Over the decades, I have learned that caring for wild animals takes special state and federal permits, particular skills and knowledge— and space. Various species require special enclosures at each stage of their recovery that allow them to safely regain their health before being returned to their natural habitats. Caring for even moderate numbers of a large variety of native species requires ample space.

The search for land brought me to a seventy-five-acre property in Boone County with great potential. It had been saved from becoming a hog confinement facility in the 1980s, instead becoming part of an organic cattle farm until it was sold to us at a bargain price in 2007. The woodland-savanna-grassland-wetland complex we now call WildWay lies between Ames and Des Moines, just south of Ledges State Park, and is connected to publicly owned and privately protected land. WildWay itself is protected in perpetuity by a conservation easement and, with the help of volunteers and funding, we are restoring the savanna and woodland, reconstructing the prairie, and allowing wetlands to re-form. WildWay serves as a growing home for our operations and as an outdoor classroom for learning how to heal wildland.

Beyond stewarding land, we care for orphaned, injured, or otherwise distressed native wild animals and release healthy individuals back into their appropriate habitats. With the help of a couple dozen trained volunteers, we care for more than 300 birds, mammals, reptiles, and amphibians each year. While this number reflects only a fraction of the number of animal-related calls and emails we receive, it is significantly larger than what I had been able to accept in previous decades as an independent licensed rehabilitator—perhaps because of the advent of e-communications or because more people know about wildlife rehabilitation or both.

The reality of how wildlife must struggle to survive on this shared human-centered planet can be overwhelming. We receive dozens of calls, emails, and social media posts weekly from frantic people who have found animals that need someone with compassion, skill, and knowledge to help them. Wild lives are suddenly shattered by a felled tree, free-roaming cat, glue trap, windowpane, looming power line, or discarded fishing line. Human rescuers intervene when they shouldn't, and we continue to educate these well-meaning people about all the different wild parenting styles.

Large-scale natural disasters produce an onslaught of fractured lives. We raise orphans, glue shattered turtle shells back together, and set limbs. We provide drug therapies for infections, parasites, and pain. We offer species-specific nourishment, heat, light, humidity, and housing in special enclosures during each stage of recovery. Too often, we must offer the gift of humane death.

Given all the time, energy, and money devoted to caring for individual animals, you might ask, Couldn't we make a greater impact by investing in habitat acquisition and species population management? It depends. Certainly, without wild healthy land, wild lives can't be sustained in healthy and diverse populations. Without that diversity of wildlife acting upon their natural habitats, the land begins to change, often not for the better. But individual animals matter, too—to the people who find them, to those who care for them, to the animal itself, and maybe to the larger population of animals. We still have much to learn about the full lives of animals on this shared planet, and distressed animals can teach us a few things if we are willing to listen. We can all become active participants in helping wildlife by going far beyond packing them up and driving them to the nearest rehabilitator. We can become part of nature again rather than humans set apart from nature. We can deepen our relationships with the natural world as we come to understand the effect of our daily lives on wildlife.

At the Iowa Wildlife Center, our work begins when we receive a call for help. Every caller becomes a student. Those minutes talking with people are perfect opportunities to empower them to make a difference in the lives of animals and to help them see natural history playing out in front of them. The child who finds nestling mourning doves on the ground learns that we can replace the original flimsy nest with a basket and hang it back in the tree so the adult birds can finish raising their young. The college student with a box of bunnies learns to look for the shallow grass- and fur-lined depression and put the bunnies back in their nest. Arborists learn to avert the need to bring in a box of screech owlets or squirrel kits by looking for nests *before* they cut the tree down or, after an ill-timed cut, by erecting a new cavity nearby for the owls or leaving the squirrels in a box on the tree stump for mom to retrieve. Homeowners learn to safely rescue the bat in the house and release it outside during insect-rich months or bring it to us in other months. And they learn to patiently await fall migration before installing exclusion devices to evict bats just in case their chimney houses a colony of moms and pups. And all these individuals learn that we must keep dogs and cats under control. "Watch, listen, enjoy," we preach. "The dramas that unfold around us are played out quickly and the actors are on and off the stage before we know it. Being able to bear witness to these events is a privilege."

No, we can't help every animal in need, nor should we. But knowledge is power. And each animal's story can teach us at least one lesson about what it means to be a wild one living in this altered landscape we call Iowa.

The Iowa Wildlife Center is a 501(c)(3) nonprofit organization. Donors and volunteers are crucial to our continued success. While Iowa has numerous individual licensed wildlife rehabilitators throughout the state, the Iowa Wildlife Center is the only center that has such a deep and broad focus. Our volunteers provide help in many critical areas, including veterinary and general animal care, land stewardship, fundraising, community outreach, and more. We require certain vaccinations, in-house training, and a commitment of at least three months for our animal care volunteers. We provide a network of kindred spirits for other tasks. We are funded primarily by individual donors, but family foundations and grants are increasingly crucial as we build our capacity to achieve even more. For more information, visit our website or find us on Facebook.

CHAPTER 16

Iowa's Rich Biodiversity Legacy
A Vision for the Future

Thomas Rosburg

IT IS REMARKABLE how clearly images remain etched in memory despite a distance of five or six decades. But there they are. I can see with surprising detail the farm in western Iowa where I grew up. The small white three-bedroom, one-bathroom farmhouse was home to my family of ten. The farm buildings, large garden, and trees in the yard and in the grove guarding the farmstead on the west are all like I was there just last week. I can easily recall collecting, washing, and packing dozens of eggs from our 300 chickens for the weekly visit from the egg man. Summer days often included time weeding the garden or helping my mother pick peas or beans. There was the daily winter chore of filling a five-gallon can with kerosene from an outdoor tank for the stove that heated the north half of the house. For a few years, I shared a bedroom off the kitchen with my older and younger brothers, the three of us making do with a double bed.

I was the only one in my family who succumbed to an inner biophilia. I guess I was the lucky one. Exploring Rush Creek, a quarter mile west and on the other side of a large loess hill, was a favorite place to be. A beaver dam made it seem just as wild as a mountain stream in the Rockies. At my grandparents' home, on land my parents farmed a mile and a half away, a two-acre planted woodlot was a wild forest to me, a home for squirrels, rabbits, opossums, raccoons, and who knows what else. A favorite assignment was roaming the fifty acres of hilly pasture with a spade in hand to cut thistles. I didn't know anything about grasslands, but I was intrigued by the many plant species that lived there as well as the gophers, ground squirrels, occasional snakes, and numerous unknown birds and insects.

Mine was a life ripe with time in nature. It fostered the growth of my biophilia and fed the curiosity of a farm boy. It may be that nature was, at least in part, a way to escape from the anxiety created by farmwork and a home that offered little if any privacy. But without doubt it steered me in the right direction. Experience is an unrelenting teacher and childhood is a time when foundations are poured. I'm sure I don't fully realize just how much those years led me toward my deep-rooted love of nature. Nonetheless, I feel very fortunate to have had a childhood that nurtured love and respect for the natural world.

THE CHALLENGE FACING US

The loss of Iowa's biological diversity and the environmental dilemmas it has caused have been rightly described in previous chapters of this section. Through millions of years of evolution, nature had perfected a model of productivity, diversity, efficiency, and sustainability. The lives of countless numbers of species were supported and enriched while they maintained and improved the health of soil, water, and air.

But today the native Iowa landscape and its amazing bounty of life, its glorious complexity, and its creative resourcefulness exist only in my imagination. Iowa is near the top of the list when it comes to states with the greatest loss of natural ecosystems and biodiversity. Our once-pristine landscape with its incredible abundance of species has been transformed into a species-poor biological desert. Simultaneous with the loss of native species has been the loss of life-sustaining ecosystem functions and processes. It's the native species and their complex interactions that build the soil, cleanse the water, and purify the air. The transformation from natural to unnatural, from Native American to Euro-American, from species-rich to species-poor, from complex and ingenious to simple and uninventive, from fertile and nutrient-protective to eroded and nutrient-leaky happened in less than a hundred years, far less than the lifetime of a stalwart bur oak. Generations of Iowans are growing up with very little understanding about what Iowa once was and should be. But it doesn't have to be that way.

Do we want places where shooting star flowers burst into a wild constellation of pink and lavender blooms, where dancing sandhill cranes forge lifelong bonds with one another and their bugle-like calls reverberate from sky and land, and where 200-year-old white oaks live out their potential 500-year life spans? I think we desperately need those places—for our spirits, our planet's health and resilience, and our long-term survival. I have spent my life thinking about, studying, and teaching about the protection of Iowa's biodiversity as well as thousands of hours working to restore Iowa's rightful natural heritage. I have witnessed seemingly miraculous recoveries after invasive shrubs and trees were removed from dying remnants. I have watched five- to fifty-acre parcels that were farmed for decades return to complex, biologically diverse, and beautiful ecosystems that provide protection for soil, water, and air. My vision is that we can and must meet the challenge before us by engaging in an agricultural and ecological transformation that effectively turns the clock back to a time when Iowa's landscapes were sustainable for both humans and native biodiversity.

WHAT CAN WE DO?

Acclaimed biologist E. O. Wilson began advocating for biodiversity with the 1985 publication of "The Biological Diversity Crisis" in *BioScience*. He coined the acronym HIPPO to educate people about the biggest causes of declining biodiversity: Habitat loss, Invasive species, Pollution, Population growth (human overpopulation), and Overconsumption (or Overharvesting). These five factors aptly summarize the problem and are interconnected. While the last four are important in their own right, each essentially contributes to habitat loss. It's not difficult to see that the fundamental pathway to protecting biodiversity is land conservation. Animals, plants, fungi, protists, and even microbes need habitat. They simply need places to live.

We can reverse the perilous decline in biodiversity and begin to repair our landscapes by following three important strategies: find and protect remnant ecosystems, manage conservation lands to restore ecosystem processes and functions, and most importantly transform ecologically damaged landscapes into conservation landscapes. (Conservation lands are defined as those that retain enough natural diversity and function to provide conservation value to native plants and animals.)

My research over the last thirty-five years has taken me to tens of thousands of acres of both public and private landscapes. Perhaps my most remarkable discovery has been the downright stubbornness of nature. Despite all that's been lost, transformed, or degraded, bits and pieces of nature still persist. These remnants, these magical islands of hope and inspiration, are nature at its best. Remnants are the heart and spirit of our natural heritage and the crucially needed models for reconstructing healthy native ecosystems. They are a testament to nature's resiliency. Imagine my excitement when after fighting my way through a tangled web of invasive shrubs, I emerged from dense shade onto an open sunny prairie remnant where I was greeted by the smiling faces of lead plant, fringed puccoon, and blue-eyed grass. Protecting such remnants must be a high priority. The challenge is how to find and identify them on private lands and how to muster the will and the way to make protection happen. In a state where over 97 percent of land is privately owned, it is clear that native biodiversity can be protected for the long term only if conservation occurs on private as well as public lands. There must be a public and private tag-team approach.

There are many places in Iowa where landscapes look fairly wild and natural. They appear to be good places for nature, good homes for native flora and fauna. But just looking wild does not mean that a landscape is a well-suited home for native biodiversity. Many areas lack the management needed to maintain them in a natural condition. The amount of public land needing management far exceeds the capacity and resources of existing conservation staff. The problem is much greater on private land, where the percentage of properly managed land is far lower. Many of Iowa's natural-looking landscapes are overrun with invasive species. These silent killers of native biodiversity can be stopped only with effective, stubborn, and usually costly management.

Iowa's native landscape was the product of multiple environmental factors choreographing the evolutionary pathway of flora and fauna over millions of years. Two important examples are natural fire and grazing by ungulates including bison.[1] Take these processes away and an ecosystem is susceptible to degradation and loss of species. Consider Kalsow Prairie State Preserve in Pocahontas County, a very fine complex of wet-mesic tallgrass prairie and pothole wetlands. Northern prairie skinks and smooth greensnakes scamper and slither beneath the deep orange-red pinwheels of wood lilies and the yellow-studded statues of compass plants. Uncommon butterflies such as regal fritillaries and arogos skippers flitter about searching for prairie violets and big bluestem, the food plants for turning the butterflies' eggs into fully grown larvae.

The preserve is mostly protected, but is the prairie functioning as it should and therefore affording protection to the entire ecosystem in the way that nature designed? Bison and elk have not grazed on Kalsow since the 1860s. Prescribed burning has occurred, but the occasional April burn does not have the same ecological effects as the lightning-caused fires of late summer that fashioned prairie organisms during centuries of evolution. Here and on other public and privately owned conservation landscapes, the absence of these and other ecological processes lessens and, in some cases, completely jeopardizes their ability to support native biodiversity.

MY VISION: A LAND TRANSFORMED

How much land is needed to adequately protect and maintain biodiversity? The Half-Earth Project, spearheaded by E. O. Wilson in his book *Half-Earth: Our Planet's Fight for Life*, advocates for protecting 50 percent of Earth's lands and seas in order to reverse the current species extinction crisis and ensure the planet's long-term health. Wilson contends that by maintaining 50 percent of Earth for nature, 85 percent of its biodiversity can be protected. The 30×30 conservation initiative, introduced in 2018 by the Wyss Campaign for Nature, is an ambitious plan to protect 30 percent of Earth's lands and waters by 2030. Equally important is the effort to marshal funding to ensure proper management and to structure conservation strategies in ways that respect and integrate indigenous cultures.

Both Half-Earth and 30×30 recognize the urgent need to stop the ongoing destruction of natural habitat—over 1,500,000 acres of nature are lost each year in the United States—and both are certainly doable on a global or a national scale.[2] However, attaining 50 percent protection in Iowa would be nearly impossible for two reasons: first, the loss of each original prairie, wetland, savanna, and forest ecosystem already greatly exceeds 50 percent, and second, thanks to the Wisconsin glaciation, Iowa is blessed with some of the richest soil in the world, making agriculture a high priority.[3] Nonetheless, land conservation must remain our primary goal.

Since the early 2000s, a model of conservation and sustainability called Working Landscape has gained popularity. A good definition has been developed by Iowa PBS: "A working landscape is an approach to managing land and natural environments that balances social, economic and ecological needs. Business and social activities are done in a way that minimizes the disturbance of native plants and animals. A working landscape is an area where humans work as responsible members of a natural ecosystem. Ideally, all of the people within a working landscape are balancing their own needs with the needs of the environment. Striking that delicate balance is defined as mutual sustainability—everyone's needs are met in a way that will maintain the landscape into the future."[4]

A working landscape in Iowa must be built around a regenerative agriculture economy that supports the livelihood of humans in ways that are more compatible with biodiversity and resource protection. Land that is marginally productive, susceptible to soil erosion, or frequently flooded can still be used for agriculture but not for row crop production. Where row crop agriculture is maintained, sustainable practices such as low-till or no-till, buffer and prairie strips, cover crops, and crop rotations should become routine.

In the early 1980s, my wife and I made our living for five years on my family's 160-acre farm in western Iowa, first farmed by my great-grandfather. I wanted to see if small-scale sustainable agriculture was a viable alternative to conventional agribusiness. I attribute our success to my philosophy that a farm should be regarded as an ecosystem using nature as a model. An ecologically in-tune farm has all the major ecosystem players: primary producers, diverse crop species; primary consumers, livestock; secondary consumers, us and our customers; and detritivores, organisms such as earthworms that contribute to healthy soil. The soil organisms, sometimes referred to as soil livestock, form the soil food web and are hugely important. A farm's soil, like the soil in a native tallgrass prairie, should support uncountable numbers of bacteria, fungi, protozoans, nematodes, algae, microarthropods, worms, insects, and mites.

Diversity is important. We raised pigs, chickens, turkeys, ducks, and cattle. We milked a dairy cow, kept honeybees, grew a third of an acre of fruits and vegetables, rotated crops among corn, soybeans, oats, and alfalfa, maintained crop residues on overwintering fields, added livestock manure to row crop fields, and reduced our chemical fertilizer and herbicide inputs to zero. Pastureland, hayfields, grass terraces, waterways, a woodlot, and fencerows provided habitat for native species. During those five years, I learned that agriculture need not be an enemy of biodiversity. We know how to make agriculture more compatible with native biodiversity. Doing so transforms the land and increases its resilience even as it provides strong support for smaller family farms—farms under 500 acres are better suited to what we can call ecosystem farming.

I envision an Iowa transformation occurring on two levels. The first transformation is from conventional agriculture to regenerative or sustainable agriculture. This will help improve the conservation value of land used for agriculture.

The second transformation is ecological. Ecosystem reconstruction—the conversion of human-altered landscapes to a designed version of nature—is needed to reverse the massive loss of native ecosystems that has occurred in Iowa. There are already thousands of acres of reconstructed prairie and wetland in Iowa. Restoration ecology is a well-studied science dating back to the 1930s. We know how to do decent reconstructions. We simply need to do many more of them. Ecosystem reconstruction, especially reconstructed prairie and grassland, is a significant component of making agriculture more sustainable. It will accomplish five crucial tasks: increase habitat for native biodiversity, decrease soil erosion, improve water quality, provide rangeland for beef production, and perhaps most importantly reverse the current carbon flux so that carbon is removed from the atmosphere and stored in the soil.

Climate change and greenhouse gas emissions are globally complex problems, but there is one clear and straightforward hope. We must do as much as possible to encourage plants to do what they do best: remove carbon from the air and put it into forms of long-term storage such as organic matter in the soil or woody tissues in growing trees.

THERE IS HOPE FOR THE FUTURE

Moving forward to a time when biodiversity and humans share the land in a more equitable way is fraught with uncertainty and challenge. But there are beacons of hope lighting the way. More and more, private landowners and land trusts are becoming protectors of biodiversity, engaging in ecological restoration and using their lands as homes for flora and fauna rather than for making money. Friends groups provide volunteer workdays to control invasive species in county and state parks. Successful reintroductions of extirpated wildlife species have returned river otters, prairie-chickens, and wild turkeys to Iowa's landscapes. Native plant nurseries are well established in Iowa and neighboring states, a result of the high demand for native seeds. The Natural Resources Conservation Service's highly popular Environmental Quality Incentives Program helps landowners establish buffer zones, install pollinator habitat, increase soil organic matter while minimizing erosion, develop grazing plans and supportive livestock practices, and enhance cropping rotations and nutrient management. Iowa's Integrated Roadside Vegetation Management program serves as a national model for replacing bland nonnative roadside flora with corridors of diverse native vegetation. Some Iowa counties have implemented natural resources inventories to identify privately owned conservation lands. These inventories can be used to better guide land-use planning, formulate conservation strategies, and allocate county resources for land acquisition and management.

The Working Landscape model provides a realistic path forward for Iowa. It recognizes the importance of landscapes that support humans and economies as well as biodiversity. While the Half-Earth Project's 50 percent goal is too high for Iowa, the 30 percent goal put forth by the 30×30 conservation initiative is possible. That means we need a total of 10.8 million acres of conservation land. In 2021, we had approximately 4.7 million acres of conservation land in Iowa; thus we need an additional 6.1 million acres.[5] This huge amount of additional land, equaling one-sixth of the state, can be found only by looking at private ownership and farmland. But with almost 26 million acres of Iowa cropland there is a lot of potential, especially when we consider that more than 7 million acres are classified as marginal—land that is either too wet and floods often, too steep and erodes easily, or too dry and infertile due to gravelly, sandy, or rocky soils to be successfully farmed—and 6 million acres currently have erosion rates twice as high as the sustainable rate.[6] This means that Iowa has huge amounts of farmland that should not be row-cropped and could be converted to grasslands, wetlands, and woodlands.

Some of the marginal farmland occurs on floodplains that are frequently flooded for extended periods. Conversion of these lands would create larger and more ecologically viable riverine corridors. Aside from providing habitat, the continuity of corridors facilitates gene flow and the migration of individuals among populations. These are landscape processes that are vital to the long-term survival of species and that are essentially nonexistent today. This new rangeland could support all the beef cattle currently raised in Iowa's concentrated animal feeding operations.[7]

Let me be clear. This proposed land conversion would *not* take 7 million acres of land away from agriculture and someone's potential income. It would instead transform agriculture to fit the model of a working landscape. *It would make land become both economically and ecologically viable, thereby ensuring the long-term health of both agriculture and land.*

These numbers indicate that there is a realistic pathway to a future that promises hope for biodiversity. Of course, none of this can happen—not the saving of remnants, not the proper management of conservation land, and certainly not the transformation of marginal agricultural land into landscapes that support biodiversity—without new policies, regulations, funding, and buy-in from farmers for government-based initiatives. The ultimate fate of biodiversity in Iowa depends on our political landscape. While reconstructing 7 million acres is a tremendous challenge, it could be easy compared to the political and legislative work needed. None of our big environmental goals has a chance without representatives, senators, and a governor who fully understand how and why protecting native biodiversity is essential to make agriculture sustainable and to improve the quality of life for future generations of Iowans. The ultimate fate of biodiversity in Iowa depends on you and the rest of the citizens of Iowa. We can make it happen by making biodiversity, sustainability, and resilience a high priority in the voting booth. And like so many things in our lives that demand consequential decisions, education is imperative and must always be a priority.

So we must decide. Do we value a landscape where pale green orchids, red-backed voles, Dakota skippers, western hognose snakes, freckled madtoms, king rails, blue-spotted salamanders, and slippershell mussels—all endangered Iowa species—are able to live their lives? Will we insist that the ecosystem services that supply clean water, maintain healthy soils, and protect and pollinate food crops are a high priority? You owe it to yourself to visit a prairie, forest, or wetland. See for yourself what nature offers. Think about each species' place, about the long evolutionary history that has shaped it into the organism you see today.

When I visit such a place, for example, Kalsow Prairie, it is like taking a trip back in time. Here I can walk among plants that have maintained their populations for thousands of years. Think about that for a moment. There is an amazing obduracy in the life surrounding me. It's like entering a church and becoming overwhelmed by respect and admiration. So it's not surprising that each fall when I see the wine-red colors of native grasses on a hillside being overrun by the dark green cones of eastern red cedars, I know there are prairie plants on that slope crying out for help, for a breath of sunshine. I know that if I can get there in time, I can save another native prairie community. It's something we can all help do by making the right choices.

A few weeks ago, in early September, I burned half of an acre of native tallgrass on my farm that had been planted by the former landowner. The burn was done to help set back invasive bird's-foot trefoil as well as dense grasses and thus prepare the site for an interseeding of twenty-five to thirty native prairie forbs, in other words, to reconstruct a more diverse prairie. So was it a coincidence that about forty-five minutes after the fire was out, with the dense scent of smoke lingering in the air and the sun sinking nearer to the horizon, a pair of sandhill cranes appeared suddenly, flying low and quick? They passed over my burn and landed in my neighbor's adjacent cornfield. Coincidence? We have never seen sandhill cranes on or near our land in the eighteen years we have lived here. Or could it be that the cranes were reacting to the fire? Following the scent of smoke with expectations of grilled grasshoppers? Acting on instinct, as generations of cranes inhabiting the tallgrass prairie region have done for centuries?

This is nature. We must make protection of it and the organisms that fill it with amazing diversity and complexity our highest priority. It's what makes living on Earth so special.

NOTES

1. See T. R. Rosburg, "Iowa's Prairie Heritage: From the Past, through the Present, and into the Future," in N. P. Bernstein and L. J. Ostrander, eds., *Proceedings of the Seventeenth North American Prairie Conference: Seeds for the Future, Roots of the Past* (Mason City: North Iowa Area Community College, 2001), 1–14.

2. Conservation Science Partners, "Methods and Approach Used to Estimate the Loss and Fragmentation of Natural Lands in the Conterminous U.S. from 2001 to 2017," 2019.

3. Data on the loss of Iowa's original ecosystems were derived from the following sources. Woodland and forest loss ≈ 75 percent, from Earl C. Leatherberry, W. Keith Moser, Charles Perry, et al., "Iowa's Forests 1999–2003" (Washington, D.C.: USDA–Forest Service, 2006). Wetland loss ≈ 92 percent, from V. Evelsizer

and J. L. Johnson, "Wetland Action Plan for Iowa," Iowa Geological and Water Survey, Special Report No. 4, 2010, Iowa Department of Natural Resources. Prairie loss ≈ 99.9 percent, from F. Sampson and F. Knopf, "Prairie Conservation in North America," *BioScience* 44, no. 6 (1994): 418–421.

4. Iowa PBS, *Explore More: Working Landscapes*, https://iowa.pbslearning media.org/collection/explore-more/t/exm-working-landscapes.

5. I estimated the 2021 amount of Iowa conservation land by adding the following figures, given in acres, and calculating 80 percent of that sum, which was my estimate of the amount of land with actual conservation value. Publicly owned land in natural areas: federal: 122,600, from Ballotpedia, "Federal Land Policy in Iowa," https://ballotpedia.org/Federal_land_policy_in_Iowa; state: 425,000, from Sierra Club, "Iowa Public Land—By the Numbers," https://www.sierraclub .org/sites/www.sierraclub.org/files/sce/iowa-chapter/wildlands-wildlife/IA PublicLand.pdf; county: 208,882, from MyCountyParks, https://www.mycounty parks.com/county/default.aspx. Land owned by NGOs: Nature Conservancy: 10,572 owned, 6,607 in easements, Suzanne Hickey, personal communication, May 4, 2021; Iowa Natural Heritage Foundation: 10,000 owned, 22,000 in easements, Joe McGovern, personal communication, May 2, 2021; Whiterock Conservancy and Bur Oak Land Trust: 5,900 owned, from https://www.whiterockconservancy .org and https://buroaklandtrust.org. Privately owned land: in the Conservation Reserve Program: 1,700,000, from USDA–Farm Service Agency, https:// www.legis.iowa.gov/docs/publications/FCTA/860716.pdf; in the Wetlands Reserve Program: 175,000, from USDA–Natural Resources Conservation Service, https://www.nrcs.usda.gov/wps/portal/nrcs/ia/programs/easements/acep/ NRCS142P2_008107; forests: 2,490,000, from USDA, "Forests of Iowa, 2016," https://www.fs.fed.us/nrs/pubs/ru/ru_fs111.pdf. Grasslands: 776,125 (25 percent of total), from Iowa State University, Extension and Outreach, Soil and Land Use, https://www.extension.iastate.edu/soils/crop-and-land-use-statewide-data.

6. Of the 25.9 million acres of cropland in Iowa, 18.4 million acres are categorized as prime farmland, meaning they have the best combination of physical and chemical characteristics for agricultural production. Another 7.5 million acres are considered marginal. See Iowa State University, Extension and Outreach, Soil and Land Use, https://www.extension.iastate.edu/soils/crop-and-land-use-statewide -data. See also C. Cox, A. Hug, and N. Bruzelius, "Losing Ground" (Washington, D.C.: Environmental Working Group), 2011, https://static.ewg.org/reports/2010/ losingground/pdf/losingground_report.pdf.

7. This statement is based on the Iowa Beef Industry Council report of 1,722,000 yearly fed cattle marketings for 2020, "Iowa Cattle Industry Facts," https://www.iabeef.org/raising-beef/cattle-industry-facts, and on 2017 average stocking rates from Iowa State University, Extension and Outreach, "Iowa's Pastureland and Grazing 2013–2018," https://store.extension.iastate.edu/product/ Iowas-Pastureland-and-Grazing-2013-2018. Contact me for details.

Regenerating Our Future
A Call to Action

Jerald L. Schnoor

GROWING UP IN Davenport in eastern Iowa, I never thought of myself as a nature boy. But looking back on it, I kind of was. I often lost myself for entire days in the pools and shallows of Duck Creek, which ran for miles through Davenport and Bettendorf. One stretch of the creek was only six blocks from my home, an easy bike ride for a day of play. It afforded me countless hours of immersion and fantasy. Deeper pools allowed unsupervised time for swimming and occasionally fishing for bluegills. Most thrilling was a dark backwater pond, rich with turtle species, in the forested area directly behind Duck Creek. Fascinated by—yet fearful of—the big snapping turtles, I kept my distance. When I glanced at the spiked ridges on their tails, I imagined prehistoric dinosaurs.

My favorite activity at the creek was catching minnows. My brother Jim and I made nets from old window screens; four corners tied with twine and laced to an old wooden clothesline pole allowed a singular sweeping pull to capture all the bounty. We smeared wet oatmeal onto the center of the screen, crawled onto a fallen cottonwood across the creek, lowered the net, and waited for those churning masses of chub minnows to feed on the oatmeal. My heart leaped as we yanked the chubs onto the shore, where they made superb bait for a weekend of fishing for the "big ones" in the Mississippi River.

PROBLEMS AND PROMISES

Today Duck Creek has been straightened and only a few wild sections remain. But the future abounds in those vestiges of wild nature. This book is a tale of promise for such remaining bits of the natural world—and of the road map they create for simultaneous regeneration of land, water, air, and diverse nature. Ecosystem remnants like Becky's Fen, ancient patches of diverse prairie and savanna, and working landscapes with healthy soils such as Francis Thicke's organic dairy and crop farm or Levi Lyle's smaller-scale niche-crop operation—these sustainable landscapes show us our history and help point our way forward. Restored and reconstructed native ecosystems, once they have regained healthy native diversity and functions, can release their cleansed waters and air to benefit surrounding landscapes. This doesn't mean that restored and reconstructed landscapes will be exactly the same as the systems that dominated Iowa a brief 200 years ago, before Euro-American settlement, but they will be richer and more biologically diverse, adaptive, sustainable, and resilient than the majority of Iowa's lands today, and they can point us toward an environmentally healthy future.

Agriculture and its intensification have caused a tragic loss of soil and biodiversity, a torrent of runoff with subsequent flooding, and the degradation of Iowa's water quality. We fail to rotate our crops, and we deplete our soils, flood our lands, and leak nutrients and greenhouse gases into the water and atmosphere simultaneously. But suppose we could reverse these mistakes and, in the process, create positive outcomes? Reviving nature and returning biodiversity to the landscape, including to agricultural lands, could set in motion a healing of many of the thorny problems discussed in this book.

As an engineer, I can imagine a double circular diagram with Iowa's four major environmental problems on the inside—biodiversity loss, poor soil health, water degradation, and climate change—and encircling those problems, on the outside, a ring of positive solutions. Our call to action begins when human intervention and innovation set regenerative agriculture in motion and reestablish diverse native vegetation and perennial cover on the landscape. These efforts initiate a process of healing all our interconnected problems. Diverse prairie and other perennial plantings, properly managed, start to increase soil depth and permeability and also restore a functional soil food web. And they create much-improved habitat for biodiversity. The plants also draw carbon compounds down into roots that store the carbon as soil organic matter, which helps offset climate change.

These actions together build healthier soils that hold rainwater and nutrients in place, lessen flooding and erosion, prevent fertilizers from running off the land, and improve the water quality of our lakes and rivers. As carbon and nutrient retention markets become more widely established, farmers will profit from the monetization of these best management practices by receiving payments for storing carbon in the soil and reducing nutrient runoff. Once we reestablish nature's diversity on the landscape, we will begin to address all the complex problems central to this book.

To energize this process, we need a land conservation movement in which every citizen can play a role. If you own a small bit of land, make it your dream ecosystem. Plant native species and flowering perennials, attract pollinators, reject pesticides and the overuse of fertilizers. Make nature your heaven on Earth, a personal testament to the movement. If you don't own land, help your local school green its playground or volunteer at a community garden or local church that's working to grow a dream ecoplot. When we shop for groceries, let's appreciate the ecological resilience that regenerative agriculture provides and choose sustainably grown products. Regarding our eating habits, could we possibly take the next step and modify our diets to fit this small planet? And don't forget to let your legislators know that you value conservation, and vote for those who understand its critical importance.

All these types of effort guide us toward Aldo Leopold's concept of a land ethic—that is, toward an expansion of our sense of awareness and moral responsibility beyond humans to include Earth's soil health, air and water quality, and plant and animal diversity—what Leopold called collectively the land. As he first defined the concept in his 1949 book *A Sand County Almanac*, all these natural features then become part of our home community. And the caring relationships between people and the landscape become intertwined and inseparable.

As we become more aware of our role in the landscape, we may wish to join citizen-science projects like the Iowa Department of Natural Resources' Volunteer Wildlife Monitoring Program to track the abundance of frogs and toads or nesting raptors or participate in the National Audubon Society's Christmas Bird Count, which has been held annually from 1900 to the present. Some of us may volunteer with our county conservation board to plant gardens for pollinators, fight invasive species, regenerate prairies, and collect native prairie seeds. Perhaps most importantly, many ecocauses and organizations need our financial support, including land restoration and preservation efforts like those of the Bur Oak Land Trust and SILT, the Sustainable Iowa Land Trust.

Conserving water and energy and recycling materials in our homes, churches, workplaces, and communities immerse us more deeply in Leopold's land ethic. And saving energy helps decrease greenhouse gases, reversing the frightening rapidity of climate change. Each of us can live the change that is needed by treading lightly on the earth, reducing our individual carbon footprints, growing and buying local food, installing solar photovoltaics on our roofs, purchasing electric vehicles, using mass transportation whenever possible, and voting with conservation in mind. We may even get to know our neighbors in the community a little better! It takes a diverse, equitable, and inclusive community to pull us all together in challenging times.

My childhood dinosaur-looking snapping turtles have endured on Earth for over 70 million years. If humanity is to survive and thrive even another 70 years, we must cherish our ecological remnants and attempt to weave them into a sustainable network for future generations. These and other sites that retain native biodiversity are the embryos for regenerating a more resilient landscape and life.

TRANSFORMATIVE ACTION

Cherishing the environment began for me when I was a student in chemical engineering at Iowa State University. The year 1970 was tumultuous. I felt depressed by the Vietnam War's senseless and deadly conflict, by the social injustice and brutal racism that ignited riots in our cities, and by an environment of burning rivers and dead lakes. It was this last problem that won my professional devotion that year.

The first Earth Day—April 22, 1970—ignited a spark of environmentalism in me and many others. How could we not be hopeful when 20 million people, the largest public demonstration in U.S. history, marched on that day? Farmers and businesspeople, Republicans and Democrats, students and teachers, legislators and preachers protested peacefully together to declare that Earth must be saved. Back then, the environment was not a partisan issue—it seemed that we were all on board. In 1968, *Apollo 8* astronaut William Anders had snapped an iconic photo of Earth rising over a lunar landscape. Two years later, for the first time, folks recognized that our beautiful blue dot floating through this infinite universe was itself finite and that we could not continue to mine, mold, consume, and discard it without end.

Now I wonder, How could we have gone on to damage the planet so quickly? Since 1970, deforestation has increased at an alarming pace. We have commandeered the atmosphere as an exhaust pipe for burning fossil fuels and spewing out greenhouse gases. Global average temperatures have risen, many wildlife populations have plummeted, sea levels have been elevated, oceans acidified, and coral reefs decimated—all in one person's working lifetime. On that first Earth Day, if anyone had predicted such deterioration of the environment in just fifty years, I would have said, "You're crazy." I reasoned that the earth was too large and wondrous to be affected so calamitously in such a short time. But somehow it happened. I guess that our 2021 world population of 7.9 billion and world gross domestic product of around $93.9 trillion are quite formidable consumptive and destructive forces.[1]

So our ecological remnants are our hope, but they are not enough. To restore a high-quality environment for humans and all other living species, we must devote ourselves to launching another moon shot, as we did in my youth. But instead of going to the moon, we need a devoted massive effort focused on regenerating Earth, our home, as a planet that will remain habitable for the foreseeable future. We know how to do this, and we still have a chance to do it, but time is running out. By weaving a network from nascent ideas, scientific evidence, and Iowa's remaining natural vestiges, we have an opportunity to reconfigure our state in a new way as a sustainable living landscape that will lead us safely into a dependable and robust future. This book provides a guiding vision. Here we sound a clarion call for the systemic transformation of our uses of Iowa's soil, water, air, and native biodiversity.

What would this massive transformation entail? Let's listen to our authors. Iowa already leads in agricultural productivity and technology. As Lisa Schulte Moore writes in chapter 4, "Iowa is one of the few places in the world where climate, soil, and human ingenuity have conspired to create agricultural abundance on a vast scale. The combination of these factors has enabled our state to lead the nation in the production of corn, pork, eggs, ethanol, and bioproducts." But that leadership has come at the cost of degraded soil, water, air, and native communities. Can we now lead the renewal of these features on agricultural lands? Schulte Moore describes the regenerative agriculture movement, based on practices such as minimally disturbing the soil and keeping it under plant cover year-round, increasing plant diversity including native plants on farms, and reintegrating pastured livestock into the farmscape. These practices can restore soil and landscape health and lead us toward agricultural sustainability. Iowa's magic could continue through perpetuity.

Schulte Moore believes that Iowa's efforts could help launch a global soil health revolution that would move the entire world toward sustainable agriculture—a shift that is sorely needed. Our stature as an agricultural leader, our technological and educational finesse, and our built, social, and financial infrastructure place us in a unique position for leading the rest of the world. Schulte Moore feels that demonstrating to other nations how to move toward more resilient, sustainable agriculture is an obligation as well as an opportunity. If we Iowans, with our many resources, cannot reverse the degradation of our soils and leave the land better than we found it, then who can?

The vision for our water is framed beautifully in chapter 8 by Larry Weber, who calls us to "slow the flow of water across the landscape, allowing it to percolate through the soil as it did when Iowa was covered with prairies, filtering out pollutants and reducing downstream flooding." How do we do this? By removing row crops from Iowa's most fragile and frequently flooded farmlands and instead planting these in perennial cover, preferably native plant communities. With such a vision, we simultaneously recharge our depleted aquifers, decrease the overfertilization of lakes and rivers, prevent soil erosion, minimize flooding, and generate precious income for everyone working the land.

Gregory Carmichael in chapter 12 writes eloquently about dealing with climate change. He believes that a soft climate change landing for humanity and nature is still possible but that we need to act with vigor and urgency or the possibility will slip away. In addition to leading the nation in moving toward renewable energy, Iowa also must expand efforts to reduce agricultural greenhouse gases. Carmichael explains how controlling agricultural methane can produce an especially rapid response in lowering greenhouse gases and their temperature-raising effects. In addition, Iowa's universities and colleges could and should educate all students about climate issues and instill in them an environmental ethic.

What about the loss of native biodiversity? Thomas Rosburg in chapter 16 proposes a two-part solution: implementing regenerative agriculture practices on row-cropped farmland and restoring healthier native biodiversity on Iowa's nonfarmed land and marginal farmland. Our needs cannot usurp nature's or the environment's. Rosburg reminds us that food must be produced and that farmers must be paid for their efforts but only as long as the soil prospers, lest we kill the goose that laid the golden egg. In his chapter, I hear echoes of Leopold's land ethic and its central concept statement: "When we see land as a community to which we belong, we may begin to use it with love and respect."

To many, such as Elizabeth Lynch in chapter 13 and James Pease in chapter 15, preventing the continuing extinction of Earth's wondrously diverse plants and animals is an overriding priority because of extinction's profound and irreversible implications. As renowned biologist E. O. Wilson wrote in his 1996 book *In Search of Nature*, "when we debase the global environment and extinguish the variety of life, we are dismantling a support system that is too complex to understand, let alone replace in the foreseeable future." How can we then curtail today's unprecedented, forever loss of Earth's irreplaceable biodiversity? Again we turn to our authors. Rosburg's Working Landscape model is a slimmed-down version of Wilson's Half-Earth initiative, which he described in a 2016 book by that name. According to Wilson, protecting half of the lands and half of the oceans for nature by 2050 could preserve up to 85 percent of Earth's biodiversity, a small price to pay for the preservation of countless species, including humankind.

But Wilson speaks not of "half of each continent." Rather, he envisions preserving carefully chosen key interwoven habitats along corridors that offer promise. In *Half-Earth*, he identifies existing bird flyways, marine sanctuaries, and ecosystem gradients that can be connected to one another to form a global network. James Pease also supports this idea in chapter 15, where he emphasizes that river corridors offer the most opportunity for protecting species in Iowa and throughout humid continental regions everywhere. These natural corridors can connect larger biodiversity restorations on the landscape. Iowa's biodiversity improvements outlined in this book will fit nicely into the mosaic of longer natural corridors promoted in Wilson's Half-Earth Project.

Rosburg admits to being an unrepentant biophiliac. "Biophilia," a term coined by E. O. Wilson in his 1984 book by that name, is defined by *Merriam-Webster* as "a hypothetical human tendency to interact or be closely associated with other forms of life in nature: a desire or tendency to commune with nature." I suspect Rosburg is in good company with many of the authors in this book, myself included. Many of us who have been observing Earth's changes and challenges sense that our planet's native communities and processes are in some way sacred and feel that this sense of the sacred has not been lost. Biophilia ardently abounds in so many people that this humble call to action, I pray, will fall on fertile ground. We yearn for a more restorative, resilient relationship with the natural world and landscape.

Such yearnings and our roots run deep. René Dubos, who is credited with the phrase "think globally, act locally," also wrote of our deep attraction to the natural environment and our need for a sense of place in his 1972 book *A God Within*. Today I picture myself returning once more to my roots at Duck Creek in my hometown of Davenport. Yes, the creek has been straightened and has lost much of its natural character in the past sixty years. But I would be remiss if I ignored the treasures of its remaining turtles and fish and birds. Two Baltimore orioles fly over its banks. Then a great blue heron greets me as if to say, "Don't despair—don't give up." Life still abounds and opportunities still remain for nature's healing, restoration, regeneration, and rebirth. To me, that's the transformative message of this inspiring volume. A rebirth has begun in small patches of restored native prairie, no-till land, riparian zone plantings, and many other places in Iowa, and these are documented in this book. But we must magnify and multiply that effort. Our call to action: Iowans have a unique opportunity and an obligation to succeed with regenerative agriculture, to slow and infiltrate our rainfall, to incorporate atmospheric carbon into our soil, to enhance our landscape's native biodiversity, and to export all that we learn to our global community. This, I feel, is our collective vision for the future.

NOTE

1. See Statistics Times, 2021 projected world gross domestic product, https://statisticstimes.com/economy/world-gdp.php, and 2021 projected world population, https://statisticstimes.com/demographics/world-population.php.

CONTRIBUTORS

Understanding the long reach of air pollution and its effects on humanity and the environment has been the focus of **Gregory R. Carmichael**'s career, expressed both in his international research and leadership and in his position at the University of Iowa, where he is a professor of chemical engineering and codirector of the Center for Global and Regional Environmental Research. Greg's research focuses on air pollution and climate change; he uses comprehensive computer models to simulate the interactions of air pollutants with weather and climate. He serves on numerous international advisory boards and is chair of the World Meteorological Organization's Environmental Pollution and Atmospheric Chemistry Scientific Steering Committee.

Pauline Drobney's passion is learning about and being in the natural world. Her four decades of professional life started when she became an assistant manager of a university preserve. She was a founder and the first president of the Iowa Prairie Network and conceived of and chaired the first Iowa Prairie Conference. A prairie consulting business led to an opportunity to become the first biologist for Neal Smith National Wildlife Refuge, where she guided the ecological restoration of the 8,654-acre refuge. Now as prairie and savanna zone biologist for the Midwest region of the U.S. Fish and Wildlife Service, Pauline continues active research efforts even as she guides the work of others.

Ronald Eckoff arrived in Iowa in July 1965 on a two-year assignment with the U.S. Public Health Service, and he never left. After thirty-five years with the Iowa Department of Public Health, including two periods as acting director, he looked forward to an active retirement and purchased seventy-five acres (later joined by forty-one more) of pastureland in southern Iowa. Prior to this, he had not been actively involved with Iowa's native ecosystems. But once he started exploring his pastureland, he discovered a prairie remnant, a bur oak savanna, and woodlands and embarked on a twenty-year (so far) adventure of rescuing and restoring these remnants. Ron certainly got his active retirement!

Marlene Warren Ehresman picked up a sick robin when she was in grade school in the early 1960s and a sick turkey vulture in the late 1970s while working on a wild turkey restoration project. She's still picking up distressed wild animals, but she now knows how to care for them better. A graduate of Iowa State University with degrees in fisheries, wildlife biology, and environmental studies, she has been a volunteer naturalist and wildlife rehabilitator and a staff member of a state land trust; she is the cofounder and now director of the Iowa Wildlife Center in central Iowa. Along with her wildlife biologist husband, Marlene has raised two sons to respect and appreciate wild places and wild lives.

Ken Fawcett grew up on a diversified grain and livestock farm in the middle of the last century, enjoying every aspect of being a farm kid from a large family. He has always had a passion for growing crops, livestock, fruit trees, and garden produce. He remains active in the family's crop farm with nephew Kent Stuart and son-in-law Troy Vincent. His wife, Helen, grew up in Amana and brings her family knowledge to their mutual enjoyment of the bounties this land produces. The family has hosted many field days, farm groups, and friends from around the world, sharing their conservation efforts. Ken and Kent were named Iowa Conservation Farmers of the Year in 2021.

In 2018 **Jim Furnish**, former deputy chief of the U.S. Forest Service and author of *Toward a Natural Forest: The Forest Service in Transition*, returned to his boyhood home in Iowa after a career in western national forests. His turning point came during the spotted owl crisis of the 1990s in the Pacific Northwest, when he did a slow burn watching committed environmentalists question Forest Service abuse of spectacular lands. Jim found his own land ethic then and transformed Oregon's Siuslaw National Forest from a tree farm to a model of restoration forestry. As a consultant, he remains active in forest policy issues, causing good trouble as needed to keep the Forest Service honest.

Even though **William J. Gutowski, Jr.**, grew up in the Connecticut River's farming valley, he had much to learn about Iowa's agriculture and landscape when he moved to Iowa over thirty years ago to join the faculty at Iowa State University, where he is now a professor of geological and atmospheric sciences. With degrees in meteorology and physics, he has focused on Iowa's climate and ever-changing weather. Bill has shared his appreciation of Iowa's communities, heritage, and landscape through his teaching and global research, including work with the U.N.'s Intergovernmental Panel on Climate Change and the World Climate Research Programme. His leadership in climate research has made him a fellow of the American Meteorological Society.

Brian Hanft got his start in local public health in 1994 as an intern with the Black Hawk County Health Department. After graduating from the University of Northern Iowa, he worked in various roles with the same agency until he moved to Des Moines, where he transitioned to the Polk County Environmental Health Office. While there, he completed his master's degree in public administration at Drake University. Searching for new challenges, Brian accepted a management position with the Cerro Gordo County Department of Public Health, where he served as the director of public health. He is now the health protection manager for the Broomfield Department of Public Health in Broomfield, Colorado.

Andrew Johnson grew up milking cows, shearing Christmas trees, running in the woods, and pondering change. From teaching agroforestry in the mountains of Guatemala to facilitating sustainable agriculture in Georgia, he understood natural systems easily—people systems, a bit less so, until he began to learn about the importance of identity and culture to the functioning of the land community. Returning with his family to the home place farm in Winneshiek County deepened Andy's understanding of the power of localism—and locally owned institutions—in rural places. He teamed up with others to harness that power through the creation of the universal-local Clean Energy District model and movement.

Christopher S. Jones is a research engineer with IIHR–Hydroscience and Engineering at the University of Iowa. He received his Ph.D. in analytical chemistry from Montana State University. He has worked at the nexus of Iowa agriculture and water quality as a consultant, in a commercial laboratory, in the municipal water and wastewater industry, with an agricultural commodity organization, and now in a university research institute. Chris's research interests include contaminant hydrology, water monitoring, and municipal drinking water; he has published fifty scientific journal articles on these topics. His favorite leisure activity is fishing on the Upper Mississippi River of northeast Iowa and southwest Wisconsin. Chris's blog on Iowa's water-quality and agricultural issues helps educate Iowans across the state.

As the youngest child of northeast Iowa farmers, **Rebecca L. Kauten** experienced dramatic physical, social, and economic changes in the world around her from an early age. These influences led her from Iowa's farm fields to tea plantations and banana groves in southern India, to the archipelagoes of Sweden, and back again to Iowa and to her Ph.D. research examining links between the physical and social dimensions of water. Rebecca's publications range from technical manuals on water-quality monitoring to writings on social conflict in recreation. Her work currently connects young people to the natural landscape at Iowa Lakeside Laboratory's field station in northwest Iowa.

Hydrologist **Witold F. Krajewski** is the director of the Iowa Flood Center and professor of civil and environmental engineering at the University of Iowa. His current research focuses on understanding the genesis and evolution of floods through field data and modeling as well as the measurement and estimation of rainfall using radar and satellite remote sensing; he has published over 250 journal articles on these topics. In 2021, Witek was elected to the National Academy of Engineering "for advances in flood prediction and mitigation." He lives near Iowa City, where his house is located high on the divide of two watersheds, making it immune to riverine floods.

Levi Lyle grew up on a farm near Keota, Iowa. He earned a master's degree in education from the University of Northern Iowa. After ten years in human services teaching, counseling, and coaching, Levi and his wife, Jill, returned to the family farm to raise their four children. Among other activities, Levi and his family grow and distribute aronia berries to local markets, which he feels brings balance to his other agricultural endeavors. Levi has worked as an organic inspector and now consults on transitions to organic farming. The author of two books of poetry, he has been a local leader in conservation no-till farming.

Elizabeth A. Lynch is an associate professor of biology at Luther College in Decorah, Iowa. Alongside her students she has spent much of the past two decades learning about the natural history of northeast Iowa. When not teaching or doing research, she enjoys exploring and foraging in the forests, fields, and streams around her home, often accompanied by a reasonably well-behaved dog. During the spring and fall, Beth obsessively patrols hundreds of acres of public land to control the spread of garlic mustard.

Cornelia F. Mutel has had a passion for nature since childhood. Her earliest memories are of the plants around her home in Madison, Wisconsin. She studied biology and music at Oberlin College and plant ecology at the University of Colorado. Until retirement, she was a senior science writer with IIHR–Hydroscience and Engineering at the University of Iowa. Connie has written or edited many books on natural history, restoration ecology, flooding, and climate change, among other subjects; those focusing on Iowa include *Fragile Giants: A Natural History of the Loess Hills*, *The Emerald Horizon: The History of Nature in Iowa*, and *A Sugar Creek Chronicle: Observing Climate Change from a Midwestern Woodland*. Connie walks daily in the oak woodland north of Iowa City, where she lives with her husband and which she is restoring to its pre-1830s diversity and health.

James L. Pease grew up along the Mississippi River in southeast Iowa exploring the rivers, woods, and other wild areas with his brothers. Jim has nearly half a century of experience as a front-line naturalist, extension wildlife specialist, and professor of interpretation at Iowa State University. Since retiring from ISU, he has continued to teach, write, and speak widely and has led natural history trips to Central and South America and other wildlife-rich areas. He has paddled and reported on over 2,000 miles of Iowa rivers and written brochures for the public. He continues to hold leadership positions in several conservation organizations.

Thomas Rosburg has been a section hand for the railroad, a farmworker on a hog and grain farm in eastern Iowa, a farmer in western Iowa, and a wildlife biologist in Iowa, Wyoming, and Colorado; he is currently a professor at Drake University teaching ecology and botany. His work has engaged over 250 students in hands-on ecological restoration projects.

Tom has acquired grants of over $1.6 million to investigate the ecology of grassland, forest, and wetland ecosystems. The recipient of many awards including the Distinguished Iowa Scientist Award and the Governor's Iowa Environmental Excellence Award, he raises free-range hogs and chickens, organic fruits and vegetables, and prairie on a small farm in central Iowa.

Keith E. Schilling is the state geologist of Iowa and director of the Iowa Geological Survey at the University of Iowa; he is also a research engineer at UI's IIHR–Hydroscience and Engineering and an adjunct assistant professor at both UI and Iowa State University. He received his master's degree in water resources from ISU and his Ph.D. in geology from UI. Keith's over 200 scientific journal articles have focused on Iowa's water-related issues, including groundwater flow and quality, water pollution, and floodplain processes. He enjoys tennis, golf, biking, hiking, and other outdoor pursuits in his leisure time.

Jerald L. Schnoor first realized a passion to preserve the Iowa environment as a child and decided it would be his lifelong pursuit on the first Earth Day in 1970. For forty-five years he has devoted his teaching career to spreading the word. Jerry is the Allen S. Henry Chair in Engineering, professor of civil and environmental engineering, professor of occupational and environmental health, and codirector of the Center for Global and Regional Environmental Research at the University of Iowa; his research interests include phytoremediation, water sustainability, and climate change. He is a registered professional engineer and a member of the National Academy of Engineering.

Lisa Schulte Moore's favorite days at work are those when she is able to bring farmers, scientists, students, and other stakeholders together to talk about Iowa's agricultural future. She is a professor of natural resource ecology and management and associate director of the Bioeconomy Institute at Iowa State University. Lisa has served on the board of Practical Farmers of Iowa and as an adviser for Iowa Smart Agriculture. With her family, she co-owns and manages Heritage Knoll Farm in Wisconsin. Lisa is a fellow of the Ecological Society of America, the Leopold Leadership Program, and the MacArthur Foundation.

Mary P. Skopec grew up in a large and opinionated family. She spent her formative years hiding from her older brothers in the lilacs by her family's home. From there, she learned to observe the world and spent many hours watching grasshoppers, dissecting acorns, and daydreaming. Pursuing a career in natural resources was an easy choice, and she eventually earned an interdisciplinary Ph.D. in environmental science from the University of Iowa. After spending eighteen years with the Iowa Department of Natural Resources managing water-quality programs, Mary found her dream job as director of Iowa Lakeside Laboratory, a biological field station near Milford.

Brian Soenen was fortunate to have an outdoor-oriented family and county conservation board environmental education program that laid a solid foundation for his future endeavors. He started cleaning up Iowa's lands with his 4-H club and the Adopt-a-Highway program. But his first water-based cleanup was Iowa Project AWARE—the river-focused program that he imagined, planned, and founded. After fifteen years working in environmental education with the U.S. Army Corps of Engineers and the Iowa Department of Natural Resources, Brian found his dream job as a stay-at-home father of four. If his growing family doesn't catch the cleanup bug from him, it won't be for lack of trying!

Charles O. Stanier is a professor of chemical and biochemical engineering at the University of Iowa who researches links among energy, pollution, health, and climate. He assists the National Oceanic and Atmospheric Administration with long-term greenhouse gas measurements in Iowa and has participated in many atmospheric field studies. Charlie served on the USDA's Agricultural Air Quality Task Force and received the College of Engineering Service Award for technical assistance to public officials during the 2012 Iowa City landfill fire. He is a five-time recipient of the award from his department's senior class for his excellence in teaching and dedication to student success.

After growing up on a farm in southwest Minnesota, **Eugene S. Takle** went on to earn a B.A. in physics and mathematics from Luther College and a Ph.D. in physics from Iowa State University. Gene has conducted research and taught classes on weather and climate at ISU for over forty years; he coauthored the 2014 and 2018 U.S. National Climate Assessments and the 2007 report of the U.N.'s Intergovernmental Panel on Climate Change. He is a fellow of the American Meteorological Society and a certified consulting meteorologist. His 2020 paper in *Physics Today* describes how global climate change is providing new challenges to Iowa agriculture.

Carole Teator has lived on a wooded acre in Cedar Rapids since 2003. Here she has battled garlic mustard and other invasive plants, buoyed by the delight of identifying dozens of native woodland species growing just outside her door. Carole's commitment to nature led to a sixteen-year career with Trees Forever helping communities and landowners plant and care for trees. In 2017, she became the eastern Iowa program director for the Iowa Natural Heritage Foundation, working to permanently protect and restore land to benefit wildlife, water quality, and future generations. She is now the program manager for ReLeaf Cedar Rapids, overseeing the reestablishment of the city's urban forest that was so extensively damaged by the 2020 derecho.

Francis Thicke grew up on a dairy farm in southeast Minnesota. After completing a B.A. in music and philosophy, he returned to work on the family farm for nine years. In 1975, he helped convert the farm to organic. He went on to graduate school in 1982, completing M.S. and Ph.D. degrees in soil science. He then worked in Washington, D.C., as the national program leader for soil science for the USDA's extension service. In 1992, he returned to farming, this time in Iowa. Francis and his wife, Susan, own and operate an organic grass-based dairy farm with on-farm processing and local marketing of dairy products. He is the author of *A New Vision for Iowa Food and Agriculture*.

When he was ten years old, **Seth Watkins** nursed a chilled calf back to health, an event that sparked his interest in farming and ultimately led to today's career as a successful cattle farmer. Seth is the fourth generation to care for Pinhook Farm, his family's heritage farm near Clarinda, Iowa. His passion is stewardship and the regeneration of the natural resources that sustain us. He is achieving these goals through rotational grazing; protecting and restoring riparian areas, woodlands, and prairies; and rebuilding his soil by using cover crops and multispecies crop rotations, grazing cattle, and most of all by working with—instead of against—nature.

With his twenty-eight years of water resources research, **Larry Weber** is considered a national leader on water resource issues. A University of Iowa professor of civil and environmental engineering and the Edwin B. Green Chair in Hydraulics, he cofounded the Iowa Flood Center and the Iowa Nutrient Research Center and served for thirteen years as the director of IIHR–Hydroscience and Engineering. Larry spends much of his personal time working on the conservation of his hundred-acre property. Old Man's Timber includes a restored stand of timber, reconstructed tallgrass prairie, a pond, floodplain wetlands, remnant river oxbows, an orchard and apiary, vegetable gardens, and a reconstructed nineteenth-century barn.

Kathleen Woida hails from a Michigan farm homesteaded by her great-grandfather in 1873. After a brief career in bustling Chicago, unable to resist the calling of the land, Kathy studied geology at the University of Iowa, where her Ph.D. research into an ancient buried soil in southwest Iowa engendered a fascination with the complex beauty of soils. She later joined the USDA's Natural Resources Conservation Service, working in Utah and New Mexico before returning with the agency to Iowa in 1999. Evaluating soil and stream erosion across Iowa and assisting soil scientists on mapping and soil health projects led her to a deep appreciation of the state's soils and landscapes. Her book *Iowa's Remarkable Soils: The Story of Our Most Vital Resource and How We Can Save It* was published in 2021.

ACKNOWLEDGMENTS

THIS COMPLEX BOOK came together in a bit over a year, a feat that would have been impossible without the dedication of many talented people. Primary among them are the book's twenty-eight authors. I don't think these brave souls realized what they were signing up for when they committed to the project. The authors of the science-based chapters—Iowa's experts and leaders in the subjects at hand—are polished writers, yet most had not explored the first-person storytelling form that I suggested. The authors of the essays—each a champion activist in his or her own right—also strove to tell personal stories that placed a lifetime of achievements within a larger matrix. All the authors poured their hearts into their writing. They hung in there through multiple revisions. And throughout the process they continued to believe in this book's possibilities and worth, which in turn fed my energy and enabled me to keep going. The authors' dedicated work pulled this diverse assemblage into a united whole. No editor could have asked for more. Many thanks to all of you for your fine efforts and for your patience with me.

Four of the authors—Kathleen Woida (soil), Larry Weber (water), Eugene Takle (climate change), and Thomas Rosburg (biodiversity)—stepped forward to become regular consultants whom I contacted when struggling with direction, content expression, or theme development. Their on-the-spot responses to my countless pleas for help were critical to the book's completion.

Holly Carver, editor extraordinaire, was equally crucial to this project, encouraging me and discussing specifics from the beginning. I told her this was *our* book, and I meant that. The professional support of University of Iowa Press staff members was also so very helpful and uplifting. In addition, Jackie Stolze provided crucial editorial assistance. Our Lady of the Prairie Retreat Center in Wheatland, Iowa, gave me a quiet space where I completed the book's final chapters. Although I am now retired, IIHR–Hydroscience and Engineering, my long-term professional home at the University of Iowa, continued to provide support services and collegial encouragement.

Numerous reviewers helped ensure each chapter's content accuracy and clarified expression of important ideas. These chapter reviewers included E. Arthur Bettis, Joe Bolkcom, Allen Bonini, Eric Bradley, Richard Cruse, Jeffrey Dorale, Kate Giannini, Erin Irish, Erwin Klaas, Hiram Levy, Lyle Luzum, Gerald A. Miller, Eric O'Brien, Teresa Opheim, John Pearson, Dean Roosa, Richard C. Schultz, Lynette Seigley, Daryl Smith, Scott N. Spak, Gabriele Villarini, and Mark Vitosh. In addition, several of the book authors reviewed each other's chapters. Other professionals who also helped clarify concepts and content included Neil Bernstein, Allen Bonini, Elizabeth Hill, Laura Jackson, J. Elizabeth Maas, Jessica Meyer, Teresa Opheim, John Pearson, Pat Sippy, and Mike Todd. I express heartfelt and unfailing gratitude to all those mentioned above and to anyone I may have unintentionally overlooked. I do hope that each of you takes well-justified pride in any contribution this book may make toward a more resilient and sustainable Iowa.

Also deserving thanks are the countless Iowans who, through past decades, have laid the groundwork for this book and for our future by working toward the visions expressed in this book. And, to quote from my 2016 book *A Sugar Creek Chronicle*, I'd like to "remember the natural world and its many inhabitants who have always formed the ground base of my life, stretching my curiosity and presenting me with inspiration and visions of abundant beauty." I think that all of this book's authors would echo this form of gratitude.

Finally, thanks to the numerous families and friends who supported and encouraged the book's many authors in their efforts. That includes my ever-patient husband, Robert, our sons and their families, and my personal friends. You know who you are. A big hug to each and every one of you!

While gratefully acknowledging everyone's contributions, I alone take responsibility for any errors, misinterpretations, or omissions in *Tending Iowa's Land*.

INDEX

livestock; sea level rise; soil health; winds, extreme

BUR OAK BOOKS

All Is Leaf: Essays and Transformations
by John T. Price

Between Urban and Wild: Reflections from Colorado
by Andrea M. Jones

Booming from the Mists of Nowhere:
The Story of the Greater Prairie-Chicken
by Greg Hoch

The Butterflies of Iowa
by Dennis W. Schlicht, John C. Downey, and Jeffrey C. Nekola

A Country So Full of Game: The Story of Wildlife in Iowa
by James J. Dinsmore

Deep Nature: Photographs from Iowa
photographs by Linda Scarth and Robert Scarth
essay by John Pearson

The Ecology and Management of Prairies in the Central United States
by Chris Helzer

The Emerald Horizon: The History of Nature in Iowa
by Cornelia F. Mutel

Enchanted by Prairie
photographs by Bill Witt
essay by Osha Gray Davidson

Fragile Giants: A Natural History of the Loess Hills
by Cornelia F. Mutel

Green, Fair, and Prosperous: Paths to a Sustainable Iowa
by Charles E. Connerly

An Illustrated Guide to Iowa Prairie Plants
by Paul Christiansen and Mark Müller

The Vascular Plants of Iowa
by Lawrence J. Eilers and Dean M. Roosa

A Watershed Year: Anatomy of the Iowa Floods of 2008
edited by Cornelia F. Mutel

Where the Sky Began: Land of the Tallgrass Prairie
by John Madson

With Wings Extended: A Leap into the Wood Duck's World
by Greg Hoch